STREET
SEX WORK
AND CANADIAN
CITIES

SHAWNA FERRIS

STREET SEX WORK
AND CANADIAN CITIES

RESISTING A
DANGEROUS ORDER

CITIES

THE UNIVERSITY
of ALBERTA PRESS

Published by

The University of Alberta Press
Ring House 2
Edmonton, Alberta, Canada T6G 2E1
www.uap.ualberta.ca

Library and Archives Canada
Cataloguing in Publication

Ferris, Shawna, 1973–, author
        Street sex work and Canadian cities :
resisting a dangerous order /
Shawna Ferris.

Includes bibliographical references
and index.
Issued in print and electronic formats.
ISBN 978-1-77212-005-9 (pbk.).—
ISBN 978-1-77212-019-6 (epub).—
ISBN 978-1-77212-020-2
(Amazon kindle).—
ISBN 978-1-77212-021-9 (pdf)

        1. Prostitution—Social aspects—
Canada. 2. Prostitutes—Canada—
Social conditions. 3. Cities and
towns—Social aspects—Canada. I. Title.

HQ148.F47 2014   306.740971
C2014-906639-2
C2014-906640-6

Index available in print and PDF editions.

First edition, first printing, 2015.
Printed and bound in Canada by Houghton
Boston Printers, Saskatoon, Saskatchewan.
Copyediting by Lesley Peterson.
Proofreading by Joanne Muzak.
Indexing by Adrian Mather.

The University of Alberta Press is
committed to protecting our natural
environment. As part of our efforts, this
book is printed on Enviro Paper: it contains
100% post-consumer recycled fibres and is
acid- and chlorine-free.

The University of Alberta Press gratefully
acknowledges the support received for
its publishing program from The Canada
Council for the Arts. The University of
Alberta Press also gratefully acknowledges
the financial support of the Government
of Canada through the Canada Book Fund
(CBF) and the Government of Alberta
through the Alberta Media Fund (AMF) for
its publishing activities.

This book has been published with
the help of a grant from the Canadian
Federation for the Humanities and
Social Sciences, through the Awards to
Scholarly Publications Program, using
funds provided by the Social Sciences and
Humanities Research Council of Canada.

Canadä   Canada Council   Conseil des Arts
              for the Arts   du Canada

Alberta
Government

This book is dedicated, with deep respect,
to the missing and murdered women of this
place we now call Canada.

May we respect and honour you as we strive
to eliminate the forms of violence that have
taken you from us.

CONTENTS

FOREWORD
AMY LEBOVITCH

I'M AMY; LOVER OF ANIMALS AND TEA, activist and sex worker. As of writing this foreword, I've been working as a sex worker for the last sixteen years. I live in a world that either victimizes or vilifies me.

As a sex worker, I am told many things. I'm told how I should feel about my experience within sex work, how I should view my clients. I am told I am blinded by false consciousness and that my experiences are not representative of the majority of sex workers. No matter what those who speak for us want you to believe, there are no "representative" sex workers. We are not just one type of human being who all share the same experiences.

More often than not, sex workers get spoken about as being "damaged," called "prostituted women," demeaned and degraded for our jobs and for the issues others see around our jobs. My voice—sex workers' voices—are not valid. Unless we speak about our experiences within sex work the way some feel we should, framed through their lens, our words are not valid. Our words are not meaningful. "You are the exception—your voices don't count." This is the exact kind of exclusionary language that creates the environment where our voices continue to be discounted. For a long time I was isolated, like many other sex workers. For some, this work can be quite isolating. When I realized that I was not alone, when I realized that I was able to speak up, get organized, and get angry, I did just that.

As sex workers, we are often over-researched and given little, if any, control over how our contributions are used. Often our very selves are erased by the research. All too often, little respect is paid to us. Our voices scrubbed out and forgotten. There are those who research and write about sex workers who often forget we are human. These are often the same people who have the ear of many powerful groups and individuals, including policy- and lawmakers. People look at their research as very significant. They are seen as the experts. I think many of these same people don't recognize the true power they have in their writing. We give our stories, our voices, and our experiences, and then continue about our days. Working, surviving, living, and loving. Sometimes information they have gathered is made to fit their agenda around sex work. All too often sex workers are not consulted from the ground up on these research papers and projects. We are used for our knowledge and then have it presented by people who very well may consider themselves sex-work allies, but who don't reflect on the importance of having those who have lived experiences right from the get-go. Regularly, very little care is given to how this research process contributes to the stigma we face on a daily basis. It is infuriating to be studied and spoken over, to be treated as though we are not the true experts in our own lives and work.

Society should no longer expect us to be victims of violence; yet our current dangerous Canadian prostitution laws prevent us from working with support staff, working from our homes, from co-ops, from rented spaces, or on the street. These laws, in conjunction with stigma and independently, and our dehumanization have created this society that gives not even basic legal and human rights to sex workers. It fosters our continued stigmatization and dehumanization. It allows and condones violence against us, which goes unreported to the police for fear of arrest and further stigmatization by the police, the courts, the media, and society. The police are the enforcers of these bad laws and sometimes take advantage of their power to perpetrate violence against us, to extort from us, and to intimidate us.

The pervasive view in Canadian society that we are victims who need saving is paternalistic and maddening. Current laws reflect this frustrating—and frankly, dangerous—paternalism.

Many things came to mind when I first heard the title of this book, the phrase *Dangerous Order* in particular. The Ontario constitutional court case to strike down provisions in the *Criminal Code* around prostitution, in which I am a plaintiff, connects the violence that sex workers face with the laws which impact us in very real ways, daily.

The laws being challenged are directly connected to the way society and religion view us: as disposable and undesirable. As sex workers, we are not seen as part of the greater community but rather on the fringes, needing rescue or pity.

There are prohibitionists and others who speak publicly about this case and on sex work in general, pointing out, with their presumed authority, that violence is inherent within prostitution; therefore a case such as this will do nothing to "save" sex workers. We don't want or need to be saved. Sex workers are savvy, knowledgeable, and wonderful human beings, who work and live within a system and society that has, at every turn, not only violated our rights as human beings, but enacted laws that validate the stigma and violence we experience. A way this type of advocate is seeking to "protect" and "save" us is by supporting and bringing to the public's attention what is known as the "Nordic Model." This model was first introduced in Sweden in 1999; since then, Iceland and Norway have adopted similar legislation. The Nordic Model views all prostitution as violence against women, and views men who purchase and profit from these sexual services as predators who are the ones who need to be arrested. Male and transgendered sex workers are not even acknowledged. Sex workers who are working on the street are targeted by the police who go after their clients, making it very difficult to get work. Those working indoors have the police, social workers, etc. show up at their door when a suspected client has entered, to arrest him and "save" the worker. Their goal with this model is to curb demand. Sex work is not seen as work in Sweden, but rather as something that "happens to us." As sex workers, our agency is completely removed and we are turned into victims, regardless of our own lived experiences and voices.

Shawna builds on the strong evidence of these connections in this book, seeing us as full human beings who face stigma and human rights violations here in Canada today. She recognizes that we are real people, who should be honoured and respected as experts. That our contributions are important for you, the reader, to learn more about.

ACKNOWLEDGEMENTS

DEEPEST GRATITUDE AND RESPECT to those whose experience, research, and activism have made my own work possible: sex worker activists and advocates for missing and murdered women across the country. Thank you for the work that you do, and for all of your contributions to this and so many other anti-violence initiatives. Heartfelt thanks to my current research partners and friends, Ms. Amy Lebovitch and Dr. Kiera Ladner, for your encouragement in relation to this manuscript, and your expert counsel and work on our ongoing projects.

My sincere thanks as well to my editor at the University of Alberta Press, Peter Midgley, and to the all of the other wonderful folks at UAP for believing in this book project. Thanks, too, to friends and colleagues Drs. Elizabeth Millward, Susan Frohlick, and Sherry Farrell-Racette, for your encouragement and advice during the extensive writing and editing process for this manuscript. To my former supervisor, Dr. Lorraine York, for your invaluable mentorship, and to Drs. Susan Searls-Giroux and Danielle Coleman for your guidance, during the first five years of this project: thank you so very much.

I can only begin to express my appreciation for the support and encouragement of friends and family in this and so many other parts of my life. To my parents, Jim and Marian Ferris, to Rod, Lynn, and Lesley Martin, to Toni Walker,

Penny Ferris, and Wilma Reuben: thank you. To Ms. Jennifer Miller, and to Drs. Suzanne Rintoul, Stephanie Morley, Andrew Griffin, Emily Johansen, and Kaley Joyes: I could not ask for more enthusiastic, capable, understanding, or hilarious friends.

To my partner, Doug Martin: sweet friend and patient editor, I love you.

INTRODUCTION

THE DISCUSSION THROUGHOUT THIS BOOK considers the effects of transnational free-market economics, ongoing urbanization, and growing concerns regarding home and homeland security on contemporary representations of and responses to street-involved sex work in Canada. Canadian leaders regularly cite the rigorous policing or elimination of the street-involved sex industry as key components of urban "cleanup" projects that will make cities into attractive, or "safe and clean" global investment centres. Analyzing a combination of legislative initiatives, media representations, police and sex worker activist-produced texts, and literary texts, I interrogate such sanitizing urban agendas, especially the seeming requirement that many street-involved sex workers in Canada give up their basic human rights, and even their lives, for the orderly global cause. Foregrounding the current legality of prostitution in Canada, as well as the growing number of serial kidnap and murder cases involving inner-city sex workers across the country, this project brings together two broader cultural debates: one regarding the moral and cultural legitimacy of prostitution in Canada and one regarding the socio-economic disposability of the poor and other culturally marginalized populations in an emergent global order. I thus work to expose and interrogate the necropolitics, or privatization of the right to secure, police, or take deadly action against private citizens who are considered "disposable,"[1] which I find at work in these cases; and the subsequent cultural portrayal of already marginalized victims as enemies of the state.

TERMINOLOGY

As literary theorist Terry Goldie poignantly observes, "All of the terms in any analysis are of course themselves 'loaded'" (4). This is especially true in discussions of sex work and sex workers. Indeed, a number of the terms used throughout this extended analysis of the increasingly fraught relationship between sex work, sex workers, and Canada's cities require definition.

More than ten years of research and discussion have led me to believe that sex work's current legality in Canada is not common knowledge. This ignorance would seem, in part, to reflect popular understandings of the terms we use to discuss the sex trade. Despite ongoing efforts to reconnect prostitution with its origins in pre-historical pagan cultures wherein priestesses had intercourse with religious celebrants in order to facilitate their experience of the divine,[2] the words *prostitute* and *prostitution* retain their modern, pejorative, and morally inflected connotations. Literally denoting—in the necessarily culturally inflected *Oxford English Dictionary*—"a person, usually a woman, who engages in sexual activity for payment," the word *prostitute* invokes a historically informed moral repugnance toward female sexual transgression. The special disgust reserved for prostitutes—especially those perceived to be willing participants in the sex industry—in contemporary European and North and South American settler societies reflects two thousand years of patriarchal Judeo-Christian and colonial investment in the regulation of women's bodies and the social enforcement of monogamous heterosexuality. International sex workers' rights activist and feminist scholar Gail Pheterson refers to this repugnance as "whore stigma," a conflation of sex for sale as "selfhood" for sale (*Prism* 11). Often described as prostituting one*self*, the selling of sexual services thus connotes perpetuation of and participation—willing or no—in an especially abhorrent form of slavery.

My own analysis follows that of researcher and activist Elya Durisin, who contends that "in analyses of sex work...a distinction between the commodification of labour power and the commodification of the body in its entirety, as in slavery, should be maintained." As Durisin explains, "Sex work exists within the gambit of wage relations, whereas slavery is premised on property relations and is the 'legal ownership of one human being by another'" (130). Indeed, sex workers and their feminist allies identify the stigma associated with workers' perceived sexualized enslavement as "one of the central issues, and major burdens, for people working in the sex trade" (Jeffrey and MacDonald 136). As Leslie Ann Jeffrey and Gayle MacDonald remind us in *Sex Workers in the Maritimes Talk Back* (2006), "Sex worker advocates have long maintained that it is the stigma attached to the sex trade, not the sex trade itself, that is the cause of suffering for sex workers" (136).

In recognition of the ideological underpinnings of these terms, then, I use *prostitution* and *prostitute*—terms still in use in Canada's *Criminal Code*—when discussing or quoting from national legislation, sex-industry-related media reports, or public anti-sex-trade initiatives. In most other instances, I use *sex work* and *sex workers* to describe the business of and people involved in the provision of sexual services in exchange for financial or other recognized forms of remuneration. Occasionally, following the terminology of a particular group under discussion, I use the terms *sex professional, experiential woman/man* (a phrase that describes persons currently or formerly involved in sex work), or *whore* (a term some sex workers have begun to reclaim, vigorously disavowing the label's negative connotations). I use *sex work* and *sex worker* preferentially, however, in part to signal my position in ongoing debates within feminism, the academy, and public culture more generally about the rights and wrongs of prostitution. Implying as they do that the exchange of sexual services for money constitutes a form of labour equal to other types of employment for which one receives remuneration, these terms at least partially reject whore stigma.

There are, however, noteworthy objections to such terminology. Critic Sherene Razack argues that a universalized position on sex work at this time inevitably privileges the experiences and voices of white women over racialized women—thus too often reconstituting the race privilege, patriarchy, and systemic violence feminists work to resist and subvert. While I acknowledge this point, I do not accept her subsequent position that the term *prostitution* should be used precisely because it names the violence that too many women, particularly Indigenous and other racialized populations, experience in the exchange of sexual services for remuneration. Indeed the class, race, and geographic as well as urban location of a woman involved in the sex trade significantly increase or decrease her risks of being a victim of extreme violence. The overrepresentation of women who trace their ancestry to North America's First Peoples among the victims in current mass or serial kidnap and murder cases in Vancouver, Edmonton, and Winnipeg, for example, reproduces the statistics recorded by Andrea Smith and those involved with the Native Women's Association of Canada's research initiative, Sisters in Spirit: statistics that definitively demonstrate that Indigenous women are significantly more likely to experience extreme violence than white women of the same class and profession.[3] Such details must be figured into any analysis of a victimized woman's plight and in the arranging of any assistance she requires. Nevertheless, I do acknowledge that the terms *sex worker*, *experiential woman*, and *sex professional* do not effectively name race-related differences in women's experiences.

Having uncovered no options that are less contentious, however, I employ these terms when examining literary and cultural representations of sex workers who trace their ancestry to Indigenous peoples. As well, throughout these portions of my analysis, I identify these women using the terms *Aboriginal* and *Indigenous* interchangeably. I do so with the recognition that, in Canada, *Aboriginal* is a constitutionally recognized category that includes First Nations, Inuit, and Métis people.[4] Connecting these women's identities to the legislative system of a colonial nation-state, however, is perhaps not always appropriate or respectful. Therefore, to signal my awareness of the politically charged nature of the term *Aboriginal*, I use the term *Indigenous*: this may respectfully refer to all persons descended from First Peoples in spaces now known as Canada and the United States (as well as other nations around the globe). In concert with, when applicable or available, the name of a woman's particular Indigenous nation, *Indigenous* acknowledges both the specificity of the experiences of colonized peoples in Canada as well as transnational connections between First Peoples and ongoing de-colonization initiatives globally.

My use of the terms *sex work* and *sex worker* is meant to distance my discussion from current cycles of combative and repetitive debate in and outside of feminism regarding the symbolic and "real world" function of prostitution.[5] This is not to say that the positions put forward by participants in these debates are without merit. For example, Razack argues that prostitution plays a significant role in "securing racial patrimonies in today's transnational world" ("Race" 376). She explains, "To suggest as I have that the john [man who purchases sex] is enacting a hegemonic masculinity does not preclude that a prostitute is exercising agency, but it does mean that how we read the collective impact of her action (as opposed to its individual dimension) changes from resistance to systems of domination to accommodation" ("Race" 354–55). In order to make this argument, however, and thus to align herself (in some key ways, at least) with feminists and Indigenous activists and scholars who consider prostitution to be inevitably linked with violence, status quo misogyny, and racial hierarchies, Razack must disregard an ever-increasing body of writing by experiential women that argues against such readings and focuses instead on the myriad of ways that sex work can and does often resist and undermine hegemonic masculinity. Significantly, such work includes writings by racialized and/or poor women whose voices, as feminism (particularly in its second- and third-wave incarnations) has learned, must not be ignored. In an effort to maintain a critical distance from the above-noted debates about prostitution as a social issue, then, I try to maintain focus on the personhood, voices (where they are on record), and social as well as racial conditions of labour of those involved in sex work.[6]

Also important to my discussion is a necessary differentiation between forms of sex work. Though "there are no statistics to indicate how many people are currently employed as sex workers in Canada" (Pivot Legal Society, *Beyond* 18), it is estimated that approximately 20 per cent of the sex trade takes place at street level (Benoit and Miller 5–7). Street-involved urban sex workers are my primary concern throughout this book.

The discussion that follows also acknowledges that a significant portion of street-involved sex workers are "survival" workers, persons who use sex work to survive on the streets, who work to support a debilitating addiction, or who have been forced into the sex industry by others (Nagle 2). Given the heightened visibility of street-involved sex work and the overrepresentation of survival sex workers in this population, it is not surprising that these workers have become the veritable face of prostitution in both traditional and contemporary discourse. Significantly, street-involved and survival sex workers have long been associated with images of city life, particularly life in the modern industrial city.

CONNECTING GLOBAL CAPITALISM AND URBAN STREET-INVOLVED SEX WORK

That global capitalism is changing the modern city is evident in the increasing cultural influence of powerful transnational corporations as well as growing international focus on developing economically safe physical and corporate infrastructures, and in the subsequent regulation of urban spaces via increased policing of certain (often already marginalized) populations. As the socio-political structuring of nation-states comes increasingly to reflect the interests of neoliberal transnational economics, however, the spotlight that shines on urban centres operates in uneven and contradictory ways. While Amsterdam and Bangkok, cities where sex work is an accepted part of the local economy, continue to attract global investment capital, officials in Canadian cities such as Vancouver, Edmonton, and Winnipeg cite the rigorous policing and/or elimination of the sex industry as key components of urban cleanup projects that will make these cities into attractive, safe and clean investment centres and orderly urban sites for the headquartering of major transnational corporations.

This discussion interrogates the tension between globalization's sanitizing neoliberal and neoconservative agendas in Canadian urban centres and Canada's current reputation as a liberal democracy concerned with the rights of all of its citizens. In my analysis of significant sex work-related cultural and literary texts, I note that prostitution and capitalism's supposedly shared interests in our corporate global climate may have produced a newly legitimate subject position for sex workers in the national socio-political imagination. However, escalating violence against sex workers in cities across Canada—violence that appears, upon closer examination, to be state-facilitated, if not overtly state-endorsed—exposes the contradictory and hierarchical web of interests behind this liberal nation-state. Though sex workers, especially street-involved and/or survival workers, are overrepresented among victims of violent crime, current statistics suggest that, overall, violent crime rates are steadily decreasing across Canada. For example, Statistics Canada notes that police-reported crime rates dropped in 2004 and, while there was a 12 per cent increase in homicides (after hitting a thirty-six-year low in 2003), violent crime overall declined by 2 per cent, "continuing a general decline since 1992" ("Crime Statistics"). More recently, in 2007, violent crime rates decreased, again, by 3 per cent, a decline that "continued the downward trend in violent crime evident since the early 1990s and marked the lowest rate in nearly 20 years" (Dauvergne). Nonetheless, governments continue to promise (some) city residents more policing and protection against so-called urban dangers; and the street sex trade has come increasingly to be represented as a particularly urban menace. Current commitments to law and order seem inevitably to accompany efforts to improve urban business infrastructures, to protect private interests in newly gentrified inner-city neighbourhoods, and to narrow definitions of legitimate citizenship, so that the poor, the homeless, and those who otherwise work or live on city streets seem no longer to be entitled to the civil rights, liberties, protections, and social supports that liberal democratic nation-states like Canada promise.

As critic Rosa-Linda Fregoso observes, at the global and local levels, neoliberal readings of the economic as the political have resulted in "the privatizing and downsizing...in particular [of] those institutions responsible for defending the public welfare and guaranteeing citizenship rights including access to work, social services, food, shelter, and civil rights" ("'We Want'" 111). In these contexts, as theorist Zygmunt Bauman notes, individuals, not national governments, are increasingly held responsible for social welfare despite the not inconsequential effects of racism, sexual chauvinism, and self-perpetuating class hierarchies—powerful forces that underpin contemporary cultural/economic systems—on a growing underclass (Work 65–67). We see evidence of this reconfiguration and appropriation of public life in Canada, for example, in recent governments' willful erosion of the tax base and the parallel disintegration of social programs—programs that employ and are used disproportionately by women, particularly racialized women. In addition, as poorly funded public education systems are forced to rely more and more heavily on private funding to renovate crumbling buildings, produce textbooks, provide cafeteria services, and fund research and scholarships, cost-cutting measures and corporate interest in profitability too often result in oversized classes led by overworked and underpaid instructors. As many of the most underfunded institutions are found in the socio-economically depressed areas of cities, urban spaces generally understood to be quite racially diverse, such a system would seem to perpetuate certain classed, raced, and colonial social hierarchies.

Currently, state governments tend to do more to protect private property than to ensure the rights and public welfare of their state citizens (Fregoso,

"'We Want'" III). According to thinkers such as David Harvey and Zillah Eisenstein, neoliberalism facilitated the rise of neoconservativism. Neoconservatism, "its primary objective...the establishment of and respect for order...coupled with the construction of a hierarchy of power that is both secure and clear" (Harvey, "Consent" 190), sells, fences off, or increases police presence in formerly "open" spaces in the name of public safety, and "cracks down" on petty criminal activities, especially in poorer urban areas. Dire consequences for already disenfranchised populations are, then, the result of contemporary incarnations of neoconservatism, combined with the effects of almost four decades of neoliberal politics on Canadian cities.

In recent years, as urban theorists such as Neil Brenner and Nik Theodore note, "cities have become increasingly central to the reproduction, mutation, and continual reconstitution of neoliberalism," a process that has resulted in the emergence of "leaner and meaner urban geographies...throughout the older industrialized world" ("Cities" 375). Such emergent cityscapes have generally been the end-result of so-called urban revitalization projects that set out to achieve "the optimum re-arrangement of urban things. Crumbling, vacant, and stagnant properties and places are to be reconfigured while desired forms of inhabitants' conduct are cultivated and mobilized" (Lippert 29). As Randy Lippert succinctly observes, "security is to serve as a key channel through which these elements flow, their institutional movement promising to catalytically transform inert property and people" (29).

In their respective book-length studies, Mike Davis and Christian Parenti similarly examine how the "renewal," or gentrification and re-settlement, of once-defunct industrial strips and once-poor inner-city neighbourhoods often parallels the criminalization of poor and disenfranchised populations. Discussing this phenomenon in late twentieth-century Los Angeles, California, Davis argues that enthusiastic political endorsements of so-called "urban renaissance" or the creation of a "city of the future" gloss over the simultaneous "brutalization of inner-city neighbourhoods" that such renewal projects entail (City 227–28). Davis further observes, "The city, self-consciously adopting the idiom of urban cold war, promotes the 'containment' (official term) of the homeless in Skid Row along Fifth Street east of the Broadway, systematically transforming the neighborhood into an outdoor poorhouse....Every night on Skid Row is Friday the 13th, and, unsurprisingly, many of the homeless seek to escape the 'Nickle' during the night at all costs, searching safer niches in other parts of Downtown. The city in turn tightens the noose with increased police harassment and ingenious design deterrents" (City 232–33). Examining corresponding trends in cities across the United States, Parenti credits this "polarization of urban space and social relations" with the development of a "new layer of regulation and exclusion" and with the rise of zero-tolerance policing. This form of policing advocates strict monitoring, even criminalizing, of petty thievery, vagrancy, prostitution, and other formerly minor social offences in an effort to, in effect, fix the chinks in the legislative armour that would otherwise lead to larger, more serious crimes.

Furthermore, as cultural critic Henry Giroux notes in *The Terror of Neoliberalism*, "The breathless rhetoric of the global victory of free-market rationality spewed forth by the mass media, right-wing intellectuals, and governments alike has found its material expression both in an all-out attack on democratic values and in the growth of a range of social problems including virulent and persistent poverty, joblessness, inadequate health care, racial apartheid in the inner cities, and increasing inequalities between the rich and the poor" (xix). In this context, Giroux argues, "human misery is largely defined as a function of personal choices, and human misfortune is viewed as the basis for criminalizing social problems" (xviii). In addition, with the abundance of corporate tax holidays that governments around the world provide, tax burdens fall more and more to middle-class taxpayers, who, Bauman notes, are learning to resent the welfare state and its accompanying "big government" and elaborate tax structures. Increasingly, then, mainstream ideology blames the poor for their neediness, even as post-industrial capitalism increases the ranks of persons living below the poverty line and makes their poverty key to the perpetuation of the current economic system. As Bauman writes, "The desperate attempts [by national governments worldwide] to reach what passes today for the standard 'economic health' are widely seen as the major obstacle against doing anything really effective to raise employment levels through job creation" (Work 65).

Bauman also makes clear the long-term consequences for the poor of the resentment this ideology produces in the middle class: "The recent renaissance of work-ethic propaganda serves the 'separation of the deserving and non-deserving poor, putting the blame on the last, and justifying thereby society's indifference to them,' and hence 'the acceptance of poverty as an inevitable plague due to personal defects, and an ensuing insensibility towards the poor and the deprived.'

In other words, while no longer supplying the means to reduce poverty, the work ethic may yet help to reconcile society to the eternal presence of the poor" (*Work* 65). As corporations work to maximize shareholder profit by minimizing labour, downsizing, outsourcing, cutting benefits packages, and capping pay, middle-class workers, those who do not own shares in their employers' companies, find themselves in an increasingly precarious economic/cultural position. This kind of class precariousness may then effectively fuel fears of what one may become: the poor, the very class one has learned, on the one hand, to accept as an eternal, inevitable presence, and on the other, to blame and despise for their impoverishment.

Such inter- and transnational analyses can be applied all too easily to contemporary Canadian contexts. In the name of urban safety and orderliness, increased police budgets are sold to the public in cities like Toronto, Vancouver, and Winnipeg; and the drug-addicted, the poor, the homeless, those who work in the survival sex industry, and others our society has failed through systemic racism, inadequate health care, and an increasingly ragged social safety net are further criminalized and victimized as police move them off city streets and into court. Despite a recent more hopeful turn, in terms of street sex work in Canada, particularly stringent legislation over the past three decades (a summary of which appears in Appendix 1) has had dire consequences for already racialized and otherwise disenfranchised populations of street-involved sex workers. The free-market economics that seems so often to precede the emergence of renewed interests in urban law and order moved many sex workers onto city streets as brothels, or "bawdy houses," were outlawed in the late 1970s and early 1980s. Former brothel properties, now prime real estate in downtown cores, were taken over by less socially contentious businesses, and anti–bawdy house legislation in cities across Canada paralleled international urbanization trends in the late twentieth century.[7] Subsequent Not In My Backyard, or NIMBY, activism in Canada that responds to prostitution as a social problem and resulting zero-tolerance policing parallel the rise of neoliberalism and neoconservatism in North America.

Furthermore, that more and more street-involved sex workers of all races are being harassed, bullied, or otherwise targeted by police as well as private citizen groups *and* violent criminals illustrates contemporary necropolitics in Canada with alarming clarity. Canadian criminologist and longtime prostitution law researcher John Lowman observes, "After 1985, the year in which the communicating law was enacted, there was a large increase in British Columbia of murders of women known to prostitute" ("Violence" 18). Lowman's work interrogates parallels between escalating violence against sex workers, increased criminalization of prostitution, and a more and more insistent public and legislative "discourse of disposal" regarding the most visible members of the sex industry ("Violence" 18). Furthermore, despite the current rash of serial kidnappings and murders of street-involved women in cities such as Vancouver, Edmonton, Saskatoon, Regina, and Winnipeg, anti-prostitution neighbourhood policing and activism continues to proliferate in these same centres.

COLONIZATION AND INNER-CITY STREET-INVOLVED SEX WORK IN CANADA

The overrepresentation of Aboriginal people among poor urban populations in Canadian cities means that such criminalization and victimization is distinctly racialized as well as classed and gendered. As Razack discusses in her analysis of the 1996 murder in Regina, Saskatchewan, by two young white middle-class men of Saulteaux woman Pamela George, interactions between certain raced, classed, and gendered bodies within these urban spaces, particularly within the context of prostitution, often function to shore up historically violent and deeply racist, colonial, and patriarchal power structures. More specifically, Razack argues, the meeting between George and the men was predisposed to be a violent one not only because the men were unpredictable and prone to violence, but also *because* they met George in inner-city Regina, *because* the men were young, white, and middle-class, and *because* George was an Indigenous woman working as a street-involved sex worker. "White settlers displaced Pamela George's ancestors, confining her Saulteaux nation and others to reserves," Razack reminds us. "Pamela George's own geographies begin here. Colonization has continued apace. Forced to migrate in search of work and housing, urban Aboriginal peoples in cities like Regina quickly find themselves limited to places like the Stroll. Over-policed and incarcerated at one of the highest rates in the world, their encounters with white settlers have principally remained encounters in prostitution, policing, and the criminal justice system" ("Gendered" 126). As Razack's discussion begins to make clear, then, Canada's racist colonial history and present too often place Aboriginal persons in the bottom levels of urban social and geographical hierarchies. As a result, laws that criminalize and victimize the poor may be seen to disproportionately target urban Indigenous populations.[8]

It is well recognized that Indigenous peoples are overrepresented in socio-economically depressed inner-city populations in Canada. Jim Silver et al. note, for instance, that "Inner-city residents, and in particular Aboriginal residents, experience lower incomes, higher rates of unemployment, higher rates of poverty, a higher incidence of single parenthood and domestic violence, and lower (although rising) levels of educational attainment than is the case for cities as a whole" (16). Silver et al. further observe that "the spatial distribution of Aboriginal people in cities...parallels their spatial distribution outside urban centres, i.e., their marginalization from the mainstream of Canadian life by their historical confinement to reserves" (17). As the greatest proportion of First Nations populations in Canada lives in the western provinces, "the spatial location of more aboriginal persons within specific inner-city areas in Vancouver, Edmonton, and Saskatoon effectively reproduces the reserve system" (Silver et al. 15), a system that initially enabled "the nearly absolute geographical separation of the colonizer and the colonized" (Razack, qtd in Silver et al. 17). Such social exclusion—what Silver et al. describe as "the relative absence from the labour market and the core institutions of society...of a large proportion of the urban aboriginal population" (17)—pushes more Indigenous peoples into marginalized and sometimes illicit industries or activities. It is not particularly surprising, therefore, that what research we have in this under-investigated area indicates that Aboriginal women make up a significant portion of the street-involved and survival sex trade.[9]

However, as Silver et al. acknowledge, such socio-geographical analyses only begin to explain the high numbers of kidnapped, assaulted, raped, and brutally murdered Aboriginal women in Canada. Archetypal colonial images of conquest and domination also inform the violence that many Indigenous women experience, both inside and outside Aboriginal households. First Nations and postcolonial critics, academics, and activists regularly critique the construction in Euro-American society of the inherently "violable," or "rapable," Aboriginal body. Examining the roots of this damaging archetype for Aboriginal women, Kim Anderson writes, "In both western and Indigenous frameworks, Native women have historically been equated with the land. The Euro-constructed image of Native women, therefore, mirrors western attitudes towards the earth.

Sadly, this relationship has typically developed within the context of control, conquest, possession and exploitation" (*Life Stages* 100). Anderson also discusses in this context the emergence and subsequent disintegration of virginal "Indian princess" imagery that connects the unexplored wilderness with North American Aboriginal womanhood in colonial narratives. Perhaps one of the best-known examples of this particular mythology is the ever-popular Pocahontas myth—extrapolated and modified significantly from an actual series of events—wherein the daughter of an Indigenous chief becomes romantically involved with a white European explorer, thus facilitating a positive relationship between their two races and cultures, a relationship that in turn helps the Europeans to acclimatize to life in the Americas.

Of course, as Indigenous and postcolonial critics have long argued, such a harmonious melding of disparate cultures—of First Nations pantheism, reverence for womanhood and the natural landscape, and less sexually oppressive social structures with European monotheism, male godhead, patriarchy, and desire to possess and exploit natural resources—exists only in colonial myth. Instead, European imperialism, with its accompanying racism and fears of miscegenation, quickly modified popular understandings of Indigenous women, with the result that the eroticized violence of colonial exploitation came to be more overtly represented. Put another way, "Once Indigenous peoples began to resist colonization...Indigenous women worldwide became symbols of the troublesome colonies, and in the Americas the squaw emerged" (Anderson, *Life Stages* 102). Sarah Carter discusses the subsequent promotion of "dirty squaw" imagery in mainstream pre-confederation Canadian culture, examining how this powerful archetype facilitated the violent oppression of Aboriginal populations, and particularly Aboriginal women, during this period and beyond (160–93). Goldie observes a similar pattern of gendered racial violence in colonial representations of race and womanhood in literature. Tracing connections between imperial policies and representations of Indigenous characters in non-Aboriginal North American, Australian, and New Zealand literatures, Goldie explains, "Both maiden and squaw are manifestations of the white culture's felt temptation by the indigene and by what the indigene represents in the land" (72). As a consequence, "whether she remains the distant [virginal] image or becomes the reality of miscegenation," the squaw "must die, must become of the past, in order for the white to progress toward the future and move beyond the

limitations of his sexual—or at least romantic—temptation and achieve possession of the land" (73).[10] Portrayed as symbolic representations of the rich "new
world" landscape and as sexually available, promiscuous "primitives" whose
unfamiliar, "uncivilized" nature threatened to overwhelm, engulf, and thus
culturally maroon European men, Indigenous women became symbolic and
literal "bearers of a counter-imperial order and pose[d] a supreme threat to the
dominant culture. Symbolic and literal control over their bodies" was, therefore, "important in the [subsequent] war against Native people" (A. Smith 15).[11]
Having been othered so completely by imperial nations, Indigenous women
captured by or inhabiting areas near colonial forces—soldiers, explorers, and
settlers—often suffered especially sexualized forms of violence and mutilation at
the hands of their captors or neighbours.[12]

In Conquest: Sexual Violence and American Indian Genocide, Andrea Smith examines official historical documents in the Americas as well as other lesser-known
past and present colonial records. Smith argues that sexualized violence
against Indigenous and other racially marginalized populations, particularly
women, remains status quo in historical and contemporary contexts, while the
same acts—rape, sexual mutilation, torture, and murder—committed against
Caucasian populations, particularly white middle-class women, remain causes
of mainstream cultural concern.[13] In a recent study, Shari Huhndorf and Cheryl
Suzack emphasize that, as an integral part of colonization, "The sexualisation
of Indigenous women...worsened the effects of governmental policies and left
women particularly vulnerable to violence" ("Indigenous Feminism: Theorizing
the Issues" 5). In the context of recent events in Canada and the damning
evidence collated in Amnesty International's 2004 report, Stolen Sisters: A Human
Rights Response to Discrimination and Violence Against Indigenous Women in Canada—
their first critical analysis of Canadian officials' inadequate responses to the
Vancouver case and other cases involving more than five hundred confirmed
disappeared and murdered Indigenous women across the country (statistics
confirmed by Sisters in Spirit)—Smith and Huhndorf and Suzack's arguments
prove alarmingly accurate.

By way of an explanation for these glaring differences in mainstream
responses to violence against white and Indigenous women, Smith offers the
following analysis that, again, voices a particularly harsh truth: "Because Indian
bodies are 'dirty,'" she writes, "they are considered sexually violable and 'rapable,'

and the rape of bodies that are considered inherently impure or dirty simply does not count" (10). Smith goes on to discuss a series of disturbing accounts of sexualized violence in colonial North and South America, highlighting the ways in which thousands of rapes, sexual mutilations, and murders of Indigenous women appear common, even mundane, in the imperial age and beyond.

STREET SEX WORK AND CANADIAN CITIES
RESISTING A DANGEROUS ORDER

In the chapters that follow I analyze cultural incarnations of and responses to the discourse of disposal about prostitution in Canada, noting ways that even those who seek to prevent more kidnappings and deaths often perpetuate the linguistic, imagistic, and cultural conditions that call this violence and murder into being. Chapter 1 examines the many important ways in which "literary, artistic, and mass media discourses not only document a compensatory imagination, but also serve to record the city's dramas, what is lost in the city and what is trans-formed" (Canclini 65). The gradual disintegration of the traditional synecdochic relationship between the sex worker body and the city in this case, I argue, signals the ongoing dissolution of socio-political ties between the nation-state and its citizenry, particularly those who are already culturally and/or racially marginalized.

This chapter further establishes the theoretical and methodological framework for the book. Toward this goal, I trace the intimate relationship between serial killers and sex workers from mid-nineteenth-century London's Whitechapel, or Jack the Ripper, murders, to contemporary Vancouver's Downtown Eastside multiple Missing and Murdered Women.[14] Examining both similarities and key differences between these two oft-compared cases, the chapter explores how the contemporary Canadian city registers both the ongoing violence of colonization and the changing role of the human—or the humane—in relation to the revisions to urban imagery and infrastructure that global business often demands.

With at least fifty-nine women considered missing—twenty-six of whom are confirmed murdered, many of whom were survival sex workers, and more than half of whom were visibly Aboriginal or multiracial—from the city's socio-economically depressed Downtown Eastside, a struggle has emerged over their representation and memorialization. Anticipating the more in-depth analysis in Chapter 2, this chapter also introduces a variety of journalistic and community activist responses to the Vancouver case, exploring the ways that sex workers' synecdochic relationship to the modern city has become, in contemporary contexts, dangerously fraught.

As a number of critics have noted, reports on the Vancouver case from a variety of news media outlets from 1996 onward resonate in disturbing ways with the individualizing neoliberal project (that is, the growing cultural tendency to hold the disenfranchised responsible for their disenfranchisement). However, as a direct result of vigilant advocacy on the part of an unprecedented number of sex worker activists, First Nations leaders, feminists, journalists, and other social advocates, socio-political analyses that advocate governmental and widespread social responsibility for the plight of Vancouver's Missing Women have begun to appear. Nonetheless, ongoing efforts by certain conservative reporters—examples of which are analyzed in this chapter—to further stigmatize the women's lives, and to manufacture a culture of fear surrounding their disappearances and murders, threatens to overwhelm more sympathetic and commemorative responses to this extreme violence. Such representation encourages private citizens to fear not the structural or ideological inequalities that often lead to survival sex work, illegal drug addiction, and/or violent murder, but the repercussions of these women's supposedly irresponsible choices and lives. Under this manufactured culture of fear, the murdered women themselves become the threat, not the victims, of a particularly heinous form of violence.

My discussion in Chapter 1 draws on previous academic findings that such mainstream news sources rarely feature the views of politically active sex workers, let alone average "worker-on-the-street" concerns about conditions in particular neighbourhoods. The current exception to this choking off of sex workers' voices in the news is the interviews with sex workers that occur immediately following incidents of violence against persons involved in the sex trade. Nonetheless, when reporters and the politicians and police they routinely interview turn from bloody stories of mutilated bodies in Edmonton, Saskatoon, Regina, and Winnipeg, or haunting tales of human DNA on a farm outside Vancouver, to report the voices of those who may have known the victims, they rarely focus on the need to interrogate and take apart whore stigma.

Chapter 2 examines how sensational stories about metropolitan crime waves, about the allegedly inherent dangers of street prostitution for sex worker and non-sex worker neighbourhood residents alike, and about the criminal or pitiable nature of street-involved sex workers provide little analysis of either legislative or socio-political factors contributing to, for example, the high visibility of prostitution at this time in Canadian history, or the growing numbers of Aboriginal women and youth in the survival sex industry. The chapter thus begins with analyses of two popular images of prostitution in Canada's contemporary mainstream media, images that multiply and are reproduced in multiple news venues and mediums: "the Lone Streetwalker" and "the Missing Woman." Here I focus primarily on exemplary pieces in newspapers from major cities in western Canada, where serial murder cases involving sex workers have been in the news since the early 1990s. The chapter also briefly examines national print news on these cases, and provides close readings of sex worker representation in alternative (non-mainstream) news sources before going on to examine growing anti-prostitution activism in cities across Canada as a defining characteristic of the ongoing neoliberal renewal of the modern metropolis. This chapter thus concludes by highlighting and exploring the influences of prostitution-related legislation and stigma-laden cultural ideology on private citizens' groups, police, and other public institutions that promote increasingly exclusive visions of legitimate citizenship and of the safe streets to which such legitimate urban inhabitants are supposedly entitled.

As the discussion in the first two chapters indicates, cultural violence against sex workers takes many forms, not the least of which is the exclusion of sex trade participants from discussions regarding what is to be done about escalating violence against people who do this work. In Chapter 3, I analyze how some sex worker activist groups have begun to intervene in mainstream narrations such as those discussed in the first two chapters, providing alternative images of sex work and sex workers and promoting counter-discourses about the need to decriminalize prostitution.[15]

Whereas in Chapters 1 and 2 I analyze dominant media representations of sex workers and murdered women, I focus in Chapter 3 on sex worker activists' use of web-based media to respond to these violent and stigmatized representations. Given that sex worker activists in the period under consideration speak, through their websites, to wide but often silent communities, their cultivation of community and education through this representative forum appears to constitute absolutely central components of their community activism. Cultural texts produced by marginalized and oppressed groups such as sex worker activists are particularly rich and significant works for feminist cultural critics like myself, who are trained in the humanities.[16]

Following sex worker activism to the Internet, one of the few public spaces freely available to sex workers, I analyze the ways that groups like SWAV (Sex Workers Alliance of Vancouver), SPOC (the Toronto-based Sex Professionals of Canada), and Stella of Montreal work to reclaim—at least virtually—the space of the city, insisting on positive connections between themselves, their sex work, and the cityscape. This chapter focuses on these three sex worker activist groups in particular because their online forums include a variety of photographs of group members and events that provide powerful rebuttals to the pejorative popular representations and narrations of prostitutes and prostitution discussed in previous chapters.

Sex worker online activism is prolific, rich, and interactive. However, while this activism appears to facilitate solidarity in the pro-sex-work movement and communicates important information to sex workers who might otherwise have no access to these databanks, strictly technopolitical activism potentially caters to a self-selected audience. This chapter thus also considers both the need for hybrid on-offline activism, and the substantially different levels of political power to which pro- and anti-prostitution activists currently have access.

In relation to the current numbers of serial kidnap and murder cases involving sex workers in cities across Canada, violence that sex worker activists and other advocates convincingly link to a contemporary discourse of disposability regarding street prostitution, this unequal access to power is particularly alarming. Both Chapters 2 and 3 highlight the interplay between real, imagined, and virtual cityscapes and their citizenry, and analyze ways that technology both facilitates and curbs the dissemination of these visions.

While sex worker activists and advocates regularly call for legislative change as well as reform for welfare and social support systems, these same groups too often neglect to address, directly, the racial makeup of the survival sex industry. Responding to the overrepresentation of Aboriginal women in the most vulnerable ranks of the street-involved sex trade and among the victims in the Vancouver, Edmonton, Regina, and Winnipeg cases, Chapter 4 examines in more depth some of the intersections between Canada's violent colonial history, ongoing racist public policies, and whore stigma in contemporary culture as they converge around Indigenous women working in Canada's inner-city sex trade. This chapter also discusses the visionary activist consciousness at work in the portrayal of even the most impoverished and victimized street sex workers in Maria Campbell's *Halfbreed* and Beatrice Culleton Mosionier's *In Search of April Raintree*. This activist consciousness is particularly important to take note of in the context of both sex worker and Indigenous groups' anti-poverty and anti-violence activism because Campbell and Mosionier's texts examine, in ways that only a tiny subsection of these groups have to date, the question of agency in the sex trade for Aboriginal women specifically. This chapter thus examines whether, for an Indigenous survival sex worker, "a blowjob's better than no job" (as former SPOC spokesperson, the late Wendy Babcock once argued), whether her racial heritage as well as her poverty force her to her knees and whether, in assuming this position, she unwillingly embodies a culturally pervasive, historically damaging, and degraded stereotype of Indigenous womanhood.

Through these readings of the sex-worker body—and character—in contemporary culture and literature in Canada, remarkably contradictory visions of citizenship and the city emerge. We learn that current incarnations of liberalism and conservatism are as gendered, raced, classed, and colonial as their historical predecessors. What also becomes evident, however, is an emergent privatization of the nation-state's former right to identify, police or secure, and take deadly action against those perceived to be enemies of the state. Increasingly defined as menaces to orderly neighbourhoods, as disorderly presences whose elimination from city streets can only contribute to the collective good of corporate and other "legitimate" urban residents, street-involved sex workers have come to embody a form of dangerous criminality against which private citizens are empowered to take collective or individual—and often deadly—action.

CITY/WHORE SYNECDOCHE AND THE CASE OF VANCOUVER'S MISSING WOMEN

FROM 1975 UNTIL 2001, AT LEAST SIXTY-FIVE WOMEN—
more than half of whom were Aboriginal, and many of whom were street-involved—disappeared from Vancouver, British Columbia (Amnesty International, 2004; Pivot Legal Society, 2004, 2006). Their disappearances from within Vancouver's Downtown Eastside, a small neighbourhood that has been labelled Canada's poorest postal code,[1] were treated with little interest by Vancouver police and municipal officials for two and a half decades. After a time, and as more women disappeared seemingly without a trace, "the moniker (and group identity) 'Missing Women' was attached to these cases and has stuck, even though, for many of the missing, the name is no longer apt" (McNeill 378). In the summer of 1999, in response to increasing pressure from media, family members, friends, and other supporters of the so-called Missing Women, a joint Vancouver Police Department and RCMP task force was formed to investigate the disappearances. In February 2002, the task force charged Robert Pickton, a farmer from Port Coquitlam, BC, with the murder of seven of the Missing Women and, from February 2002 until October 2004, performed excavations on the farm grounds, examining soil samples and looking for evidence of those who had been reported missing.[2] As more DNA, bone shards, and other physical evidence of these women were found, more murder charges were laid against

1

the now infamous farmer. He has now been convicted of murdering six of the Missing Women: Marnie Frey, Georgina Papin, Brenda Wolfe, Sereena Abotsway, Mona Wilson, and Andrea Joesbury. In June 2009, the Court of Appeal for British Columbia upheld this conviction; and, because Pickton was already serving the maximum time in prison before he would be eligible for parole, crown prosecutors opted not to try him for the pending twenty additional counts of murder—a decision that is not without significant public controversy ("BC Court"). Most recently, the Supreme Court of Canada has also rejected Pickton's appeal, so his conviction and his life sentence with no chance of parole for twenty-five years stand (Greenaway and Skelton). Today, however, many of the disappeared women are yet to be accounted for. Moreover, Downtown Eastside (DTES) residents and activists report that more women—some estimate as many as twenty by 2008—had gone "missing" from the area since the start of the Missing People Trial in 2002 (Culbert, "'Nothing's Changed'").

The case of Vancouver's Missing Women, people who are often described in media reports as prostitutes and drug addicts, can be understood as a cultural text. This text brings into high relief the recurrent conflation in post-industrial Canadian culture of, on the one hand, what might be called the "character" of city streets and, on the other hand, the character of the women who work those streets. Significantly, however, this case also highlights ongoing re-evaluations of modern images of the city and sex work. Indeed, the traditional synecdochic relationship between the prostitute body and the great metropolis becomes more complicated, even precarious, as the ongoing effects of colonization and the interests of global capitalism, increasingly reflected in the policies of national governments here in the (over)developed global North, intensify urbanization across the country.

The discussion that follows examines the evolving relationship between sex workers and the city, and suggests that the emerging global city in Canada, no longer the Great Whore or "sin city" of nineteenth- and early twentieth-century moralists' imaginations, has reached a pivotal point in its development. This is a point at which global capitalism either effectively incorporates sex workers into its logic of saleable market niches or begins to express its more socially exclusive, systemically racist, and excessively security-conscious agendas more overtly and with terrifying consequences for some of the most vulnerable populations in Canada. Given the similarities between the case of Vancouver's

Missing Women and other cases involving increasing numbers of disappeared and murdered women that have recently made the news across the country,[3] I study the Vancouver case in order to interrogate the ways sex worker advocacy and right-wing concerns with so-called urban "cleanups" and policing of colonized and other marginalized populations both respond to and reflect the more alarming effects of global capitalism.

A serial killer who targets sex workers is not a new phenomenon. What is new in the case of Vancouver's Missing Women are the economic and political forces at play in contemporary urban culture. Post-industrial capitalism's utter devotion to the free market creates a potentially emancipatory space for sex workers as producers, consumers, and investors in a deregulated consumer culture. However, with increasing calls for law and order and social control, this political space becomes dangerously fraught. Consequently, traditional whore stigma persists in the practice of describing sex work as "bad business," as "bad for business," or as a particularly untenable form of social disorderliness. The modern trend toward the creation of clean, regulated Canadian cities is reflected, then, in contemporary concerns with sanitizing spaces that citizens—increasingly addressed as consumers—perceive as dangerous, and with freeing the modern metropolis from any forces that might inhibit market growth or challenge the social hierarchies perpetuated by contemporary corporate/consumer culture. Disturbingly, in this political context, and as I elaborate below, the near-eradication of the Vancouver women's bodies suggests that as the city, the traditional Great Whore, changes her image, it may now be open season on her former synecdochic relations.[4]

THEORY AND METHODOLOGY

I approach this analysis from the position of a feminist cultural and literary critic analyzing racialized, classed, and sexualized violence and its connections to historical and contemporary institutions and ideological frameworks. I am particularly concerned to pursue, therefore, a combined structuralist and post-structuralist analysis not only of individual missing and murdered women's stories (and the cases connected to them), but also of how the *telling* of these stories—about the victims, the perpetrators, the contexts, and the violent acts themselves—has the power to change or to reinforce cultural structures that produce and respond to extreme violence against marginalized women.

I begin from a position akin to that of author, satirist, and literary critic Thomas King, who argues, in his Massey Lectures, that "the truth about stories is that that's all we are" (2). In other words, the stories we tell ourselves and each other enable us to know who and what we are; stories thus become the means through which we orient ourselves in culture. There is no "me," "you," "us," or "them" without the narratives that introduce and elaborate these concepts. Such an understanding of culture (and ideology, in the Althusserian sense of the word) highlights the powerful effects of exclusive, racist, or misogynist stories—as well as the widespread cultural changes that the dissemination of less destructive narratives could enact and perpetuate. As Nigerian storyteller Ben Okri writes,

> One way or another we are living in the stories planted in us early or along the way, or we are also living the stories we planted— knowingly or unknowingly—in ourselves. We live stories that either give our life meaning or negate it with meaninglessness. If we change the stories we live by, quite possibly we change our lives. (A Way of Being Free, qtd in King 153)

In the contexts of news media and popular cultural representations, a number of critics have analyzed the ways that news-gathering and reporting constitutes a process of storytelling. Many contemporary critics consider much current news reporting to be a type of "creative non-fiction": "factual accounts— products of extensive research and reportage, combined with dramatic story-telling techniques" (Masse). Journalists must, therefore, be understood as members of a larger population of storytellers whose narratives tell us who and what we are. In so doing, they, too, "plant" stories in their readership, stories that have the potential to "either give our lives meaning or negate [them] with meaninglessness."

As Robert Entman observes, journalists engage in a process of "selecting and highlighting some facets of events or issues, and making connections among them so as to promote a particular interpretation, evaluation, and/or solution....Those frames that employ more culturally resonant terms have the greatest potential for influence." Entman continues, "They use words and images highly salient in the culture, which is to say *noticeable, understandable,* memorable, and emotionally charged" (417, emphasis in original). Elaborating on Entman's conception of media frames, James Ettema argues, "If these frames are to construct reality effectively...they must resonate with what writers and readers take to be real and important matters of life" (132). In other words, "while pre-existing beliefs constrain frames, coherent and compelling story-telling, among other activities, animates them" (Ettema 133). Ettema explains further: "Resonance is not simply there, in the world, to be appropriated from a cultural repertoire. Like salience, it must be enacted in the processes of message production. And like salience, which promotes certain moral evaluations and hinders others, resonance is a key element of journalism as a moralistic, if not always moral craft. Resonance elevates news to myth and deepens it into ritual" (134). Journalists, as Ettema stresses, are storytellers and therefore mythmakers: "Understood as the production of a textual effect, the crafting of resonance draws upon narrative structures and rhetorical strategies available to writers of both fact and fiction" (134).

This concept applies specifically to representations of stigma, as Helga Kristin Hallgrimsdottir, Rachel Phillips, and Cecilia Benoit demonstrate: "Resonant framing means using contextually available cultural tools—relevant and salient metaphors, recognizable stereotypes, and familiar story templates—to render news stories immediately accessible and satisfying to audiences. In essence, fulfilling the resonance requirement of a media frame leads authors to privilege certain kinds of characters and storylines; this not only helps us understand how stigma representations in the media come to be filled with socio-historically specific content, but also how stigmas come to be important narrative tools in media stories" (268). Especially pertinent to my own work is Hallgrimsdottir, Phillips, and Benoit's argument that "shifts in both the content and scope of stigmas as found in media narratives are...likely to reflect socio-historical changes that pertain to the social location of stigmatized subjects" (268). In his 2010 book Missing Women, Missing News: Covering Crisis in Vancouver's Downtown Eastside, human geography critic David Hugill likewise reminds us that cultural systems of domination extend beyond journalists while, at the same time, cultural phenomena are reflected in news reporting (14). In the case of Vancouver's Missing and Murdered Women, my own analysis seeks to investi-gate the ways in which such a shift as Hallgrimsdottir et al. describe might be inspired by rather than reflected in media representations.

The possibility of positive change arises from such work as Ettema's. Applying social movement theory to journalistic storytelling, Ettema argues that, like social movements, journalism has the potential to create change through the telling of alternative stories. Subtly crafting their stories to frame certain issues as salient, and to cultivate counter-hegemonic ethical responses—to violence against sex workers, for example—journalists, like other storytellers, can simultaneously access and change dangerously exclusive cultural myths and rituals.[5] In thus changing the stories their audiences "live by," journalists then have the potential "quite possibly [to] change our lives" (Okri, qtd in King 153) in ways that may begin to destigmatize sex worker populations.

Despite this potential, as research across the fields of media studies, sociology, anthropology, cultural studies, and women's and gender studies has found, mainstream news too often functions as a form of "communications ISA," or ideological state apparatus (Althusser), disseminating and reinforcing hegemonic conceptions of class, race, gender, and sexuality.[6] As Marian Meyers argues in "Crack Mothers in the News: A Narrative of Paternalistic Racism," mainstream news often "supports the status quo...as well as its role in shaping social and political policy" (195). Under such a system, poor racialized women—particularly those deemed to be sexually transgressive—are represented in ways that perpetuate their cultural exclusion and the violence that often accompanies such marginalization.

In terms of Vancouver's Missing and Murdered Women, Yasmin Jiwani and Mary Lynn Young's study of case-related print news between 2001 and 2006 analyzes the "frames used by the mainstream media in covering the issue, particularly how hegemonic discourses about Aboriginality and prostitution play out within the larger framework of reporting on violence against women" (896). My own research of case-related print news in Canada also begins with reports written in 2001, the year prior to the first charges laid by the Missing Women Taskforce, and concludes with the commencement of the Missing People Trial in January 2007. I examine this body of case-related print news, discussing in particular reports in the *Vancouver Sun*, the *Province*, the *Globe and Mail*, *National Post*, *Ottawa Citizen*, and additional Canadian Press archives from the same years, as well as a wider array of local responses to this and other similar cases during this period.[7] While my findings parallel some of Jiwani and Young's findings regarding media discourses of sensationalism and violence in relation to the "larger framework of reporting on violence against women," my analysis is more immediately concerned with mediated representations of and responses to urban street-involved sex work, especially those members of this marginalized industry who are subjected to extreme violence. Such narrations of violence indeed tell an imagined public how to respond (or not) to these events, and how they—and we—are implicated (or not) in the same.

I am also concerned with understanding such contemporary representations and responses within the contexts of traditions of anti-prostitution actions and storytelling in England and her former colonies. I thus analyze in this chapter historical and contemporary hegemonic and discursive frameworks that produce and respond to extreme violence against street-involved sex workers, focusing in particular on the (dis)connections between the Whitechapel murders (or Jack the Ripper case) in Victorian England and the case of Vancouver's Missing and Murdered Women. While cultural representations of and responses to the serial murder of women believed to be inner-city sex workers have changed very little in the last 120 years, changing attitudes toward the city have, I find, resulted in subtle but significant changes in the ways that urban street-involved sex workers are understood.

Representations of Vancouver's Missing Women most often locate them very specifically in the city's Downtown Eastside, a geographical space that "includes the poorest census tract in Canada, and is the site of high concentrations of drug addiction, prostitution, HIV/AIDS and Hepatitis B" (Pratt 1058). Such representations mark the women as inhabitants of what Geraldine Pratt refers to as a "zone of exception" (1058), an urban space constructed hegemonically as a degenerate zone (Razack, "Gendered" 127). Labelling the women as Downtown Eastside inhabitants, then, these representations construct them in specifically classed terms. In this way, the violence they suffer here is simultaneously normalized (and thus rendered invisible) and sensationalized (and thus rendered hypervisible). The women's violent fates in this way become both public spectacle and moral object lessons for a wider Canadian public.

Moreover, in its repeated focus on the disappeared women as urban street prostitutes and drug addicts, dominant print media coverage of Vancouver's Missing Women constructs the victims as criminals who are classed, racialized, and of poor moral character. As such, the women become what Pratt understands as a gendered and racialized form of "bare life": existing on the abandoned margins of contemporary neoliberal political structures, joining a population that, in Giorgio Agamben's words, "somehow cannot be integrated into the political system" (qtd in Pratt 1054). Yet this abandoned population remains important, as their fate makes clear what citizens must not be or do if they wish to occupy the political centre, with all of the state rights and protections that accompany such a symbolic and literal position.[8]

Although not all of Vancouver's Missing Women were sex workers, grouped together under this moniker, all of the women are assumed to have been similarly involved in the street-involved or survival sex trade. As a result, much of the ongoing controversy over the case reiterates debates about prostitution that have played out in a number of serial murder cases involving sex worker victims over the past two centuries in Britain and North America. In this chapter I argue that the similarities and differences between this and previous serial killer cases are of unprecedented importance at this time. Through analysis of exemplary representations of Vancouver's missing and murdered women, I examine competing portrayals of these people. Such a discussion exposes the sinister underpinnings of mainstream socio-political responses to sex work as a public or social issue, and highlights the immense cultural resistance sex workers and their allies face today as they struggle to destigmatize prostitution and thus to prevent the extreme violence to which members of this industry—as well as those who are assumed to be sex workers—are subjected.

RESISTING DOMINANT REPRESENTATIONS

Community-based, province-wide, and nation-wide efforts to remember the Missing Women, to demand justice in the name of the Missing, and to reconceptualize the place of sex work and sex workers in contemporary urban Canada have grown out of the Vancouver case. Numerous material and virtual memorials as well as sociological, criminological, cultural, and some exceptional journalistic analyses[9] remember the Missing Women as valuable members of local communities, work to find solutions to the socio-economic conditions that lead women into the survival sex trade, and attempt to counter grisly, sensationalist media reports and prejudiced public responses to sex work in general and to this case in particular. Activists fight against whore stigma within their own ranks and in wider society, struggling to foreground the missing and murdered women's humanity, emphasizing the circumstances of their lives and the relationships the women had both with and as caring friends, sisters, daughters, and mothers.

The most politically engaged of such initiatives address the racist component of the whore stigma that led to the murders of too many of Vancouver's women. Given that the majority of the missing and murdered women in Vancouver as well as those in Edmonton, Saskatoon, and Winnipeg are Aboriginal or mixed-race, their kidnap and murder cases collectively underline the sexual exploitation and socio-political exclusion of Indigenous women that mark the effects of historical and ongoing colonization. In March 2004, the Native Women's Association of Canada (NWAC) launched their "Sisters in Spirit" research campaign. In November 2005, Sisters in Spirit (SIS) secured federal funding to work in concert with the Canadian government and other Indigenous women's organizations to "conduct research and raise awareness of the alarmingly high rates of violence against Aboriginal women and girls in Canada." Sisters in Spirit also set out "to increase public knowledge and understanding at a national level of the impact of violence against Aboriginal women, often leading to their disappearance and death" (NWAC, "Sisters in Spirit"). Likewise emphasizing federal responsibility for what they estimate to be more than five hundred unsolved missing and murdered Aboriginal women cases in Canada over the past two decades alone, Amnesty International (AI), in their October 2004 report, *Stolen Sisters: A Human Rights Response to Discrimination and Violence Against Indigenous Women in Canada*, indicts and shames the Canadian government for ignoring these cultural realities. Noting the continued "absence of accurate national statistics" regarding the ethnicity of victims of such extreme violence—and, again, advocating further government-led initiatives to prevent the same[10]—AI cites NWAC/SIS's list of missing and murdered Indigenous women in Canada in their 2009 report, *No More Stolen Sisters: The Need for a Comprehensive Response to Discrimination and Violence Against Indigenous Women in Canada*. "As of July 2009," the report reads, "the list included more than 520 women who have gone missing or been murdered in the last three decades" (1). As I revise this chapter once more, NWAC has recorded closer to six hundred missing or murdered Indigenous women and girls, most of whom were based in urban centres in Canada's western provinces (*What Their Stories Tell Us* 25–26).

As I discuss in more detail in Chapter 4, Sisters in Spirit and many of the Aboriginal women's agencies with which NWAC partners address the plight of

Indigenous women in prostitution via analyses of colonization, racialized sexu-alized violence, spiritual and economic impoverishment, and urban marginaliza-tion. AI provides a similarly intersectional sociocultural analysis, emphasizing that "the isolation and social marginalization that increases the risk of violence faced by women in the sex trade is often particularly acute for Indigenous women" (*Stolen Sisters*). Both AI's 2004 and 2009 reports highlight "The role of racism and sexism in compounding the threat to Indigenous women in the sex trade" (*Stolen Sisters*). Both reports also include comments by Justice David Wright, who, at the 1996 trial of John Martin Crawford for the 1992 murders in Saskatchewan of Eva Taysup, Shelley Napope, and Calinda Waterhen (all of whom were Indigenous women), observed the following: "The man responsible for the killings saw the victims as vulnerable for four reasons: one, they were young; second, they were women; third, they were native [*sic*]; and fourth, they were prostitutes. They were persons separated from the community and their fami-lies. The accused treated them with contempt, brutality; he terrorized them and ultimately he killed them. He seemed determined to destroy every vestige of their humanity" (*No More 2*).

Nevertheless, despite efforts like these to foreground the plethora of connections between Aboriginal women and urban poverty and violence, the plight of Indigenous women in the survival sex trade remains under-analyzed in many contexts. One of the most visible of these contexts is mainstream print news media. As I discuss in Chapter 2, print media responses to Vancouver's Missing Women case rarely stray from two archetypal tropes: the Missing Woman and the Lone Streetwalker.[11] Such representations regularly examine real or perceived breaking points between individual Missing Women and their families—often indicating that a woman's illegal addiction, her move into the street-involved sex trade, or both, precipitated such breaks. These reports rarely analyze larger historical and cultural structures that push so many women, Indigenous or otherwise, into poverty and survival sex work.

Despite their under-representation in print news, as the NWAC and AI reports make clear, significant efforts to combat the many desperate circum-stances faced by street-involved Indigenous and non-Indigenous women have gained *some* credibility since the Vancouver case began to make headlines. While NWAC launched Sisters in Spirit, others continued the work they had done for years in this area of the city. For example, the Vancouver-based PACE Society and the now-defunct PEERS (the Prostitutes' Empowerment, Education and Resource Society) Vancouver,[12] either are or were advocacy, research, and outreach groups established by current or former sex workers and community supporters; as more and more of their community members were taken from Vancouver streets, these organizations increased their efforts and garnered further support and legitimacy in their community as they worked to prevent more tragedies like the Vancouver case. PEERS Vancouver in particular tried to address the needs of Aboriginal sex workers in the city. As the late Jannit Rabinovitch, one of PEERS' founders, wrote in 2003, "acknowledging unique needs [of Indigenous women and girls], PEERS Board and staff hired a First Nations survivor (or former survival sex worker) to coordinate the development of community workshops that highlight the experiences of Aboriginal women in prostitution" (251).

However, while groups like PACE and PEERS—whose mandates extend beyond the Vancouver case—have worked to eliminate survival sex work and to help the most vulnerable members of the street-involved sex trade, the differences in the groups' mandates poignantly illustrate the pervasiveness of ongoing popular debates about the rights and wrongs of prostitution. For example, PEERS, a non-profit organization that received funding from the federal and British Columbian governments, described themselves as "dedicated to the empowerment, education and support of sex workers." The group's mandate further states that the organization "respects those involved in the sex industry and works to improve their safety and working conditions" (PEERS Vancouver). Their numerous "exit strategy" programs, however, indicate that PEERS directed a significant portion of its resources toward decreasing sex industry populations.

Such exit strategies, complete with retraining opportunities, drug rehabilitation programs, peer support, and counselling are indeed valuable community programs for sex workers. Nevertheless, such a mandate risks dividing PEERS from other groups like the PACE Society whose members work to "promote safer working conditions" and who "envision a future where all Sex Workers...may enjoy the same rights as all other Canadians" ("About Us"). PACE has offered on-street, all-night outreach programs, counselling, legal support, and a host of other invaluable services—including exit strategies—for sex workers. But their mission statement more clearly refutes whore stigma; and programs like their cookbook for people living with Hepatitis C, their "Tips" pamphlet for those considering involvement as subjects in community or academic studies, and their "Confrontation Management" project for workers involved in "high risk environments" demonstrate the Society's dedication to making sex workers' lives and working conditions better ("Violence Prevention").

CONTAINING THE MURDER VICTIMS

Even as many groups and individuals struggle to combat the conditions that place women in the survival sex industry at high risk of violence, there is a significant cultural push to contain the effects of such consciousness-raising efforts and to defend and reaffirm state policies that criminalize sex workers and individualize the Missing Women's misfortunes. Reports on the Vancouver case from a variety of news media outlets from 2001 onward resonate in disturbing ways with the individualizing neoliberal cultural project, or the growing cultural tendency to hold the disenfranchised responsible for their disenfranchisement. Many journalists' portrayals of the Missing Women also reflect and reinforce neoconservative concerns with the control, regulation, and criminalization of the urban poor.

In addition, the majority of such representations focus on the Missing Women's families and friends, not the Missing Women themselves. To be sure, some of these family members and friends do try to contextualize the women's lives in important ways. For example, in the days leading up to the release of Métis filmmaker Christine Walsh's critically acclaimed documentary Finding Dawn in 2006, a number of print media sources carried stories in which family members of Missing Women tried to understand how their mothers, sisters, or daughters ended up on the streets of the DTES. In addition, a number of reports from 2002 onward include statements from Sto:lo leader Ernie Crey, whose sister Dawn Crey's story was among those featured in Walsh's documentary.[13] Ernie Crey's comments often focus on current and historical structural hierarchies that place Aboriginal people, especially Aboriginal women, at risk of violence in Canada.[14] However, concern for the women and the connections between colonization and racialized misogynist violence is restricted, even in representations like these. In such narratives, "signifiers of Aboriginality"—such as references to Crey's national affiliation, for example, or to other Indigenous communities and cultural rituals—"fix" the Missing Women's identities, constructing them as other or abject (Jiwani and Young 910). "As fixed entities, the reasons underlying" the women's "migration to the urban core of the Downtown Eastside remained unexplored and taken for granted" (Jiwani and Young 910). With the exception of Dawn Crey, for example, no other Missing Aboriginal Woman is regularly identified in mainstream sources via her national affiliation. Providing fuller, more nuanced information about a Missing Woman's identity offers the possibility of moving beyond "signifiers of Aboriginality" that assume sameness; it could, for example, lead to an exploration of colonization's direct effects on specific First Nations, or to an examination of urban versus rural reserve systems.

Reports during this period are more likely to examine or condemn police indifference to violence against Aboriginal women than to explore connections between such indifference and the violence of colonization. Moreover, the majority of print news from this period seems primarily to be concerned with reporting what sensational bits of the cases can be gleaned from the trial, with cataloguing trial procedures and participants' facial expressions (particularly Pickton's), or with reiterating families' grief after taking in details of their loved ones' grisly deaths.

As noted above, with few exceptions, much of the print news between 2001 and 2006 includes at least a sentence or two about the Missing Women's involvement in drug addiction and street-involved sex work. Such reports also regularly include statements from family members who express regret about victims' residing in the DTES, and claim to have little knowledge of their sisters', daughters', or mothers' activities in this area. Statements such as the following are customary and were, initially, rarely followed by any discussion of socio-economic factors that may have contributed to the women's circumstances before they disappeared. Noting Campbell River woman Marnie Frey's drug addiction,[15] one report explains that, "before long, Marnie was headed to Vancouver's Downtown Eastside, where she got caught in the cycle of working the streets to support her addiction." In a similar report, "She was the out-of-town girl going to Vancouver," says Rick Frey, Marni Frey's father. "Well, God, they are so vulnerable down there" ("Missing Women's Families Remember"). Erin McGrath, whose sister, Leigh Miner[16] (unnamed in this report), has been missing since 1994, remarks, "My sister had a drug problem. We just didn't realize how bad it was and when she went to live in Vancouver we didn't realize that there was a place like east Vancouver" (Bains and Joyce).

One of the more heavy-handed family-focused reports includes an inter-view with Marilyn Kraft, mother of Cynthia (Cindy) Feliks, who was last seen in

December 1997 and whose DNA was found on Pickton's farm in 2002. "Cindy's family and friends always held the belief that she was too street smart to be lured into anything too dangerous," *Globe and Mail* reporter Petti Fong tells us. "But their confidence faded when more time passed and no one heard anything. In 1997, Ms. Kraft reported her daughter as missing." Fong's 2006 story, entitled "Pictures Provide the Clues to a Daughter's Lost Life," begins by recording Ms. Kraft's belief that with her knowledge of Feliks's fate, she can see "things that were slightly off" about her daughter in childhood and adolescence. These things apparently include, "the rip in a stocking, running like a scar down one leg. The flash of a black slip beneath a pink taffeta dress, unnoticed because Cindy was laughing so hard. The one uncontrollable lock falling out of place in an immaculately styled hairdo." Such moralistic re-evaluations search out signs of a gendered disorderliness. Feliks thus becomes a child and then a teen whose unrestrained laughter is read, in retrospect, as evidence of a tragic character flaw; in this reading, Feliks cannot, even in childhood, adhere to (conservative) middle-class codes of feminine modesty and social decorum. And a mother finds in her child's history hints of the sexual and social transgressor that the child, in her view, became.

Fong's report notes briefly that Kraft is Feliks's stepmother, but that she "raised Cindy and three other stepchildren as a single mom after kicking out the children's abusive father." Fong thus hits a number of salient notes for readers, artfully providing us with the material we need to piece together the story Fong is *not* telling. The larger mythological framework, against which this form of fallen woman/beautiful wild-child-who-never-grows-up narrative resonates, enables Fong to offer a few basic pieces of information; we readers know how to fill in the rest of the story for ourselves. And with the careful distancing of Kraft from Feliks—via her role as heartbroken stepmother to a damaged child—Cindy Feliks becomes the force to be reckoned with in this tragic tale.

The narrative proceeds to describe Feliks as a prostitute and drug addict for whom "a child and husband weren't anchors"; thus the gendered middle-class morality informing this story becomes even more overt. Despite evidence of her violent death, Feliks is represented as largely responsible for her tragic fate. "She always thought she could take care of herself. We thought she could too, even during the bad times," Kraft is quoted as saying. "When we heard about all that stuff going on at the farm," she continues, "we told ourselves she wouldn't go out there and leave herself that wide open." The fact that Fong's narrative includes no conversations with Feliks's Vancouver friends—many of whom, the report tells us, called Kraft repeatedly looking for her daughter following her disappearance—provides some indication of the *Globe and Mail* reporter's ideological position in relation to the account she provides. But Fong implicates us, her readers, in the overt moralism of this tale. We have, after all, participated in its ritualistic construction; we have recognized its themes; and we have drawn on dominant ideological frameworks in order to understand what is being communicated.

In these and many other print news stories about the lives and deaths of Vancouver's Missing Women, key social problems are similarly translated into individual pathologies of "fallen women," archetypal storylines wherein a once "good girl" ends up living "down and out" in a "bad" neighbourhood, or tales of personal immorality facilitated by illegal addictions. In these and numerous reports like them, the DTES becomes a symbol of the women's problems, of the families' losses, and of death. Expressing their shock and dismay regarding their murdered family members' failures—symbolized, in so many accounts, by a woman's residency in the alien DTES neighbourhood, the families in these representations become the voices of a legitimate citizenry. In some ways, Rick Frey, Erin McGrath, Marilyn Kraft, and others speak for all families of the victims, and for non-sex worker citizens everywhere, in expressing their disappointment and moral outrage at being forced to acknowledge this other zone of existence—and in exemplifying the pathos that seems inevitably to accompany this awareness.

Articles like these also note families' distress over police failure to keep them informed. As PACE spokespeople, as well as Ernie Crey, Simon Fraser University criminologist John Lowman, writer and community activist Maggie de Vries (author of the 2003 memoir *Missing Sarah: A Vancouver Woman Remembers Her Sister*[17]), and numerous others have argued before and since, the initial refusal by the Vancouver Police Department (VPD) to investigate the increasing numbers of missing women is evidence of systemic cultural prejudice against sex workers, especially the poorest, and the most racially marginalized populations within this industry. However, politicians at all levels of government, as well as police and right-wing pundits, regularly ignore such scrutiny of police indifference to crimes against survival and other sex workers. Too many suggest instead that increased police presence and continued criminalization of prostitution (i.e., efforts to eradicate prostitution entirely) will prevent future serial killers from finding victims in unofficial red-light districts like the DTES.

For example, of the eleven stories about Vancouver's Missing Women from a variety of key Canadian news sources reporting on February 2, 2002, shortly after the task force revealed that they were searching the Port Coquitlam farm, only one story by Steve Mertl of the Canadian Press notes the Aboriginality of the majority of the Missing Women or contains any kind of critical analysis of this and other factors influencing either the lives or the deaths of the missing. Mertl's article is also unique in quoting from an interview with John Lowman, who suggests, "Even if recent developments help break the case...there is plenty of blame to go around the lengthening list of missing women." Lowman aims high, Mertl reports, when he "points a finger at former federal justice minister Anne McLellan, who he says opposed the reform of laws governing prostitution, keeping street hookers [sic] isolated and vulnerable to predators...What we've done is force them into more and more secluded locations," Lowman says. "The women who are out on the street are often the ones who are in the most dire circumstances on the Downtown East Side" (qtd in Mertl). But even Mertl's article sugarcoats Lowman's indictment of political and cultural forces by quoting him only selectively.

In "Courting Death," part of a series on sex work and Vancouver's Missing Women by Ottawa Citizen reporter Dan Gardner, published in June 2002, Gardner includes Lowman's more comprehensive cultural indictment: "The law is killing people," he's quoted as saying here. Gardner explains, "Mr. Lowman [sic], a criminologist at Simon Fraser University and one of Canada's leading experts on prostitution, believes that stings such as those run by the Vancouver police, and other forms of law enforcement, set in motion a chain reaction. At the end of that chain, says Mr. Lowman, is the mass murder of prostitutes." In May 2003, Vancouver Sun reporter Doug Ward interviews Lowman and, like Gardner, communicates the crux of Lowman's message: "The rhetoric of the '80s and early '90s was: 'We'll get rid of the prostitutes.' Lowman said public policy has sidestepped the crucial issue of where and under what conditions prostitutes can meet their customers. Because we haven't answered that question, over 100 women are dead. The prostitution laws have created a 'discourse of disposal' in which prostitutes, according to Lowman, were seen as a public nuisance to be moved from one neighbourhood to another. 'Their physical marginalization occurred as police used the communicating law in combination with other harassment laws to displace prostitutes out of residential areas into darkly lit industrial back streets'" ("Morality"). Relatively rare in mainstream arenas in 2002, critiques like Lowman's—available in articles like these as well as Lowman's comprehensive body of peer-reviewed research on the topic of prostitution law[18]—provide pivotal analyses of the increasingly fraught relationship between street-involved sex trade populations, their urban communities, and the streets where they live and work.

However, laws and law enforcers are not the only ones who have been criticized for their handling of this situation. In her comprehensive 2002 analysis, "Re-Mediating the Spaces of Reality Television: *America's Most Wanted* and the Case of Vancouver's Missing Women," critic Beverley A. Pitman tracks the changes in media representations of local responses to the Vancouver women's disappearances. Pitman argues that as coverage shifted in 1998 and 1999 from local media to Fox TV's *America's Most Wanted* (*AMW*) and back again, the city-wide community initially created as a result of widespread public condemnation of police and city council's mishandling of these cases was effectively dispersed. *AMW*'s portrayal of the case is, while characteristically melodramatic, consistent with current journalistic trends, juxtaposing images of popular Vancouver tourist sites with dark cityscapes through which move shadowy DTES residents. The episode also includes a "re-enactment" of one woman's supposed abduction that replaces a Mexican/ Native woman with a blonde white woman.[19] Such a portrayal effectively erases racial differences, reinscribes class hierarchies the local community had worked hard to overcome, and functions as a "static endorsement of a white North American status quo" (Pitman 170).

Pitman further argues that this portrayal carried over into local media coverage of the case after the *AMW* episode aired. Prior to the show's airing, "For a period of three or four months," Pitman writes,

> Divisions between the two parts of the city—the Downtown East
> Side [sic] and the rest—which police practices helped to produce,
> were overcome. They were transcended by the representational
> work of the women's supporters, Downtown East Side activists,
> and local newspaper columnists, and they were transcended, too,

by Vancouverites' emotional and moral response to the women's families and friends. In the process, an uncommon kind of community was created.

By the Spring of 1999, members of the public were speaking out against the mayor's and the police department's handling of the disappearances. On 12 May, a march attended by more than four hundred people was held in the Downtown East Side. Placards carried by supporters...declared, "Prostitutes are not disposable!" Hundreds listened to family and friends speak of lost ones, and demanded that the mayor launch a search into the disappearances. (176)[20]

Pitman also notes that this community of concerned citizens subsequently convinced the mayor's office to offer a financial reward for information pertaining to any of the Missing Women or their abductor(s)/murderer(s). Also in response to community pressure, then-mayor Philip Owen and the VPD finally agreed to print and distribute a poster including photographs of the then thirty-one Missing Women to increase awareness of and extend the search for information regarding this case (see Appendix 2). After contributing $70,000 to the reward offered, the province's attorney general spoke to the *Vancouver Sun*, advocating a community where "sex workers are treated with the respect due all citizens" (qtd in Pitman 176). The community that was displaced when local media took up coverage after AMW's episode, Pitman argues, was a community "inclusive of sex workers," which "sought to dismantle status-quo community policing as it related to sex workers, and establish a safe place for sex work" (181).

One of the many criticisms Pitman levies against AMW and subsequent portrayals of the case by news agencies concerns the privileging of the grief of the Missing Women's families, which Pitman sees as effectively erasing "other forms of social belonging" to which the local community, in contrast, had given credence. Cultural theorist Amber Dean agrees, suggesting that such foregrounding of familial concerns has become a disturbing (though perhaps necessary) posthumous cultural recovery project. Drawing on Judith Butler's exploration in *Precarious Life* of "how certain forms of grief become nationally recognized and amplified, whereas other losses become unthinkable and ungrievable" (xiv–xv), Dean highlights ways that popular memorializations of the Missing Women risk "reconstituting a binary of grievable/ungrievable victims" ("'Just Another Day'" 2). She thus explores ways in which "such a reconstitution of this binary" is "in some instances brought about by mourners' (understandable) efforts to 'humanize' the missing and murdered women as a method of reconstituting their grievability" ("'Just Another Day'" 2). As Dean observes, connecting the Missing Women to their families—estrangements between victims and family members notwithstanding—is a key step in this "humanization" process. Foregrounding the women's roles as daughters, sisters, and mothers, the women's advocates offer the wider Canadian public recognizable images of the victims with whom they may then more easily identify. Significantly, this (re)connection of family members has the effect of blurring, even effacing, the other, non-familial relationships and everyday circumstances that made up the women's lives in the DTES.

Such consistent blurring of reality, while effective in some ways, in others highlights all the more clearly the marginalization of DTES residents in contemporary culture. Print media coverage between 2001 and 2006 would seem to continue to displace the cross-neighbourhood activist community Pitman, de Vries, and others describe, and to endorse a classed and raced status quo. Despite efforts by family and friends—and some local reporters—to recuperate and memorialize the women, the majority of news reports during this period refer to the Missing Women as prostitutes and drug addicts who disappeared from Vancouver's "skid row" (Armstrong, "Police Alter" A3), or Downtown Eastside, an area also described as "seedy" (Babbage), "seamy" (Gill; Saunders), "sordid" ("BC Police Search"), and "drug-riddled" (Joyce), implying that the women's families miss them in spite of their unfortunate lives and associations. Such labels also highlight the individual or personal choices of the Missing Women, always speaking to their character flaws rather than addressing such issues as colonization, evaporating social safety nets, or jobless industrial towns, forces that contribute significantly to the ranks of the urban poor as well as the survival sex trade. These representations also set the women's families up as the injured parties in these kidnap and murder cases, their grief consistently qualified by assertions that the Missing Women lived very different lives from the rest of their families. Through this process the DTES comes to signify this difference in social standing.

Perhaps as a result of the publication ban during the Missing People Trial, and certainly as a result of vigilant advocacy on the part of an unprecedented number of sex worker activists, First Nations groups, feminists, and other advocates, socio-political analyses that advocate governmental and widespread social responsibility for the plight of Vancouver's Missing Women and for those currently involved in survival sex work began to reappear, particularly in the *Vancouver Sun*, even as sensational grisly details were leaked to the public in a variety of print news venues. As Jiwani and Young observe, "when the sensationalistic bits and pieces revealed in the courtroom cannot be communicated at large, or when the results of the investigation are shrouded in secrecy... this news hole provided an opportunity for added and more critical coverage of public policy related to the murdered and missing women, stereotypes, the criminal justice system, and 'Aboriginality'" (910). Whatever the impetus behind its appearance, however, such coverage constitutes a welcome change from narratives that stigmatize Missing Women's lives.

Especially insidious are stigmatizing narratives by journalists and news sources that manufacture a culture of fear surrounding the disappearances and murders of Missing Women, as this overwhelms sympathetic responses to the women's plight. Private citizens are encouraged to fear not the social circumstances that lead to survival sex work or drug addiction, and violent death, but the repercussions of these women's supposedly irresponsible choices and lives. Under this manufactured culture of fear the murdered women themselves become the threat, not the victims of a particularly heinous form of violence.

"Individual misfortune," Henry Giroux observes, "like democracy itself, is now viewed as either excessive or in need of radical containment. The media, largely consolidated through corporate power, routinely provide a platform for high-profile right-wing pundits and politicians to remind us of how degenerate the poor have become to reinforce the central neoliberal tenet that all problems are private rather than social in nature" (xviii). Analyses like Giroux's of the culturally restrictive dangers of neoliberalism become all the more disturbing in light of, for example, the front-page headline and accompanying full-page colour photograph of the (then) alleged murderer in the October 29, 2004 edition of the *Vancouver Sun*. Under the banner "Ottawa Rates Health Risk from Human Remains in Farm Meat," *Sun* reporter Larry Pynn's article begins, "A Health Canada study commissioned by RCMP investigating alleged serial killer

Robert Pickton has calculated the odds of contracting a disease from eating pork products contaminated with human remains from the accused's Port Coquitlam pig farm."[21]

Pynn's article is one in a collection of similarly themed narratives that emerged in 2004 news coverage of the Missing Women case. Jiwani and Young discuss the "tainted meat" reportage as evidence of "the insertion of a new [media] frame—this time one of horror" (908). They are correct, of course, but a closer analysis of the ways that language and ideology combine in one such narrative further illustrate why this kind of discursive violence becomes salient, how it resonates for an imagined public, and thus implicates its readers in its discursive violence against already-murdered women. For example, the second paragraph of Pynn's "health risk" article tells readers that the risk of disease from infected pork is "negligible," that in fact there is more chance of infection from recurrent unsanitary food handling conditions on the farm than from possible ingestion of meat from animals fed with human remains. At this point the report, while predictably trading on the horrific details of the murder case, could effectively refocus public fears on the issue of meat-handling practices. Instead of pursuing this line of thought, however, Pynn turns again to the human remains in his next sentence. Here he quotes Dr. Tony Giulivi, the author of the seven-page Health Canada study, who states, "This poses no known risk to the food supply. The viruses...do not cross the species barrier and would be inactivated by the pig digestive system." Pynn then goes on to "remember" fears of infection after RCMP investigators' initial announcement more than a year before that people who had eaten pork from the Port Coquitlam farm could be at risk.

With repeated references to human remains and prostitution, Pynn lists the diseases from which some of the murdered women may have suffered; and, in a section entitled "Assessing Risk," he lists the exact negligible percentages that measure likelihood of contracting these illnesses through tainted meat. In addition, Pynn repeatedly invokes the authority of public institutions like the RCMP, Health Canada, and the medical profession. These public authorities and lists of statistics from the Health Canada report give the article a tone of scientific precision and objectivity. Pynn appears to provide only the facts most relevant to his headline; his story is seemingly unpadded by emotive or evaluative commentary about the women or their lives. But, of course, the facts he chooses tell their own emotionally volatile and inherently ideological story about the Missing Women and about sex work.

Pynn's article works to shift public concern away from the tragic circumstances of the murdered women's deaths, instead fuelling public fears about the diseases from which the women may have suffered—diseases like HIV/AIDS and Hepatitis C that are, rightly or wrongly, traditionally associated with sex work and injection drug use. These women, even in death, threaten to infect public social structures and to endanger public health. In short, Pynn's article undercuts the public platforms of Davis, Lowman, de Vries, and the murdered women's many other advocates who would highlight and change the legislative and socio-economic conditions that produce such cultural and material tragedies. Pynn's quasi-objectivity and pseudo-science instead "remind us of how degenerate the poor have become" (Giroux xviii) and frame their fate as individually, not socially and politically produced.

Like AMW's treatment of the case of Vancouver's Missing Women, then, articles like Pynn's resonate in such a way as to radically contain knowledge of the women's misfortunes, effectively limiting potential democratic change as well as anti-racist and pro-sex-work activism inspired by the women's plight. In following years, journalistic responses to the Missing People Trial—see, for example, Robert Matas's January 28, 2006 piece in the *Globe and Mail*, "Pickton Set to Plead Not Guilty Monday"; or Lori Culbert and Neal Hall's series about the Pickton murders (see, for instance, "Family, Friends Attend Court Opening") in the *Vancouver Sun*—while often more nuanced, continue to encourage such understandings of the Missing Women, cultivating public memory of pork contaminated with human remains. In discourse like this, the women's lives and their attendant problems become public issues that are not illustrative of the effects of a widespread stigmatization of those who work in the sex industry. These issues are not the result of a shrinking social safety net, ongoing colonization and its attendant racial oppression and exclusion, or any other systemic contemporary problem. Instead the issue becomes the public need for protection: the law-abiding public is urged to protect themselves and to desire state protection from these bad women and their bad choices. These kinds of representations of sex work and sex workers facilitate increased policing of sex workers' lives and encourage more talk of prostitution as a social pestilence.

The women Pynn describes have made terrible choices that have resulted in their contracting communicable illnesses and have ultimately gotten themselves killed and disposed of in one way or another on a farm where pigs were housed. Represented in this way, these women require the wider Vancouver public to face the consequences of the women's choices. As public contaminants, the murdered women are constructed as bare life, or as abject, in the Kristevan sense of this term—that is, they are completely recognizable as humans, and yet entirely repugnant as the part of humanity human beings most wish to deny (3). Or, following Butler's adaptation of Julia Kristeva's concept (an adaptation that brings us closer to Pratt's gendered and racialized understanding of Agamben's bare life), they "fall outside the human, indeed, constitute the domain of the dehumanized and the abject against which the human itself is constituted" (Butler, *Gender Trouble* 142).

Others besides myself have objected to Pynn's portrayal of the murdered women. Maggie de Vries angrily responded in a special section of the *Vancouver Sun* on November 2, 2004, four days after his article appeared. Taking issue with Pynn's remembering of public fears of contamination, de Vries accuses Pynn of writing such fears into recent history in order to promote an exclusionary socio-political agenda. As de Vries observes, "That is fear- and horror-mongering at its worst.... The piece says that the public is not at risk of disease. I was not aware that the public was afraid it was at risk." She then points out some key implications of Pynn's choices: "The story mentions that many of the women who were murdered had diseases. It is bad enough that sex workers are often blamed for the spread of disease when they are alive. (Actually, I believe that more risks are taken during casual sex than during transactions between clients and sex workers unless clients refuse to use a condom.)[22] Now sex workers are to be blamed for spreading disease even after they are dead, which is preposterous. And such a notion reduces my sister and others to bits of disease-riddled flesh" ("Harm"). Unlike Pynn's report, de Vries's response, while significant and newsworthy, is also socially responsible and usefully critical—but it was not headline news. Her indictment of the paper thus both highlights news media's adherence to the "if it bleeds, it leads" dictum (PBS) and magnifies the ways in which Pynn's creative non-fiction does more than simply adhere to sensational journalistic conventions. Those of us who seek to understand the impact of such public storytelling are left to wonder, in this case, whose version of events is or was more influential to paper readership.

Alongside the damaging influences of creative efforts to reimagine or write over the lives of the missing people (Culbert, "Sketches"), or to find and ruminate over their abject remains (Pynn), there is a more symbolic and potentially powerful interpretation of the word *missing* available in the VPD's initial assertion that they could not look for missing people if there was no physical evidence of their disappearance. Without the police focus on searching city streets or digging through dirt, without the very literal search for missing bodies, advocates could still speak to the lost nature of Vancouver's Missing Women.

In response to the former mayor's initial refusal to offer a reward for information about Vancouver's Missing Women because his administration was not financing "a location service for hookers" (qtd in Phillips), Maggie de Vries describes the women's supporters' frustration as akin to "screaming into a void" (qtd in Phillips). Indeed, faced with these official dismissals of their concern for the growing number of women disappearing from the DTES, the women's friends and families recognized an overarching moral judgement of the women they missed: culturally, these women did not matter; literally, they were (almost) not matter anymore. Already abandoned by the ranks of Canada's legitimate citizenry, they were constructed as bare life, criminal, abject, marginal, already largely invisible, and lost. Any search for these missing women was a waste of taxpayers' money and police time: why search for those who are always, already lost? And as the sluggish investigation progressed, the absence of a body count remained reason enough for Mayor Owen and other municipal officials to downplay the seriousness of the case and thus to endanger more women and facilitate more deaths.

SEX WORKERS AND THE CITY
TRADITIONAL VIOLENCE

Even the briefest historical survey illustrates that these reactions to the missing bodies of Vancouver's murdered women are perhaps best understood in the contexts of traditional city iconography in the West and the close and (until recently) abiding relationship between this iconography and popular representations of racial "others" and prostitutes in Judeo-Christian cultures in Britain and her former colony, Canada. Moreover, reactions to and representations of the case of Vancouver's Missing Women signal significant changes in contemporary images of the city and the moralistic association of the city with the body and soul of the fallen woman or prostitute in traditional Euro-American discourse.

Judeo-Christian mythology metaphorically connects the Great Whore of Whores, a manifestation of evil and vice, with a licentious, sin-ridden city. As scholar Khalid Kishtainy suggests, "The strict prohibition of prostitution was part of the banishment of the flesh and thus sex that accompanied the development of Judaism and the teachings of the prophets during the eclipse of Hebrew rule in Palestine" (20). Judaism "looked upon all manifestations of evil as synonymous with or derivative of whoredom," and Christianity "went on to equate sex with whoredom, and called for abstinence as much as possible" (21). All of this myth-making functioned to distinguish Judaism and Christianity from the polytheistic and sexually celebratory religions of ancient Babylonia and Egypt, religions that included—and often centred on—priestesses with whom worshippers would have sex as a form of religious worship and celebration.[23]

Surviving early Judeo-Christian literature reflects these initial efforts to distinguish new religions from their pagan predecessors. Perhaps the most infamous of these writings figuring sexuality, especially female sexuality in its most pagan or prostitutional forms, as the root of all evil is the apostle John's prophetic dream in the Book of Revelation, the final segment of the Christian Bible. John names Babylon the most vice-ridden city on earth, and in his dream, Babylon, a female prostitute, is both an icon of evil and a symbol of impending apocalypse. She is "Babylon the Great. The Great Mother of Prostitutes and of the Abominations of the earth" (Rev 17:5). John dreams the downfall of this Great Whore as the Biblical God invites her citizens to leave her, figuring their exodus from within her walls as a violent, matricidal birthing scene: "Come out of her," the Christian God tells his people, "so that you will not share in her sins, so that you will not receive any of her plagues....Give her as much torture and grief as the glory and luxury she gave herself" (Rev 18: 4b-6). The "Mother of Prostitutes and...Abominations" must be destroyed in childbirth, it is implied, because her very pregnancy is evidence of evil licentiousness. The city of Babylon, the Whore of Whores, thus provides us with an archetype of the synecdochic relationship between prostitution and the city in Western discourse.

This is just one of many historical points of reference for the development of what sociologist and sex advocate Gail Pheterson calls whore stigma in contemporary culture. Whore stigma is "a social and legal branding of women who are suspected of being or acting like prostitutes" (Pheterson, *Prism* 30). The historic and continuing power of this stigma makes it "contagious (i.e., public association with whores is self-incriminating)" (*Prism* 21). Political and popular discourse continues to separate whores from the rest of society—through, for example, the criminalization of prostitution—so that non-sex workers, like those who are invited to leave the Biblical Mother of Prostitutes, "will not receive any of her plagues." In doing so, as our current serial murder/sex worker tradition indicates, we have truly given whores "much torture and grief."

Of course whore stigma is rooted in more than the religious history of Western civilization. The Book of Revelation example is also a particularly vivid illustration of a patriarchal impulse to stigmatize and control female sexuality, stamping out what remained of sacred prostitution from goddess-based societies like those of ancient Egypt and Babylon (Roberts 9). Kishtainy likewise suggests that the rise of private ownership during this period contributed to a patriarchal focus on the limitation of female sexuality and the control of family bloodlines. Prostitutes' lack of dependence on a single master or sexual partner and the subsequent indeterminacy of their children's patrilineage posed a distinct obstacle for religious and state dogma that recognized a singular male godhead, and that organized socio-political structures around male family lines and male power. The rise of Judaism and then of Christianity were thus accompanied by patriarchal social and economic forces that promoted whore stigma and culturally ostracized prostitutes by stigmatizing all but a very restricted form of female sexuality.

This stigma, however, has not always been as intense or as focused as it is in Judeo-Christian mythology. Although, historically, those who have provided sexual services for remuneration throughout Europe and in European colonies have faced periods of deep persecution and patriarchal control, some reports indicate that prostitution and the Christian church were often connected in ways that necessarily diluted the ire that church dogma would otherwise direct at whores. While values like female chastity and monogamous heterosexual marriage were preached from pulpits throughout Europe in the twelfth and thirteenth centuries, in a strange conflation of virgin/whore binaries, some convent records from this period suggest that many of these establishments doubled as brothels, where monks and priests greeted clients and kept records of brothel earnings.[24] In addition, in Vatican City throughout the Early Modern and Reformation periods, church and state officials profited from and openly patronized church and state-run brothels, even as the state became increasingly concerned with policing women's sexuality, and church doctrines surrounding female chastity were translated into a more secular language of (female) sexual purity, domesticity, and motherhood.

During this period as well, as public authorities throughout Europe issued edicts allowing for the arrest, public humiliation, and imprisonment of women who were thought to be working as whores, a number of upwardly mobile working-class or peasant whores of great beauty and wit became celebrated members of aristocratic circles.[25] Such upward social mobility was relatively rare in pre-industrial Europe and her colonies. However, this kind of economic (and social) success became more widely available over time, due to a complex series of social changes, ranging from land enclosure acts in England that cut peasants off from the land they had worked for centuries to the Industrial Revolution that, in Europe and her colonies more generally, expanded market opportunities and increased access to capital for persons outside of the aristocracy, church, and government. The metaphorical relationship that early Judeo-Christian societies had established between the prostitute body and a great, sinful city, however, came to be interpreted more literally under industrial capitalism.

This traditional synecdoche became especially relevant in part because of the new attention to living conditions in the metropolis in the developing capitalist economy of the nineteenth and early twentieth centuries. Industrial capitalism increased and condensed urban populations so that, by the middle of the nineteenth century, persons from all social strata, including the emerging middle class, lived in closer proximity to one another than ever before.[26] The literal proximity of social classes in modern cities led to fears, especially on the part of the new middle class, of class contamination, often described in moral terms. Working to differentiate themselves on the one hand from the notoriously licentious and increasingly broke European aristocracy, and on the other from the overworked and underpaid working classes whose lives also often included hard-drinking and casual attention to traditional Christian values like marriage and sexual monogamy, the middle class came to understand themselves as the moral conscience of modern industrial times.[27] Historical Christian dogma surrounding marriage and sexuality; scientific and cultural research that both relied on and reproduced ideological understandings of race, gender, and class;

and especially rigid ideologies of social and sexual decorum reinforced capitalist and patriarchal class, gender, and race relations.

Such boundary policing between classes, genders, and races fuelled the more literal gendering, racing, and classing of the urban landscape and the simultaneous development of misogynist stigmatizing and colonialist racializing of prostitution.[28] With respect to gender and class, examining the relationship between "good" wives and "fallen" women in nineteenth- and early twentieth-century Europe and North America, political philosopher Shannon Bell traces what she refers to as the production of the prostitute body. Bell suggests that scientific inquiries by nineteenth- and early twentieth-century sexologists simultaneously reflected and created hegemonic biases about female bodies, women's sexuality, women's place in patriarchal society,[29] and the rights of working-class persons. The development of an essentialist[30] patriarchal ideology of gender and class—what Victorianist Mary Poovey refers to as "the oppositional economy" (9)—was based on biological differences between the sexes and "produced 'the prostitute' as the other of the other: the other within the categorical Other, 'woman'" (Bell 2). In the oppositional economy, men and women were best suited for separate but complementary cultural spheres: men for public lives in business and industrial commerce, and women for domestic lives of child-rearing and the moral education of all.[31] As public women, prostitutes were not only men's opposites, and thus others, but they also constituted another population of others in relation to the domestic (and white) middle-class feminine ideal in the industrial city.[32] The prostitute body thus became a newly classed, gendered, and particularly public symbol of otherness and of moral debasement.

With respect to the racialization of the prostitute and her body, modern unease with female promiscuity also developed out of fears of racial miscegenation and the weakening of the British Empire throughout the nineteenth century.[33] Discussing the negative racialization and correspondent relegation of non-white bodies to the urban spaces designated for nineteenth-century working and underclasses, critical race theorist David Goldberg traces the connection between certain races and degeneracy that were facilitated by social, sexual, political, and scientific ideologies, such as eugenics. Within such frameworks, "races accordingly have their proper or natural places, geographically and biologically. Displaced from their proper or normal class, national, or ethnic positions in the social and ultimately urban setting, a 'Native' or 'Negro' would generate pathologies—slums, criminality, poverty, alcoholism, prostitution, disease, insanity—that if allowed to transgress the social norms would pollute the (white) body politic and at the extreme bring about racial extinction. Degeneracy, then, is the mark of a pathological Other, an Other both marked by and standing as the central sign of disorder" (*Racist Culture* 200). Furthermore, as gender and critical race theorist Sherene Razack argues, in historical as in contemporary contexts, "racialized and poor women...presumed to be sexually available outside of marriage (in discourses of slavery and colonialism, for instance), are already thought to inhabit the space of prostitution" ("Race" 348). In other words, when we consider gender in relation to the white supremacist capitalist bourgeois ideological framework Goldberg describes, we begin to understand how the bodies of poor white women and racially othered women come (a) to inhabit the same urban spaces, and (b) to be conflated with these spaces and then read as degenerate and prostitutional. In and outside of the colonies throughout the nineteenth and early twentieth centuries, Western social fears coalesced around increasingly visible populations of urban female sex workers as negatively classed (i.e., poor), negatively racialized (i.e., Indigenous, black, brown, or Asian), and thus degenerate bodies.

Such fears resulted in an ever more literal city/prostitute conflation, a conflation that informed middle-class efforts in England and throughout the former British Empire to police class and race boundaries through the regulation of female sexuality. Overtly sexually transgressive women became particularly problematic during this period for the usual reasons: patriarchal and colonial concern with traceable (patrilineal and white, presumably Anglo-Saxon) family lines, traditional Judeo-Christian fears of the body and its appetites, as well as fears of uninhibited sexuality and the association of these fears with a wanton, negatively racialized, feminized lack of civilization. This widespread cultural unease, or dis-ease, translated into a particularly vehement fear of prostitution as a form of social disease. And nineteenth-century literary and popular culture exhibit this uneasy marriage of middle-class morality's impetus to save female sexual sinners and their fear of the contaminating influence of these social actors.[34] However, as growing working-class populations in industrial cities experienced below-subsistence wages, exploitative working conditions, and want of proper housing, more prostitutes appeared on public streets and in public parks and music halls. The public presence of these sex workers became a symbolic affront to middle-class morality, and their industrious capitalization on their own assets continued to offend what was often constructed as civilized middle-class society. The increasing visibility of public women during this period seems in fact to have facilitated the increasingly literal interpretation of the synecdochic relationship between the prostitute and the city.

Such city-whore ideology also fuelled syphiliphobia in nineteenth-century Euro-American cultural discourse. The literal proximity of so many bodies of multiple classes and races in the urban landscape inspired widespread cultural fears of disease and contamination. As cultural and literary historian Sander Gilman's work begins to make clear, additional fears of sexual transgression emerged alongside a social discourse that equated female sexual promiscuity and prostitution, particularly in working-class and poor city quarters, with a specifically urban form of social degeneracy and disease. Working-class sex workers in cities like Victorian London thus provoked cultural anxiety—especially among the middle classes—because they were seen to embody disease, degeneracy *and* every woman's potential fate (Gilman, "'Who?'" 263). For white British women, for example, in the oppositional economy, women's supposedly innate desire to comply with men's needs for comfort was assumed to create an equally innate tendency toward prostitution should *sexual* comfort be proffered even once. Black African and Indigenous women, however, were presumed to be innately sexual and licentious by virtue of their race; such ideologies resulted in the popular assumption that Indigenous and other negatively racialized women must struggle daily against their baser instincts, and that many would fail in this struggle. Thus the cultural paradox: while good middle-class women had to guard against and save others from the city's dangers, *all* women were also part of these dangers by virtue of their sex and what was understood as its natural propensity for sexual excess and transgression.

In *Soft City*, British travel writer and novelist Jonathan Raban discusses "some of the Manichean metaphors which writers in the nineteenth century tried to apply to the city": they saw it "as a pustular disease, a giant dirt trap, an embodiment of original sin, or a reincarnation of primeval chaos. These are romantic images," Raban notes, "and they stem from the passionate English discovery of an idea of Nature which led the most articulate and outspoken members of Victorian society to reject the city at the very time when cities were growing faster and bigger than ever before" (87). Indeed, massive urbanization may have effectively created the conditions for nineteenth-century Romantics' artistic investment in capital N Nature over the metropolis. And the Romantics' preference for the pastoral landscape over the industrial cityscape provided a powerful outlet for anti-urban—and anti-prostitution—discourse. For many nineteenth-century critics and reformers, only resistance to or eradication of this unnatural being—the urban prostitute—could facilitate the re-establishment of Natural order. Reformers, or "social purity" campaigners, thus focused on removing women they viewed as fallen from the streets, treating them for diseases from which they may or may not have suffered, and relegating them to significantly less visible spaces such as convents, hospitals, and workhouses.

In *The Age of Light, Soap, and Water: Moral Reform in English Canada, 1885–1925*, criminologist Mariana Valverde notes the following about early Canadian attitudes on this topic: "Insofar as there was a single issue that typified or symbolized the whole work of social purity, it was prostitution, referred to as the 'social evil.' This was not a mere euphemism: for many Canadians prostitution was really *the* social evil, the most important of a long list of social problems ascribed to modern urban life...It was not the sole focus of the purity movement, as drink was for the temperance movement; but prostitution was *the social* evil (in contrast to masturbation, the 'solitary evil') and the fight against it was an ongoing campaign that was guaranteed to unify an otherwise diverse movement" (77, emphasis in original). Reformers in England and Canada sought to cleanse the city metaphorically—in terms of whores' moral "rehabilitation"—and literally—through the removal from city streets of women whom modern industrial culture constructed as contaminants in every sense of the word.

Significantly, social purity campaigns, concerned as they often were with the worsening living conditions of the working class as well as the worsening character of city spaces, strengthened whore stigma in these cultural contexts. This had the effect of culturally isolating women whose offering of sexual services for financial remuneration had once been a relative non-issue in their communities. As historian Judith Walkowitz argues, in London, England, processes of moral policing and isolation helped create the cultural conditions for one of the most notorious serial murders of sex workers in recent history: the unsolved 1888 Whitechapel (or Ripper) murders.[35]

Equally important to this series of murders was the way that English journalistic and police representations of the working-class neighbourhood of Whitechapel, more than the city of London itself, both produced the conditions for the murders and limited investigators' abilities to solve these cases. As in *America's Most Wanted* and other journalistic portrayals of twentieth- and twenty-first-century Vancouver's Downtown Eastside, late nineteenth-century Whitechapel became, "For the respectable reading public, a stark and sensational backdrop for the Ripper murders: an immoral landscape of light and darkness, a nether region of illicit sex and crime, both exciting and dangerous" (Walkowitz, *City* 193). Whitechapel was in fact the site of the grisly murder and mutilation of at least five women, Polly Nichols, Annie Chapman, Catherine Eddowes, Elizabeth Stride, and Mary Jane Kelly.[36] However, the strength of popular efforts to confine the case to this socio-economically depressed region of London stresses the ways that fears of industrial capitalism's modern metropolis and contemporary indictments of her synecdochic relations informed the prejudices around which this notorious murder case revolved.

In addition, the moralistic tone of news reports on the case, many of which include gruesomely detailed drawings of the women's mutilated bodies, became moral object lessons for other girls and women, insinuating that a brutal fate awaited any woman who declined to follow certain codes of conduct in the city. Such instructive analogies perhaps inevitably fuelled further public initiatives to curb and control transgressive female sexuality, especially the public or prostitutional kinds evident on urban streets. As Walkowitz explains, "The middle classes of London were far less concerned with the material problems of Whitechapel than with the pathological symptoms they spawned, such as street crime, prostitution, and epidemic disease—'the whole panoply of shame' of this 'boldest blotch on the face of the capital of the civilized world'" (*City* 193). Predictably, social purity campaigns inspired by the Whitechapel case (and echoed in campaigns in cities across Canada and the United States[37]) further socially marginalized and thus endangered the already isolated women they ostensibly set out to protect.

The Whitechapel case and its accompanying social and moral panic functions as a spotlight on the ways in which widespread cultural investment in middle-class morality had begun to take hold in the popular imagination of the period in Britain as well as her former colonies, to an extent curbing working-class sexual permissiveness and effectively ejecting working-class prostitutes from communities where their means of supporting themselves had once been a non-issue. The Whitechapel murderer, a killer whose alleged letters to the *Pall Mall Gazette* suggested that "he" was particularly interested in murdering "whores," reportedly attacked, murdered, and mutilated his victims in the densely populated streets or rooming houses of East London. Though the murders took place in "areas where local residents kept close watch on each other's movements" (Walkowitz, *City* 193), no witnesses came forward, and precious few friends and neighbours knew any details about the women's lives.

Over the past century and a half, serial killers who prey on sex workers have become a kind of status quo group of urban criminals. In particular, as Roberts observes, "Since the mid-1970s, with increased police pressure on the sex industry, an epidemic of prostitute killings has swept the West" (*Whores in History* 302). Contemporary cases like that of Vancouver's Missing Women underline the enduring power of systemic moral indoctrination—the history of which in the United States and Canada closely parallels that of Britain—the resulting stigma under which sex workers continue to labour in contemporary Euro-American culture, and their perpetual vulnerability and isolation in urban settings. Significantly, Jack the Ripper remains a figure to whom contemporary news sources, police, and the public alike across Europe and North America enthusiastically compare urban serial killers who prey on sex workers.

FEMINISM AND SEX WORK

From at least the time of the Whitechapel murders, social campaigns sympathetic to the plight of murdered sex workers in Euro-American cities have attempted to advocate for them in the public sphere. However, too often these campaigns, like those that grew out of the Whitechapel case, work against sex workers and with unsympathetic police and other public officials to further stigmatize and blame sex workers—especially those who work in the street-involved industry—for the social evils that facilitate their murders. Walkowitz examines this trend in media and activist responses to the serial murder of thirteen women—Wilma McCann, Emily Jackson, Irene Richardson, Patricia Atkinson, Jayne MacDonald, Jean Jordan, Yvonne Pearson, Helen Rytka, Vera Millward, Josephine Whitaker, Barbara Leach, Marguerite Walls, and Jacqueline Hill—seven of whom worked in the sex trade, between 1975 and 1981 in Yorkshire.[38] Dubbed the "Yorkshire Ripper" case in news reports of the period, Walkowitz notes that these murders and local responses to them "appear to take their cues from the legendary events of 1888….As in the case of the Whitechapel murders, this series of murders also gave rise to complex political effects: they provoked misogynist assaults on women's freedom, in the form of widespread copycat activities and police use of prostitutes as 'live bait.' They also provoked and reinforced purity campaigns to clean up red-light districts and to outlaw smut" (City 229–30). And while British women came together in response to the Yorkshire murders in unprecedented, powerful, and often successful ways to protest against culturally sanctioned male violence and sensationalist media portrayals of "lust murders," the forms these protests took often foregrounded feminism's deeply ambivalent relationship to the sex industry. Usually intended to highlight the "forms of sexual objectification and public intimidation that confront women daily" (Walkowitz, City 234), these campaigns also featured anti-sex-shop, anti-pornography, and anti-prostitution actions.

Indeed, feminist responses to the Yorkshire murders reflect the sex wars raging within Euro-American feminism during this period, as the positions of sex worker and non-sex worker feminists became increasingly polarized.[39] By attacking sex work on so many different levels, and in speaking to a public already inclined to stigmatize those working at all levels of the sex industry, dominant feminist activists who responded to the Yorkshire Ripper case, like their moral purity campaign foremothers, further marginalized and angered sex workers. Much feminist and other political activism during this period further damaged the already troubled relationship between sex workers and mainstream culture.[40]

As noted above, dominant responses to the Vancouver case, like those in Yorkshire and the rest of Britain in the 1980s, reflect traditional sex work "advocacy" trends. Protests often centre on prostitution as a social issue, targeting socio-economically depressed urban areas and/or unofficial red-light districts, and calling for an end to the sex industry as a whole. Often even as sex workers and their supporters—feminist or otherwise—defend already dead women from further abjection in public forums, debates continue within their ranks around the cultural or moral legitimacy of prostitution.

Acknowledging the difficulties non-sex worker and sex worker feminists have had establishing useful dialogue, Pheterson claims that feminism remains one of the few political movements that—at the very least—attempts to discuss prostitution within its varying social contexts (*Vindication*; *Prism*). In her introduction to *Whores and Other Feminists* (1997), a collection of writings by women, many of whom had worked or were currently working in the sex industry, editor Jill Nagle highlights the ways that feminist attention to socially constructed binaries (for example, lesbian/heterosexual, good girl/bad girl), "compulsory virtue" for women, and "common sense" white supremacist capitalist hetero-patriarchal dogma significantly align with sex workers' concerns (4–5). Despite the groups' past and present differences, since the 1970s and 1980s more and more dialogue between sex worker and non-sex worker feminists has emerged that disallows traditional moral judgements of sex work.[41] Despite such developments, however, "New waves of social theorists, from the most sober to the most sensational, have continued to extract prostitution from its larger context" (Pheterson, *Prism* 13). Positions like Nagle's are affirmed by Lesley Ann Geoffrey and Gail MacDonald in their introduction to *Sex Workers in the Maritimes Talk Back* (2006): "Feminist theorists," they write, "should be at the forefront of defending sex workers' agency and championing their resistance because feminists recognize that the relationship between power and sexuality is powerfully gendered" (9). In other words, as a growing body of work by critics and researchers such as Laura Augustin, Melissa Hope Ditmore (with Antonia Levy and Alys Willman), Elya Durisin, Francis Shaver, and Pivot Legal Society, as well as Bell, Jeffrey and MacDonald, Lowman, Nagle, Pheterson, Roberts, Walkowitz, and others indicates, more and more feminists recognize that "'the Prostitute' is a social construction that reflects the meanings and understandings imposed by outside agents" (Jeffrey and MacDonald 5). Or, as Wendy Chapkis argues, "There is no such thing as 'the Prostitute'—only the meanings attached to her/him by others" (qtd in Jeffrey and MacDonald 5).

Despite the further establishment of these much-needed connections between sex worker and non-sex worker feminists and the urban anti-whore-stigma and anti-violence activism such connections facilitate, parallel impulses to particularize the circumstances of the murderers and their victims are evident in the Whitechapel murders of 1888, the Yorkshire murders of the 1970s and 1980s, and those in present-day Vancouver. Representations of the Whitechapel case focused on the murderer as a dangerous social deviant who killed other dangerous social deviants. The tragedy of the victims' deaths is further obscured in the historical and continuing fascination—evident even in the title by which the Yorkshire Ripper case is popularly known—with serial killers as Ripper-esque social deviants. This kind of focus on the character and psychopathology of killers in the numerous cases in which serial killer victims are sex workers indeed extracts prostitution from its larger context. The people who die at the hands of these killers become unfortunate victims whose private choice of profession inevitably puts them in harm's way—not women whose marginalization under patriarchal, misogynist, and racist culture leaves them vulnerable to attack by social actors whose racism and misogyny are products of that same culture.

About the Whitechapel murders, Walkowitz writes, "From newspaper accounts that linked a monstrous crime and a monstrous individual to a monstrous social environment, the Ripper story was reduced to a notorious case history of an individual erotic maniac, whose activities were seemingly unconnected to normal interactions of men and women" (City 228). The murderer in the case is rendered in narrow psychological terms as an individual monster operating within a specific monstrous environment, not as the outgrowth of a misogynist, classist, and deeply racist culture operating within (and effectively exploiting) a marginalized, neglected population who inhabit a disastrously inadequate urban infrastructure.

ONE MORE CASE IN A LONG TRADITION

Such flawed representations of murderer and victims come into play once more in the Vancouver case. I return, again, to images of clear-eyed reporters speaking from Stanley Park juxtaposed with shadowy figures who walk the darker streets of the DTES. In addition, exchanges like the one between Larry Pynn and Maggie de Vries over the abjection of Pickton's victims poignantly illustrate that traditional ideas about prostitution as a social disease remain powerful in contemporary Canada. Paradoxically, however, while critics object to America's Most Wanted's portrayal of the Vancouver case as a Ripper-style series of mysterious murders, advocates for the Missing Women agitated to prevent the sale of a Jack the Ripper doll in a Vancouver store, claiming the doll was insensitive given the similarities between the Ripper murders and the present-day case.[42] As well, even as advocacy groups across the nation struggle to keep the victims' identities as women, as friends and family members, and as important members of local communities first and foremost in the public eye, the women's residency in the DTES and their (alleged) connections to the street-involved sex industry are routinely discussed by all sides as causal links to their disappearances and murders—as though violence is inevitable for sex industry workers.

Discourse surrounding the Vancouver case, like that in Whitechapel and Yorkshire, intrinsically links sex-worker bodies with the darkest elements of the cityscape. In the Vancouver neighbourhood, supposedly independent social actors are separated from the culture that produced them with the result that only the woman who works as a street-involved sex worker (survival or otherwise) and her murderer are responsible for her social marginalization, for her disappearance from city streets, and for her death. Such discourse writes over and significantly inhibits illustrations of the ways that our cultural environment unequivocally shares responsibility for the monstrous crimes committed against the murdered women of Vancouver.

Again, what is new in the Vancouver case are the politico-economic forces at play in the city. Though nineteenth-century social and moral ideologies continue to inflect twenty-first-century cultures, the physical and discursive production of cities as the new sites of post-industrial capitalism has begun to supplant overtly moralistic understandings of prostitution with concerns about the urban conditions that best facilitate market growth. In this context, the most visible forms of prostitution, especially the elements of the trade connected most directly with poverty, drug addiction, and homelessness, become, simply, bad business. And the perpetrators of such damaging enterprises must not be saved or offered assistance, but rooted out and eradicated from the new cityscape.

Such substitutions of fiscal for social responsibility are facilitated by increasingly pervasive free-market and necropolitical ideologies. As globalization theorist Saskia Sassen succinctly puts it, "Global cities are the sites of the over-valorization of corporate capital and the further devalorization of disadvantaged actors, both firms and workers" (xx). In this system, market growth becomes a measure of social progress. As federal and municipal governments cut corporate taxes, invest in (some) urban infrastructure, and increase policing and security around such investments, fewer resources are made available for social programs. Under such a system, social welfare programs and de-colonization initiatives become, instead of investments that pay off in other than immediate dollar-and-cent ways, extraneous expenses. Individuals are increasingly held responsible for their own social welfare and cultural positioning despite the not inconsequential effects of colonization, racism, sexual chauvinism, and class prejudice, powerful forces that underpin and continue to inform contemporary social hierarchies.

Under post-industrial capitalism, the term *democracy* itself seems to undergo such an obscene revision that it comes to signal "free markets." In such a system, the unregulated market is envisioned as the ultimate democratic system, undeniably following the will of the majority, and transforming citizens into investors and consumers. This is, therefore, an important period for prostitution in Canada: if our culture measures the worth of a particular asset, business practice, or commodity in terms of its profitability, then sex workers from all levels of the sex industry, so long as they make money and thus contribute to the gross domestic product, could in fact be understood as legitimate, or good, citizens. Indeed, contemporary interest in market freedom in a culture that, "independent of the former real world" (Jameson 161), is in the process of dissociating itself from former ideas about morality and value, may have inadvertently produced a politically legitimate position for sex workers in the hegemonic cultural imagination. Under such a system, even neoconservative interests in law and order could conceivably advocate the protection of sex workers who could be shown to service, for example, the corporate CEOs who want a quick sexual encounter while in town on business, with no strings attached.

Of course, this potential point of entry becomes the fissure through which the moralism that underwrites such policing of borders as well as the populations they contain and divide becomes visible. Indeed, such representations of "liberation" and "protection" mask the historical, complex, and hierarchical web of interests that inform contemporary socio-political structures. Even as a joint presence in cities of private property owners, corporate investors, and colonized or otherwise marginalized populations perhaps provides an unprecedented correspondence of concerns between these groups regarding the governance of cityscapes, "this joint presence is further brought into focus by the increasing disparities between the two" groups (Sassen xxxiv). As Durisin observes, in the current capitalist neoliberal context, "the workers who experience the most severe levels of violence and exploitation are those who have the least access to employment protection or citizenship rights, and are working in gendered and racialized service and manufacturing occupations" (131).

Nowhere are the ramifications of this increasing disparity in sociocultural influence and protection more clear than in the Vancouver case. As the above-noted responses to the disappeared women indicate, longstanding cultural hierarchies, especially those imposed via colonization—as well as a long tradition of serial killer/sex worker cases—very much inform these women's lives and deaths. These structures also inform our narratives of the same. Vancouver's Missing Women are memorialized, or produced and reproduced, as abject components of a sensational and historically resonant story.

What also sets the Vancouver case apart, however, from the plethora of Ripper-style cases in recent Euro-American history is the near-eradication of at least twenty-six women's bodies. The butchered bodies of Jack the Ripper's victims were found and photographed or sketched.[43] These murders were, there-fore, attended to by police and the public because the blood and gore effectively demanded attention. As critics have argued in the intervening years, the five Whitechapel women's murders became moral object lessons for other women about the dangers inherent in illicit sexual behaviour and the sinfully sexual city. In contrast, the lack of actual bodies in Vancouver makes this case both more and less visible to police and the Canadian public. With no mutilated bodies to discuss, a nineteenth-century-style moral object lesson becomes harder to construct—not that journalists have not tried to do so, as multiple "human interest" or "fallen women" stories and the so-called contaminated meat fears would suggest.

Without the bloodied and mutilated remains of murdered prostitutes to warrant a police investigation, the Missing Women's marginalization and forc-ibly invisible citizenship in contemporary Canadian society becomes ironically, painfully clear. Despite the Canadian publication ban in place when they initially appeared, articles like Pynn's nonetheless construct images of mutilation and diseased, degenerate victims. Narratives like Fong's construct such violence as exceptional even as the victims are represented as wild girls turned wild women whose violent fates were to be expected. The impetus behind reports like these would appear to be the resurrection of the morality tales for girls and women that have traditionally accompanied these kinds of cases. Focusing on the women's possible mutilation, but suggesting that the public will never know for sure what, exactly, Vancouver's Missing Women suffered, such representa-tions communicate the horror of being rendered, violently and systematically, invisible—a condition inherently connected to one's occupation, as abject or bare life, of the abandoned (gendered, raced, classed) literal and metaphorical spaces of urban culture.

"Contaminated meat" reports, alongside recurrent stories about missing and murdered "drug addicts and prostitutes" that hint at the extreme violence victims suffered before their almost literal erasure from the streets of the DTES thus simultaneously deny and adhere to the traditional synecdochic relationship between whores and the city. I suggest two possible explanations for such tentative adherence to stereotyped associations: the recurrent focus on a particular city neighbourhood from which the women disappeared, and the literal removal of the women from the streets of this neighbourhood. While print news reports from 2001 to 2006 focus on the women as Vancouver residents, many journalists are quick to add that these were but a few drug-addicted prostitute residents of Vancouver's DTES. Even the first reward poster (Appendix 2) produced by the Vancouver mayor and police—not without controversy—identifies the missing as Downtown Eastside, not Vancouver women. This representation changed with subsequent posters; in the 2004 version (see Appendix 3) only the title "Missing Women Task Force" accompanies these controversial images (discussed in more detail in the next chapter). In these early official representations, the traditional city/sex worker connection is denied in favour of a more palatable—to those outside the area—linkage of these lost women with the small two-block radius of the DTES.[44]

Significantly, the title of the poster produced in 2007 (see Appendix 4) reconnects the Missing Women to the city of Vancouver. Despite high-profile coverage of and affiliation with extreme violence, and despite continued disappearances and ongoing violence against street-involved women in the DTES— events recorded and resisted by groups such as PACE, WISH, PEERS, and Vancouver Rape Relief—Vancouver continues to be a popular year-round tourist destination. Tourism British Columbia carefully declines the link between the Missing Women and Vancouver, returning instead to an oblique representation of the violence as DTES-specific.

Unsurprisingly, *HelloBC.com*, British Columbia's official tourism website, makes no direct reference to the city's Missing Women cases. In the summer of 2012, marketing Vancouver as "one of the world's most spectacular cities" and focusing on its role as "host city of the 2010 Olympic and Paralympic Winter Games,"

BC Tourism's rhetoric places Vancouver on a global stage. In an introductory section entitled "World Media Attention," the site enthusiastically proclaimed:

> Named "top city of the americas" in Condé Nast Traveler magazine's 2009 Readers' Choice Awards, Vancouver offers travellers both outstanding opportunities for outdoor adventure and the sophisticated amenities of a world-class city.
>
> Vancouver was also named a Top 100 World Destination pick in TripAdvisor's 2008 Travelers' Choice awards, and one of ten Best Family Vacations in Canada in the 2011 Travelers' Choice awards.
>
> Vancouver has been chosen as the world's "Most Liveable City" in 2011 by the Economist Intelligence Unit (EIU), a title it has been awarded eight times since 2002. ("Vancouver")

Visitors to this "sophisticated" and "liveable" city are encouraged to take a "*daytime* stroll" (emphasis added) in Gastown—a space down the street and around the corner from Main and Hastings, the epicentre of the DTES—as the neighbourhood is "within easy walking distance of downtown Vancouver" ("Vancouver Neighbourhoods"). In addition, write-ups for Gastown and Chinatown advise tourists to "be mindful" that while these neighbourhoods are "very safe," they are each "partially located in a more graphic part of the city" ("Vancouver Neighbourhoods"). "Graphic" would appear, then, to be tourism code for unsafe, or dangerous, and certainly less sophisticated or liveable. Once again, the threat of abject violence is contained, even as its presence necessitates the development of trite rhetorical euphemisms for the degenerate zone.

In the nineteenth and early twentieth centuries, a female prostitute's death reinscribed the synecdochic relationship between her body and the supposedly destructive forces of the city. Her death functioned as a sign of urban degeneracy and the need for the body politic to move from urban sickness and excess to rural health and simplicity. As former Toronto Mayor David Miller argued in 2004, "We are an urban nation today—a country where the bulk of the population lives in large urban centres. And we are continuously moving in that direction, not away from it" ("New Deal Speech"). Recent global market and immigration trends suggest that this urbanization process continues. The dissociation of the dead sex worker body from either the image or the fate of the city proper would appear to reflect this naturalization of urban living.

As I discuss in more detail in Chapter 2, growing urban neighbourhood activism parallels increasing urbanization trends in Canada. It would appear that city living is now inevitable, perhaps even necessary, and that a corresponding reorganization of traditional urban imagery is underway. In the emerging symbolic economy, the Canadian city—in this case, Vancouver—emerges as a shining, inherently orderly beacon of contemporary post-industrial civilization. In this new symbolic framework, the city's former disorderly synecdochic relations become abject, or bare life: populations whose violent fates prove the success of the city's new purpose and image.

ANTI-PROSTITUTION REPORTING, POLICING, AND ACTIVISM IN CANADA'S GLOBAL CITIES

AS DISCUSSED IN CHAPTER 1, street-involved sex workers have, over the past three decades, come to embody, symbolically, the danger and filth (physical and moral) that, once considered integral to the image of the metropolis, must now, according to the demands of global capitalism, be eliminated from the streets in particular urban neighbourhoods. Keeping in mind these intimate connections between contemporary global capitalism, the changing cultural and physical structures of the inner city, and growing urban populations, this chapter first interrogates two popular tropes or images in mainstream print media representations of and responses to prostitution—tropes I entitle the "Missing Woman" and the "Lone Streetwalker." Such reporting simultaneously echoes and reifies traditional anti-prostitution dogma with little attention to the effects of such dogma on the already disenfranchised populations of sex workers whom it attacks. Significantly, even as more serial kidnap and murder cases involving sex workers have become national news over the period in question, the same two problematic and stigma-laden images dominate print news descriptions of sex work and sex workers.

To examine the implications of such whore stigma further, this chapter also analyzes ties between anti-prostitution neighbourhood activism in Vancouver and Edmonton and ongoing urban renewal in these same urban centres. This analysis highlights and explores the influences of current neoliberal social, legal, and political initiatives on the mandates of anti-sex-work groups and police precincts: private and public organizations that promote relatively narrow visions of citizenship, safe streets, and urban order, which require, as a matter of course, that street-involved sex workers give up their livelihoods, their basic human rights, or even their lives for the orderly neighbourhood cause. This chapter thus explores how contemporary public discourses register changing definitions of the human, the humane, and the urban, as national politics increasingly reflect the influences of free-market ideology, the language and practices of global capitalism, and the resurgence of robust law and order rhetoric.

Culturally dominant anti-prostitution biases are, perhaps unsurprisingly, evident in print reporting across the country, as mainstream Canadian print news sources routinely use a few recognizable, even predictable stock images and story formats to represent and discuss urban sex work and sex workers. Furthermore, with the exception of the seemingly inevitable blood and gore headlines, very little has changed in the representations of sex work and sex workers by mainstream print and news media in Canada in the years since the media first began reporting serial murders of street-involved sex workers in Vancouver, Edmonton, Saskatoon, and Winnipeg. In their study of prostitution-related news in the *Vancouver Sun*, the *Winnipeg Free Press*, the *Toronto Star*, the *Montreal Gazette*, and the *Halifax Chronicle Herald* between the years of 1981 and 1995, Erin Gibbs Van Brunschot, Rosalind A. Sydie, and Catherine Krull found the following: "The depiction of the street prostitute and her (or his) work remained consistent, and there was often remarkable homogeneity in the media coverage irrespective of the political leanings of various newspapers. There were four themes that were most prevalent in the years under review: nuisance, child abuse, violence, and non-Western prostitution. Two other themes—drugs/organized crime and disease—were less nationally prevalent, but were regionally specific" (53). The researchers further observe that "reporting of prostitution as nuisance prevailed in all cities, often in reference to 'community standards' and 'property values'" (55). In such cases, Van Brunschot et al. note, "The general claim... remained the problem that prostitution represented for the 'normal,' 'average' citizen and the need for some type of regulation and control despite the recognition that it was" among "these same 'normal' and 'average' citizens that prostitutes' customers are found" (67). Analyzing sex workers' responses to fifteen years' worth of prostitution-related print news in Halifax, Nova Scotia's daily newspaper the *Chronicle Herald*, Leslie Ann Jeffrey and Gayle MacDonald also find in 2006 that "the media play a major role" in perpetuating whore stigma through their participation in processes of social "surveillance and social control" that "present simplified and stereotypical images of sex work and sex workers, make sex workers the objects of negative attention, and silence sex workers as speakers in their own right" (137).

Expanding my own survey of print news between 2001 and 2006 to include all prostitution-related reports in urban and national newspapers and their corresponding online editions during this period, I found similar patterns to those observed both by Van Brunschot et al. and by Jeffrey and MacDonald, despite the fact that the Vancouver Missing Women case significantly increased the number of prostitution-related print news reports in the years following those covered by Van Brunschot et al.'s study.

One striking similarity is that much contemporary sex work-related coverage rehearses the same stereotyped representations of sex workers that Jeffrey and MacDonald observe, as well as the polarizing rhetoric of citizens' groups versus prostitutes and johns that Van Brunschot et al. discuss. Another consistency worth noting is that reports not dealing with the numerous kidnappings and serial murders of sex workers in cities across the Canadian west continue to centre instead around the (not unimportant) issues of child sexual exploitation, human trafficking in Canada and abroad, and the nuisance and danger that street sex work constitutes, both for the workers and for those the media considers to be regular citizens, especially children, in the urban neighbourhoods where prostitutes work. Although such issues as these are not the focus of this book, they do indeed require attention; nevertheless, as I have argued elsewhere, moral panic about sexually exploited youth in Canada too often neglects the involvement of a high percentage of these at-risk youth in the *survival* sex trade.[1] Such an oversight facilitates the blaming of the sex industry for problems inherent in child welfare and family services that increase the numbers of homeless youth who, in the absence of family or state support, exchange sex for money, drugs, food, a clean or safe place to sleep, etc. Similarly failing to discriminate between survival and other forms of sex work, public concern about human trafficking as it relates to sexual slavery and exploitation again blames the sex trade for problems that are endemic to many pink-collar (woman-centred) service industries.[2]

In focusing on the indentured labour of trafficked women and children in the sex industry, such moral panic creates a hierarchy of concerns regarding slavery, implying that some forms are more (or less) acceptable than others, and thus dividing an anti-slavery movement in dire need of solidarity.[3]

Similarly, I acknowledge neighbourhood complaints about the traffic, noise, littering of city streets with condoms and needles, and the sexual harassment of non-sex workers by cruising johns that seem inevitably to accompany street-involved sex work as legitimate concerns. Unfortunately, however, too often residents take such concerns to politicians and police without discussing them with those who are arguably most directly able to address them: their neighbourhood sex workers. By excluding sex workers from discussions of the place or role of prostitution in the community, non-sex worker citizens blame sex work and sex workers for problems that are, in part, legislatively produced in Canada, and in so doing cripple their own neighbourhood initiatives.

Mainstream print news rarely features the views of politically active sex workers, let alone average worker-on-the-street concerns about conditions in particular neighbourhoods. The exceptions to this choking off of experiential voices in dominant news reports tend currently to occur after incidents of violence against persons involved in the sex trade. Van Brunschot, Sydie, and Krull found a similar trend, but noted that by "employing the rhetoric of 'safety on the job,' violent experiences are often recounted [in news reports] as a means of illustrating the risks prostitutes run in having to ply their trade in a covert manner" (61). Though violence against sex workers thus precipitates some dominant media exposure for issues of concern to people working in the industry, the voices of active sex workers and of representatives from groups like PACE, PEERS, the Toronto-based Maggie's, SPOC (Sex Professionals of Canada), SWAT (Sex Workers Alliance of Toronto), Stella (of Montreal), or the Halifax-based Stepping Stone are rarely heard in mainstream media outside of violent contexts. The rest of the time, instead, workers' bodies are photographed and filmed in predictable ways, and their comments become short excerpts incorporated into reports that may very well be written before these interviews take place.[4]

In effect, as Jeffrey and MacDonald's findings also suggest, those who work in the sex industry are rarely the knowledgeable experts whose opinions on inner-city crime, policing, or neighbourhood improvements are front-page news. More often than not, the anti-prostitution opinions of police, politicians, and other citizens outside the industry precede or offset sex-worker concerns. Pieces purporting to feature sex industry participants too often feature pictures of now-dead women who are memorialized in the words of their families and friends, but whose own words are absent.

In the next section, I offer examples of two prevalent images of prostitution in mainstream Canadian online and print news published between 2001 and 2006. The first of these images is the "Missing Woman" archetype in sex work-related news, an archetype that necessarily appears within the contexts of reporting on violence. This image is exemplified by the 2004 Missing Women poster discussed briefly at the end of Chapter 1, reproduced in Appendix 3. Throughout the above-noted period, Canadian news sources routinely use pictures either from this or earlier versions of this poster when reporting on the Missing Women of Vancouver. Many of the women pictured here were dead long before Vancouver officials finally agreed to post this reward the first time. And as the number of murder charges against the farmer grew, the likelihood that many of the women still unaccounted for were dead seemed to increase as well. Those concerned with preventing further violence, symbolic or otherwise, must therefore consider what effect images like these—both the poster as a whole and the individual pictures included on it—may have in such investigations.

THE MISSING WOMAN

As sex worker activist Kyla Kaun argues, such representations further prejudice an already prejudiced public against murdered or kidnapped sex workers. Speaking to the power the media has to "shore up the common biases of the public by focusing on sex workers as particularly problematic" (Jeffrey and MacDonald 149), Kaun, who testified in 2005 in Vancouver before the federal Subcommittee on Solicitation Laws (the SSLR), notes that mug shot or mug shot-like photos portray the Missing Women as criminals, people about whom the public is less likely to care when they are represented this way. Kaun also argues compellingly that if police and press reports on missing sex workers were to use a woman's "grad picture or a picture of her with her children or her family, then we are going to have a different feeling about that individual than from the image we see of her being arrested" (SSLR mtg. 17, 46).

Cultural theorist Amber Dean's analysis of the poster images likewise finds them unlikely to cultivate public concern. Drawing on Roland Barthes's theories of photographic images and ideological contexts, Dean suggests viewers are "'trained' [through culture] to recognize chains of signification that, for the photographs in the missing poster, might for many viewers signify something like mug shot = criminal = inherently bad or deviant person = unworthy of concern (with those images that are not mug shots presumed 'guilty by association')." Like Kaun, Dean argues that persons not directly connected to the Missing Women are unlikely to be stirred to care (and thus to action), "unless this prior 'training' is disrupted, challenging us to consider other frameworks for interpreting the poster" ("Hauntings" 142).

Kaun and Dean's critiques are well taken. Most of the Missing Women of Vancouver had or have community ties to the area. Many of them are or were mothers, and most of the women were reported missing by friends and family members. Nonetheless, the permanently disappeared women of Vancouver regularly appear in mainstream print news in groups of single-person photographs clearly extracted from the 1999 or 2004 posters, as though there are no other images available, and as though their disappearances become noteworthy only when grouped together. Moreover, "Although each woman is pictured alone, this arrangement groups the women such that they are barely separable: individual identities are wiped away as the images are swept up into a figuration of 'Vancouver's Missing Women'" (Dean, "Hauntings" 139). Because these photographs have, as Dean puts it, "been replicated so exhaustively now, in media reportage...they have come to stand in for the entire series of events surrounding the women's disappearances and murders as well as for the lives of the women pictured" ("Hauntings" 133).[5] Despite these repeated groupings, however, the actual frames of these images continue to mark off boundaries between their subjects so that the women remain separate, even from one another, set off from friends or family, away from recognizable neighbourhood landmarks, and thus visually unaffiliated even with the city streets from which they have been disappeared.[6]

As the Missing Women case in BC has developed, and following the publication ban set by the trial judge, some reports—particularly local ones—appear to respond to concerns like Kaun's, foregrounding many of the women's roles as mothers of children who are (or who soon will be) old enough to understand the circumstances surrounding their mothers' disappearances and/or murders. However, pictures like those included in Lori Culbert's January 2006 *Vancouver Sun* article set motherhood up as one of the few redeeming features of these disappeared or murdered women's existences. One of the images, clearly a family photo, shows a smiling Sarah de Vries cuddled on a chair or sofa, reading a book to her young daughter. The other image, a professional photo by Lance Sullivan, shows Marnie Lee Frey's teenage daughter, smiling and posed alongside her grandparents, Lynn and Rick Frey.[7] In this same article, Culbert describes the seventy-five children of Vancouver's then sixty-eight Missing Women as "precious reminders of lost lives," and notes that "the backgrounds of the missing women—some came from poverty, others from middle-class families—were as varied as the reasons that led them to drug addictions and prostitution. But despite their challenges, many of the women shared a common thread of dedication to their children" ("Children"). Culbert's analysis emphasizes the cost to others of the Missing Women's disappearances: she reports caregivers' concerns about the experiences and feelings of the women's children as the Missing People Trial has progressed, and includes comments such as the following from Janet Henry's twenty-year-old daughter, Debra Chartier: "My mom is an important part of my life, even though she did have some problems and wasn't there most of the time. I don't plan to follow in her footsteps. I don't plan to be better than her either. Nobody's perfect. But I do plan to fight for her until she's found."[8] Culbert also notes that "some of the missing women's children have escaped the cycle of poverty, violence, and drugs that claimed their mothers, while others have fallen into it. Their experiences are as diverse as their mothers.'" Such commentary and images do work to facilitate public concern about the fate of the disappeared and murdered women of Vancouver by suggesting that, while these women—devoted mothers or no—are lost, we must care about their fates for the sake of their children. Yet while the pictures included by Culbert indeed offer a more nuanced account of the women's lives, the accompanying article largely factors the women themselves out of public interest in this case. Having fallen into drug addiction and prostitution, Culbert implies, the Missing Women of Vancouver failed their children, and society must now attempt to make amends for this collective failure.

Kaun's argument that photos of the disappeared typically resemble mug shots rings true, again, when we recognize that some of the more flattering photographs in the various versions of the Missing Women poster appear to be cropped from pictures of larger groups. Even in significant and well-intentioned initiatives—for example, projects in which artists create portraits to "soften" the missing women's appearances (Project EDAN), or to illustrate their humanity (Masik)—the women appear together but alone. Such projects poignantly illustrate how these women's lives all too often become unimaginable and thus, in Dean's analysis, "ungrievable" ("Hauntings" 137). Or, as discussed in Chapter 1, the murdered women become important insofar as their images and life stories may be used to impart object lessons to "good" citizens about the violent fallout from cultural, especially sexual, deviance. In short, despite sex workers' and their allies' reports describing extensive networks of friends and business associates who look out for one another on the streets, print media images of missing sex workers continue to portray solitary women, women who are often "Missing," sometimes smiling, but almost always alone.

CBC Edmonton's now-concluded online series "Deadly Streets" offered a disturbing modification of the Missing Woman trope.[9] One graphic in this series featured a simple, large-scale sand-coloured map of Edmonton and the surrounding area. (Although uncredited on the website, a similar map graphic, credited to Richard Johnson, dominates above the fold and accompanies reporter Katherine Harding's article, "The Edmonton Killings," in the May 18, 2006 edition of the *Globe and Mail*.) Around the outer edges of the map were colour headshots of nine murdered Edmonton women with their names printed in small black text underneath their photos: three along the top—Ellie-May Meyer, Rachel Quinney, and Monique Pitre—three along the right side—Melissa Munch, Debbie Lake, and Charlene Gauld—and three along the left—Samantha Berg, Edna Bernard, Sylvia Ballantyne.[10] A thin black line connected each woman's photo with a red dot on the map. Only the line from Samantha Berg's photo connected to a dot within the city of Edmonton. Each of the other women's images connected to red dots outside city limits. This graphic appeared when visitors to the website clicked the "Murder Victims" button in the navigation menu in the top right panel of the "Deadly Streets" series. With the exception of the undated "Murder Victims" page, each page of this series was dated June 17, 2005. Clicking the next navigational button, "Timeline of Events," in the series menu, led to a page that confirmed that each red dot in the "Murder Victims" image marked a location where a woman's remains were found, after she was taken from the streets of Edmonton and then brutally murdered.

This version of the Missing Woman archetype would seem, then, to have repeated on the symbolic plane the removal of these women from the city of Edmonton. The city centre with which the women were quite literally associated by virtue of their street involvement was the centre of the graphic, too. And yet the lines from the red dots—even the one connected to Samantha Berg's photograph—led the eye away from the city. Or, for those who noticed the photographs at the "border" of the graphic first, the lines from the images led toward the city, but stopped abruptly with each red dot, so that the women remained outside of the city proper.

Moreover, although the pictures of the women were certainly the most detailed elements of this graphic, the replication of the cropped photos super-imposed over and connected to specific areas of a map once again suggested that the most noteworthy aspect of the women's disappearances was their similarity to one another. As links to further case-related news throughout this feature series did not function in the year prior to the series' removal from the site, later readers accessed only an incomplete overview of Edmonton's high-profile serial murder case. Furthermore, the brief summary that was accessible—always under the banner "Deadly Streets"—identified the women as "prostitutes," as "women who work in Edmonton's sex trade," and as persons who live "high-risk lifestyles." Thus the Missing Woman imagistic trope worked in concert with textual signifiers of street-involved sex workers as abject or bare life; such representations cultivated interest not in the suffering and deaths of multiple women, but in the tracking of a serial killer or group of killers who had—according to reports available in 2005—eluded Edmonton police for more than twenty years.

Significantly, the Missing Woman archetype has become a racialized figure, particularly in the years since the 2004 publication of Amnesty International and Sisters in Spirit's initial reports on missing and murdered Aboriginal women in Canada. In their 2008 article, "Women and the Canadian Legal System: Examining Situations of Hyper-Responsibility," NWAC and CAEFS describe kidnap and murder as "particular ways that Aboriginal women experience violence and victimization" (99). As I discuss in the previous chapter, however, the overrepresentation of Indigenous women among Canada's Missing and Murdered women cases tends, in print and online news, to provoke a negative process of signification that results in less, not more, public concern about such extreme violence. The additional connection—through the solitary Missing

Woman image—to street-involved prostitution and criminality would seem to cultivate even less public concern about these disappearances and murders.

THE LONE STREETWALKER

> How do race and gender intersect and interlock in the economy of
> representations circulating in the news media? And what are the
> regimes of truth surrounding their [murdered women's] status as
> worthy/unworthy victims deserving or undeserving of their fate?
> —Yasmin Jiwani, "Race and the Media: A Retrospective and
> Prospective Gaze"

The racialization of the Missing Woman archetype is ironic given the racial makeup of another pervasive image of sex work in popular print media: the Lone Streetwalker. Images featuring this similarly archetypal figure frame a solitary, usually Caucasian-looking female figure who appears to be working at night, seemingly unaware of the camera but posing seductively or otherwise dressing or walking to display her body to its best advantage for the drivers of the cars on the street she faces. The woman's face is rarely shown clearly. And while many of these photographic subjects may request that their faces not appear in news reports, precious few mainstream sources include commentary from these subjects on the ways that current legislation allows police to detain and arrest them despite their engagement in a legal exchange of sexual services for pay. Instead, their faces veiled in darkness and their comments truncated or written over in a variety of ways, these women's bodies signify criminality and victimization.

The pale skin of the Lone Streetwalker—showcased primarily through the play of light on her legs or arms (she usually wears a short skirt and/or a skin-baring top) remains a consistent feature of this archetype. Despite the fact that at least sixteen of Vancouver's murdered women, and at least five of the fifteen missing women of Edmonton, are Indigenous persons—not to mention the as-yet unconfirmed numbers of Aboriginal women taken from Winnipeg's streets, or the early 1990s case in Saskatoon in which all seven murder victims were Aboriginal women—this recurrent image of street-involved women at risk appears uniformly white. A number of disturbing interpretations of this overrepresentation of whiteness in narrations of the sex industry are possible here. For example, Indigenous groups' struggles to dissociate First Nations women from colonial representations of Indigenous women as "squaws," or whores, in concert with multicultural Canada's hegemonic denial of the legacy of such historical embarrassments, may help to whitewash mainstream contemporary images of sex work.[11] In addition, predominantly Caucasian spokespeople for the sex industry, alongside the recurrent media focus—through Sarah de Vries's adopted family, for example—on respectable white families whose daughters have gone missing from Vancouver's Downtown Eastside, signal the hegemonic culture's recurrent privileging of whiteness and the ways in which white faces function as representative signifiers of goodness, morality, agency, and personhood. Caucasian versions of the contemporary fallen woman seem, then, to provide more marketable or publicly interesting tales of tragedy and need. Such incarnations of white supremacy, alongside a hegemonic romantic investment in a rather limp version of multiculturalism, make unthinkable, or at least unrepresentable, the plight of the non-white sex worker.

Furthermore, despite community reports to the contrary, images of the Lone Streetwalker imply that the street sex trade continues, seemingly unaffected either by increasing concerns about the harm and nuisance that street-involved sex work may inflict on urban neighbourhoods or by increasing risks of violence and mounting evidence of foul play. These faceless figures continue to work alone in the dark, displaying their bodies for cruising drivers, flagrantly disregarding concerns about neighbourhood safety, and willingly risking their lives in these dangerous times. While there are workers for whom waiting for a companion to begin work, or checking in with a buddy or drop-in centre contact of some kind before and after servicing a client, remains at best a distant idea in comparison to their immediate concern with obtaining money, drugs, etc., these people do not represent the majority of sex industry workers.[12] Despite the great variety of people involved in the street sex trade—let alone the rest of the industry—news sources continue to offer these faceless pictures of lone white "working girls," as though only white women enter this industry, and as though working and simultaneously risking their lives is all they ever do. Images like these—and the stories that accompany them—rarely include street-involved and/or survival sex workers' community involvement, their dedication to their children or other dependents, their claims that they often work during the day, or their claims that they often work together, taking down license plate numbers for one another and watching each other's backs as much as possible.[13] Representations like the Lone Streetwalker instead imply that street-involved sex workers consistently and foolishly tempt both passing motorists and fate each night after dark.

All but one of the images discussed in this chapter appeared in a variety of Canadian print news venues (or their corresponding online editions) published between 2001 and 2006. The image in Figure 2.1 is taken from the November 1999 issue of the now-defunct feminist magazine *Elm Street*, in a story by reporter Daniel Wood entitled "Vancouver's Missing Prostitutes." I highlight this article first because it has been credited with helping to cultivate public concern about the growing numbers of Missing Women in Vancouver and thus to "galvanize public opinion in favour of a major investigation" (Cameron). Recognized at the April 2000 National Magazine Awards for exceptional investigative reporting ("Twenty-third Annual"; *Masthead*), Wood's article indeed received significant public attention and provides further evidence of the community-driven activism occurring during this period in Vancouver's history (activism that Beverley Pitman and Maggie de Vries also document).

The image highlighted here was commissioned from local photographer Chick Rice prior to the story's being written and was taken with the subject's permission one night on a Vancouver street (personal communication). In two other similar photographs in the article, female sex workers stand alone against a dark brick and concrete cityscape, their faces turned away from the camera or obscured by their hands or hair. The caption below this image reads, "On Vancouver's Downtown Eastside, women sell themselves for as little as $5 to buy heroin. Who'd care if a killer were stalking them? Even after 31 went missing, no one did—until their friends and families demanded the police take action."

While Wood's story sympathizes with and promotes the political agendas of the Missing Women's family and friends, his use of the morally inflected phrase "women sell themselves" instead of "people sell sex" or "workers sell sexual services" still evokes that emblem of patriarchal sexual repression, the fallen woman. Such phrasing—wording that other reports before and since regularly employ—suggests that a woman's worth relates directly to the demands she makes on those to whom she grants sexual access to her body. Another

FIGURE 2.1

Illustration for Daniel Wood's article, "Vancouver's Missing Prostitutes."

Photo by Chick Rice, used by permission.

oversight here is the failure to note that someone who provides a sexual service to finance a heroin addiction participates in the *survival* sex trade, a trade that some other members of the sex industry themselves wish to eliminate. She is not representative of the sex industry as a whole.

FIGURE 2.2

Banner included in CBC Edmonton's online series, "Deadly Streets."

Used by permission.

Figure 2.2 is the banner included on each page of the aforementioned CBC Edmonton series, "Deadly Streets." Though it is difficult to say for sure, the Lone Streetwalker image here appears to be a still from CBC TV reporter Judy Piercey's September 1, 2003 report for nightly news series *The National*, entitled, "How Police, Street Workers and Families Are Dealing with the Murders of Edmonton Women."[14] In this image, the Lone Streetwalker stands on a busy and recognizably urban street, the landmarks of which are largely obscured. By virtue of her solitude as well as her proximity to the vehicles she faces in this nightscape, in concert with the play of the bright head-and-tail lights of the cars on her pale skin, this woman's body signifies street-involved prostitution. Unlike the gritty immediacy of Chick Rice's image, this woman's perceived distance from her photographer suggests a disconnection—or lack of relationship—between photographer and subject. This staging offers a more voyeuristic perspective, as though the woman does not know she's been photographed while working. In another story, she could blend into the cityscape, functioning as context, as part of the background scenery. But this is a story about "deadly streets"; this woman-as-prostitutional-body, however distant, blurred, and voyeuristically rendered, constitutes a key element of this image as well as the story her body introduces.

In fact, the woman's form appears directly to the right of the "Deadly Streets" label superimposed over the centre of the photo. Roughly half the size of the woman and the clear focal point of the banner, the phrase transforms the Lone Streetwalker's body into a kind of punctuation point (an exclamation mark, perhaps). At the same time, the placement of the woman's body next to the word "streets" makes her form part of the text, another term to be decoded. Set to the left of the word "deadly" she might be perceived as the deadly force on these streets and as such be represented with a symbolic, if terrible, agency. Next to "streets," however, she becomes the object, the one who symbolically receives deadly street-involved violence, even as her proximity to the word "deadly" perhaps inevitably evokes the longstanding city/whore cultural trope that understands the street-involved sex trade as a form of violence against the community in which it occurs.

As noted above, the short pieces of text that appeared below this banner identified the kidnapped and murdered women of Edmonton as "women who work in Edmonton's sex trade," "prostitutes," "sex-trade workers," and "missing and murdered people who lived high-risk lifestyles." In addition, the stories focused primarily on police investigations into the women's murders. Links to related CBC reports—reports with titles such as "Police Try to Trace Dead Woman's Last Days," "Mother Begs Daughter's Killer to Turn Self In," "Prostitutes Remains Identified," and "Dead Woman Was Scheduled for Detox This Week"—that may once have provided some sense of the women's lives, not to mention their humanity, stopped functioning long before the series itself was removed. Moreover, the banner on the "Murder Victims" page of the series, including as it did in 2012 only the Missing Woman images superimposed over the map of Edmonton and surrounding area, provided viewers with an especially grisly "before and after" representation; the faceless Lone Streetwalker in the banner thus functioned as the "before death" version of each of the murdered women whose images appeared below hers. She was the "before" to their "after," despite the pale skin and lighter hair that marked (rightly or wrongly) the living woman as white, and the darker skin tones and hair that hinted at the Indigenous or mixed-race heritage of the dead.

Stepping away from news relating to murder cases involving street-involved sex workers, there are significantly fewer reports across the country during the period of my study of media materials (2001–2006), a fact that supports sex worker groups and their allies' contentions that sex work-related news rarely appears outside of violent contexts. A 2002 article in the *Ottawa Citizen*, by reporter Dan Gardner, entitled "How Cities 'License' Off-Street Hookers," discusses the ways that municipalities across Canada license massage parlours and escort agencies but criminalize street prostitution. Gardner interviews Lowman as well as a number of Vancouver politicians who debate and discuss the hypocrisy inherent in this system that targets only those who do not have the financial resources to conduct their sex-industry jobs away from the public eye. These pro-sex-worker concerns notwithstanding, however, the black-and-white photo that accompanies Gardner's piece pictures yet another woman dressed in dark coat, skirt, and high heels, facing away from the camera and toward a bright light on the relatively deserted night street on which she walks. As in other versions of this image trope, the skin of this woman's legs appears white against the dark urban backdrop. In this image, the Lone Streetwalker's body is central. By reproducing the Lone Streetwalker stereotype, this image does little to support the article's message.

Journalistic representations of the Lone Streetwalker, then, sometimes reinforce the themes conveyed in the articles they accompany, and sometimes contradict them. A more complex instance may be found in the relationship between the Lone Streetwalker image that appears on the front page of the June 16–23, 2003 edition of *Here*, Saint John, New Brunswick's self-proclaimed alternative news weekly, and the text of journalist Mark Parker's accompanying story, about clashes between sex-worker and non-sex-worker residents in a Saint John neighbourhood, entitled "Sex in the City," which appears inside on page 13. With this cover shot, and the accompanying headline, *Here*'s editors appear to foreground and interrogate the stereotypical nature of the article's accompanying picture to an unusual degree.

"Sex in the City" remains a popular tagline for prostitution-related news, drawing as it does on the seductive glamour of the award-winning American *Sex and the City* HBO television series (still on the air during this period) while simultaneously accessing the long association in the West of the metropolis with prostitution. The headline thus tellingly juxtaposes the sexual liberation of independent, wealthy, middle-class women (once considered the straight, sexual avant-garde) with the sexual transgression of more socially marginalized women in the city. The latter form of urban sexuality, represented here as elsewhere by the image of the Lone Streetwalker, does not receive rave reviews from many contemporary critics.

This Lone Streetwalker, typically faceless and seemingly unaware of the camera, stands against the backdrop of Saint John's inner city, displayed for the invisible drivers of the passing darkened vehicles. We recognize the traditional signifiers of street prostitution as she, like the Lone Streetwalkers in Figures 2.1 and 2.2, invokes a very old and particularly urban story. The tragic heroine of this archetypal tale becomes this woman whose black sling-back shoes, short black skirt, and leather jacket offer a hint of *Sex-and-the-City* sexual intrigue. But the shirttail peeking out below the jacket—a jacket that, on second glance, may not be real leather—puts a ragged edge on the woman's ensemble. This subtle suggestion of poverty, together with the woman's obscured head and face, evoke the pathos we have come to expect in such tales.

The usual signifiers of femininity as well as what John Berger describes as the broken idealism, or the particular "realism" invoked by the image of the prostitute (in the West), appear here (63). The feminine in this rubric becomes the object of the (traditionally) male gaze, the object who gives herself over to this gaze. The prostitute, as the figure who metaphorically promises herself to the male viewer and literally gives herself to any number of the men who look at her, disrupts the more traditional patriarchal artistic romance of the viewer–object relationship. In this particular image, a darkened figure stands on Cliff Street in Saint John, faces away from the camera, appearing to offer herself not to the camera's gaze but to that of the unseen drivers of the passing vehicles. The photo simultaneously denies a clear romantic connection between its viewers and the object of their gaze and foregrounds the voyeuristic nature of our looking. The image thus replicates a traditional power imbalance between object and viewer. However, perhaps because the object gives herself, as it were, to another (ostensibly) male viewership, the photograph is framed in such a way as to invite a level of comfort for other viewers with their own voyeurism.

However, compared with the images discussed previously, images Canadians regularly encounter in most any mainstream print news venue, something seems "off" in this picture. This woman's pose appears more static, as though she is less interested in moving toward the passing cars than the other lone figures. The shoes also seem wrong, somehow, the heels significantly lower than those worn by the other Lone Streetwalkers pictured elsewhere. These differences invite viewers to look again, more closely than before. In doing so, we may begin to question our initial perceptions of realism.

The street figures prominently in this photo, and so does the night, as evidenced by the bright streetlight illuminating the woman's face and body.

The image includes no trees, or gardens, bus stops, or public benches of any kind. Instead, down the street to the woman's right in the near distance is a pile of garbage next to what looks like the doorway to a pub or store. The dark, the garbage, and the pub suggest a downtown, perhaps inner-city location.

But again, something seems off. Why do the colours, especially the bright yellow light and the solid blue night, appear so cartoonish? And why can we not see even the back of this woman's head? Has this photograph been modified? If so, how much? Are we meant to recognize that the photo is staged? To my mind, the subtle but clear differences between this image and the others highlight the stereotyped nature of journalists' typical offerings in sex work-related reporting. In this context, the next line of text is telling as well. The questions, "Should they be given help? Or moved along?" point to a debate we have heard many times before, a debate with a decidedly moralistic tone that probably does not include the voices of the workers under consideration. All of the rote signifiers of a conventional human interest story—the kind that perhaps even includes the titillating details about sex work that have simultaneously fascinated and disgusted researchers and the general public alike for more than two hundred years—appear here.[15] Such signifiers invite readers into this version of the debate over where and when, if ever, street-involved sex workers like this one should be "allowed" to work in the city.

The story on page 13, however, further complicates the process of signification begun on the issue's cover. *Here*'s "Sex in the City" feature indeed discusses ongoing clashes between Saint John's Cliff Street sex workers and other neighbourhood residents. It opens by introducing "Pam," a woman who works the corner of Cliff and Coburg streets. Somewhat surprisingly, however, Pam and her co-workers, according to Parker, look "like university students" and wear scuffed sneakers and jeans on the stroll.[16] The woman on the cover does not seem to be part of this group—or in the rest of the article, for that matter—except, of course, for the cover shot, which appears again in the centre of Parker's article.

The feature moves quickly from Pam and her friends to concerned Cliff Street resident, Jackie Higgins. Higgins voices her concerns about the traffic, the noise, the public intercourse, and the discarded condoms and needles that accompany the street-involved sex trade in her neighbourhood. Higgins's concerns are those of neighbourhood associations from cities across Canada, and she has undertaken many of the same neighbourhood initiatives: she has called in license plates of sex customers to their employers, she has notified police, she has written to the mayor.

However, Higgins's not-in-my-backyard attitude, like the private and public anti-prostitution initiatives discussed below, is conflicted and contradictory. "There are 6 or 7 well known prostitutes, if that's the term you're going to use," she tells Parker. "Personally, I think that's too good a term for them" (13). But she adds, "As angry as I am that my home has been invaded, I wish I could help these women" (13). Thus Higgins simultaneously envisions Pam and her friends as violent "home-invading" criminals and as pathetic victims whose abject degradation shifts responsibility for their condition and their actions from themselves to those around them.[17]

Parker then includes a few words from Constable Jim Fleming, a community police officer who advocates a "get tough" policy in dealing with street sex workers he says are most likely drug addicts as well. Fleming's solution to Higgins's "home invasion" problem: "keep after the women until they leave the neighbourhood" (13). In advocating such zero-tolerance policing with little consideration of where sex workers will go when they are chased out of or barred from certain neighbourhoods, Constable Fleming's approach responds to and reifies the disposal rhetoric of citizens like Higgins and the neighbourhood associations they form.

Parker seems not to have consulted Pam and her co-workers on this point. Without these perspective-enhancing voices, Parker's article follows the same decades-old journalistic tropes that Van Brunschot, Sydie, and Krull observe in earlier prostitution-related reporting. The journalist continues these patterns in the next section of his article as he consults Torontonian sex worker activist Anastasia Kuzyk, who explains that "The problem is that homeowners think that their rights supersede" sex workers' "right to make a living" (13). Kuzyk's words echo those of pro-sex-work activists at SWAV, SPOC, SWAT (then Kuzyk's home organization), Stella, and Stepping Stone. Drawing on her own experiences in Toronto's Parkdale neighbourhood—where she helped establish "lock boxes where addicts could deposit used needles" (13) and where sex workers agreed to put used condoms in plastic baggies and then into the trash later—Kuzyk suggests that Higgins work with her neighbourhood sex workers to find solutions so that their continued coexistence may be more satisfactory for all involved. Finally, Kuzyk advises non-prostitute neighbourhood residents to "examine their attitude toward the women." Sex workers "aren't even considered to be human by a lot of people. We're just whores'" (13).

Parker then consults University of New Brunswick professor Leslie Jeffrey, co-author of *Sex Workers in the Maritimes Talk Back* (2006), whose research reinforces Kuzyk's position. Jeffrey also refutes Officer Fleming's position, noting, "No study has even proven that the addiction rates among sex workers are higher than those in any other profession."[18] Jeffrey further observes that, "By trade, sex workers form the second largest group of murder victims in Canada, and...policies like Fleming's get-tough approach add fuel to that fire" by pushing street-involved workers into unsafe spaces (13). Having thus reframed the sex work situation on Cliff Street to offer solutions to the systemic problems that produce such conflicts, Parker returns in the final paragraphs to Jackie Higgins who says she has no intention of ever speaking with Pam and her co-workers because, inexplicably, "that would only encourage them." However, despite her lack of friendly interaction with these women, Higgins says she "wants the public to understand the conditions the girls face and the extent of the problem in Saint John." Parker's article then concludes with a description of blonde-haired, scuff-shoed Pam climbing into another customer's car on Cliff Street.

However, despite the *Here* reporter's efforts to highlight and critique popular stereotypes of prostitution, and to reframe traditional neighbourhood debates around street-involved sex work, his article nevertheless reproduces common tropes in prostitution-related reporting. The text, together with the cover shot and headlines (both of which are reproduced in Parker's full-page article), reinforces longstanding hegemonic anti-prostitution biases. Even as Parker attempts to present both sides of the issue, the format as a whole privileges Higgins's and Fleming's anti-prostitute positions by virtue of their placement in the text: they speak first.

Furthermore, although Kuzyk provides positive models for resolving clashes between sex worker and non-sex worker neighbourhood residents, because Pam and her friends have no voice in his article, Parker effectively aligns himself with the very people and institutions he invites Kuzyk (and Jeffrey) to critique. Readers see Pam only from Parker's, then Higgins and Fleming's, then Kuzyk and Jeffrey's perspectives, perspectives that are increasingly removed from her particular circumstances. We see her only from a distance—or we see her in the anachronistic female figure featured in the cover shot. In fact, Pam would appear symbolically to keep working while Parker, Higgins, Fleming, Kuzyk, Jeffrey, and *Here*'s readers mull over the situation in her neighbourhood. She gets into a white car in paragraph two, then climbs into a red jeep in the final paragraph. Like Higgins and Fleming, and despite Kuzyk's and Jeffrey's advice that Pam and her co-workers be treated with respect equal to that offered the other parties in the dispute, the voices of the women around whom these neighbourhood issues revolve are not included in this piece. Higgins's claim that she'll not be speaking with Pam and her co-workers, placed as it is directly after Kuzyk and Jeffrey's comments that she should do exactly that, could render Higgins's words ridiculous and thus cultivate some much-needed credibility for sex workers and their supporters. However, Pam's lack of voice undoes this good work.

In thus defining Pam only in relation to her work and then only through others' perspectives on the same, the report makes Pam into an abject cultural apparition whose sole identity (as a prostitute) constructs her as a symbolic threat to her neighbourhood. In Parker's comparison of the silent Pam and her unnamed co-workers to a group of university students, and in his description of them moving in and out of cars carrying Tim Horton's coffee cups and wearing jeans and sneakers, these workers become spectres of a form of female sexuality that a patriarchal and anti-prostitute culture find particularly threatening: prostitution that masquerades as rather unremarkable everyday life.[19] Insofar as it toes the traditional line on street prostitution, then, this news source, like so many mainstream news venues, offers little hope for sex work activists who seek to humanize and decriminalize Canadian prostitutes by foregrounding their identities as everyday citizens in urban neighbourhoods.

Despite escalating violence against sex workers, despite the federal government's striking of the SSLR in response to national and international public concern over this violence, despite *Stolen Sisters*, the Amnesty International report expressing grave concern over the high numbers of disappeared First Nations women in Canada, national news venues continue to tell us the same stories and to show us the same familiar images. Experiential persons and other advocates of decriminalization, activists who discuss institutional racism and the effects of colonization, analysts who foreground the significance of high unemployment rates in the lives of many survival sex workers, and street-involved sex workers who describe the violence and sexual exploitation to which police subject them—none of these groups has the ear of the media majority in Canada.

ANTI-PROSTITUTION NEIGHBOURHOOD ACTIVISM

> Sex trade in a community gives rise to competing interests and
> difficult social pressures.
> —Elaine Craig, "Sex Work By Law: Bedford's Impact on
> Municipal Approaches to Regulating the Sex Trade"

Unlike sex workers, anti-prostitution activists in urban centres across the
country do garner extensive media coverage and significant support from city
police and municipal, provincial, and federal politicians for their concerns.
As discussed in my introductory chapter, critics such as Neil Brenner and
Nik Theodore, Mike Davis, and Christian Parenti note that the gentrification
(renewal, revitalization, and resettlement) of once-defunct industrial strips
and once-poor inner-city neighbourhoods that characterizes neoliberal socio-
political and economic engagement in a number of Western contexts is often
accompanied by an enthusiastic discourse celebrating such "creative destruction"[20] in anticipation of an "urban renaissance" that will produce a "city of
the future." Such discourse regularly glosses over the simultaneous "brutalization of inner-city neighbourhoods" that such renewal projects entail (Davis,
227–28). Subsequent efforts to contain the poor in increasingly smaller urban
areas, what Davis describes as veritable "outdoor poorhouses," are accompanied by "increased police harassment and ingenious design deterrents" such as
public benches on which it is impossible to lie down, traffic-calming measures
that reduce vehicular movement through moneyed residential neighbourhoods,
or city parks with fewer wooded paths and more flat grassy areas to facilitate police surveillance (232–33). Parenti likewise observes a "polarization of
urban space and social relations" that has facilitated the rise of zero-tolerance
policing (70). Such regulatory strategies, often referred to as "broken
windows" or "quality of life" policing, advocate the strict monitoring or even
criminalization of petty thievery, vagrancy, prostitution, and other formerly
minor social offences in order, supposedly, to fix the cracks in society's glossy
surfaces that would otherwise lead to larger, more serious breakage, or crimes.
Unsurprisingly, as Anastasia Kuzyk and Lesley Jeffrey highlight in Parker's "Sex
in the City" report, the interests of property owners are overrepresented in such
regulatory strategies.[21]

While Davis and Parenti's discussions focus on the US, such trends are evident in Canada as well. And while Canadian incarnations of neoliberalism and neoconservativism are perhaps less overtly facilitated by fundamentalist evangelical Christianity than those in the US, a disturbing moralism nevertheless underwrites widespread public support in Canada for increased police presence in major cities despite declining national crime rates; for increased policing of the homeless and the ejection of such populations from public thoroughfares, parks, and buildings; and for curfews and other initiatives that target youth and the poor. During the 2006 Canadian federal election, the Liberal Party's platform featured statements such as the following: "Canada's cities and communities are where we truly experience what it means to be Canadian. Paul Martin and the Liberal government understand this and have committed a great deal to improving where we live and raise our children. We also know that cities propel economic growth, employment and innovation. They are at the centre of our country's success" (Liberal Party). This position reflects the "New Deal for Cities" that Paul Martin's Liberals initially promoted once elected.

The New Deal proposed a relationship between Ottawa and major Canadian cities akin to that of federal and provincial or territorial governments, highlighting the ways that "Canada depends on communities that can attract the best talent and compete for investment as vibrant centres of commerce, learning, and culture" (Throne Speech, February 2004). Following the Liberal Party's defeat in the January 2006 federal election, Stephen Harper's Conservative Party declined to deal with cities directly; however, his government promised to earmark funds transferred to provinces and territories for improvements to "community" infrastructures like public transit and commuter highways (Conservative Party 16).[22] The Harper government's subsequent plans during this period primarily involved tax incentives and investment in urban infrastructures to attract more business and investment to Canadian centres. The Conservatives' additional promise to "Stand up for security" again focused on cities, promising "More police on the streets" to help deal with stereotypical urban, not rural, "drug, gang, and gun-related crimes" (22–25).

Municipal politics across the country between 2001 and 2006 and beyond— even in Liberal, Bloc Québécois, and New Democratic Party strongholds—has similarly focused on urban law and order as integral to economic growth. At the 2004 Canadian Mayoral Summit, left-leaning Toronto Mayor David Miller catalogued some of the initiatives his administration would undertake to ensure that Toronto fulfills its "pivotal" role in the global economy. Increased police presence and regulation of city streets was one of the first items on his agenda ("New Deal Speech"). Vancouver's similarly left-leaning former mayor Larry Campbell suggested, in his inaugural speech in November 2002, that his administration would focus on Vancouver's international image by encouraging foreign investment in the city. In addition, after noting decreases in violent crime in and around Vancouver, Campbell said his administration recognized that "Vancouverites are rightly demanding intensified efforts to make our streets and neighbourhoods safe," and he indicated that he would be working with Vancouver police to ensure that this increased safety was provided (Larry Campbell). After Campbell's first year in office, however, a 2003 Ipsos-Reid poll found that while 68% of those surveyed thought their mayor had done a good job, and 38% approved of his four-pillar approach to Vancouver's drug problem, "a majority" of those surveyed thought he had "been too soft on dealing with issues such as panhandlers (55%), squatters (51%) and property crime (52%)" (Ipsos Canada).

The majority of voting Vancouverites' subsequent democratic endorsement in December 2005 of Mayor Sam Sullivan is therefore not particularly surprising. During his three years in office, Sullivan expressed similar interests in improving the city's international image—especially as preparations were underway to host the 2010 Olympics—and attracting foreign investment through means that were to include the increased policing of city streets and neighbourhoods. In his inaugural address, Sullivan took Campbell's plans a step further, stating that his administration would get more police on the streets, but that they "must also look at ways to better engage communities in the fight against crime... and support streamlining the enforcement of city bylaws so that we can improve the civility, order and cleanliness of our streets and neighbourhoods" (Sullivan 2005). While Sullivan also expresses a belief that drug addiction, a now infamous problem in Vancouver that is especially associated with the city's Downtown East Side, should be treated in social programs as a long-term disability instead of a crime, his interest in enforcing civic bylaws targets many of the panhandlers, survival sex workers, and homeless poor whose addictions he seeks to mitigate.[23]

As noted earlier, in terms of street prostitution in Canada, increasingly stringent prostitution-related legislation over the past three decades (see Appendix 1) has already had some dire consequences, especially for disenfranchised populations of street-involved sex workers. The market deregulation, cuts in social spending, and corporate tax holidays that seem so often to precede the emergence of neoconservative interests in urban law and order moved many sex workers onto city streets as brothels, or "bawdy houses," were outlawed in the late 1970s and early 1980s. Former brothel properties became prime real estate in downtown cores and were taken over by less socially contentious owners, a process that suggests a significant correlation between anti–bawdy house legislation in cities across Canada and international neoliberal urbanization and gentrification trends in the late twentieth century.

Increasing urbanization, class proximity, and class anxiety (as discussed in Chapter 1) continue to facilitate the rise of powerful neighbourhood associations who work, in conjunction with an increased and distinctly less tolerant police presence, to protect their own interests. In keeping with "broken windows" neighbourhood regulation strategies, one of the first issues to which such groups apply themselves is street prostitution. As Lowman observes, Canadian "discourse on prostitution of the 1980s" was "dominated by demands to 'get rid' of prostitutes" ("Violence" 18). He also notes the following: "After prostitution was displaced out of Vancouver's West End in the summer of 1984 by a nuisance injunction, lobby groups...emerged in four other neighbourhoods (Mount Pleasant, Strathcona, Kensington-Cedar Cottage, Grandview-Woodlands) to combat prostitution displaced from other areas. Most of these organizations...simply wanted to see prostitution removed from their neighbourhood without seeming to care where it might go" ("Violence" 15). What happened next is chilling: "After 1985, the year in which the communicating law was enacted,[24] there was a large increase in British Columbia of murders of women known to prostitute" ("Violence" 18). There are, Lowman concludes, disturbing parallels between escalating violence against sex workers, increased criminalization of prostitution, and citizens' groups' more and more insistent "discourse of disposal," a discourse that demands that sex workers be removed from more and more urban streets through police arrests, restricted access laws, and the fencing off of more and more public areas.[25] Just as the "Sex in the City" article illustrates, and as numerous other dominant news sources record, despite the growing number of serial kidnappings and murders of sex workers in cities across Canada during the period Lowman studies, urban anti-prostitution neighbourhood policing and activism proliferated alongside this extreme violence.

Like Jackie Higgins, anti-sex-work groups employ a number of strategies to eliminate prostitution from the streets they consider theirs. Some, like CROWE (Concerned Residents of the West End), a Vancouver group active in the mid-1980s, or the more contemporary Grandview-Woodlands Neighbourhood Action Group,[26] may use posters, pamphlets, and letters to newspaper editors to threaten vigilante action against sex workers and thus move street prostitution out of these neighbourhoods.[27] Other residents' groups may, as a group in Edmonton's Inglewood community did in 2005, monitor neighbourhood properties, agitate to have fences put up to keep "all kinds of undesirables" out of certain areas, and help police to regulate "no go zones" for those women with prior arrests for prostitution (Inglewood Community League Newsletter). Others may, as in some controversial initiatives in Winnipeg, Ottawa, and Halifax, take down license plate numbers of johns for inclusion in police reports, or for use by private citizens intent on shaming johns. Such campaigns have also entailed impounding johns' cars and forcing attendance at john schools (discussed below), for which attendees can pay up to five hundred dollars before their vehicles are returned.[28]

Paradoxically, many of those involved in neighbourhood actions like these also have expressed concern for street-involved prostitutes and survival sex workers. On the assumption that all forms of prostitution entail the sexual exploitation of those who sell their services, some concerned groups join a long tradition of moral crusaders in setting up community outreach centres. Centres like the recently defunct Prostitutes Empowerment Education Resource Society (PEERS) in Vancouver (discussed in Chapter 1), or the former Prostitution Awareness and Action Foundation of Edmonton (PAAFE—now called the Centre to End All Sexual Exploitation, or CEASE) offer street sex workers therapeutic counselling, job retraining, resource management programs, and education with the goal of getting them out of the sex industry.

In addition, organizations like these occasionally support programs that aim to decrease demand for sexual services by educating johns about the "sexually exploitative" nature of prostitute use. For example, although this is no longer the case, in 2006, the PEERS website included links to the VPD (Vancouver Police Department) and the John Howard Society of British Columbia—two intimately connected organizations involved in administering john schools. Similarly, CEASE/PAAFE's website during this period included links to a course outline and photographic record of a john school run by Edmonton Police called POP (Prostitute Offender Program) (PAAFE, "John School," 2005). In early 2011, the PAAFE site introduced the organization as the "governing body which coordinates the Prostitution Offender Program and manages and disburses the funds generated by the Prostitution Offender Program fees" (PAAFE, Homepage, Apr. 2011). Although their mandate has expanded to include diversion programs for men and women, CEASE/PAAFE continues to oversee POPs in Alberta.[29]

Edmonton Police and the John Howard Society, like CEASE/PAAFE, take an approach that presumes sexual exploitation, disease, and violence to be inherent to prostitution. As the John Howard Society's Alberta branch reported in 2001, POPs require that in lieu of entering the criminal justice system, johns pay a fee to attend a daylong program. Such programs address issues of "damage and nuisance associated with street prostitution and its associated drug trade. Ex-prostitutes speak of the impact of prostitution on women and how they view men who buy sex....Health issues such as STDs are addressed, and psychiatrists speak about sex addicts" (*Prostitution*). Thus designed to deter men from participating in prostitution again, john schools have received mixed reviews. As the Federal, Provincial, and Territorial Deputy Justice Ministers' Working Group on Prostitution—a group that published its report in 1998 after six years of research—records, "proponents of prostitution diversion assert that the programs are effective and have been successful since they have experienced low recidivism" (Canada, *Report and Recommendations*). As the following comments by "schooled" Edmonton offenders suggest, programs like the Edmonton-run POP, at least according to CEASE/PAAFE, educate johns in the desired manner. One man asserts, "I do not want to contribute to the horrific industry." Another says, "This is more than my embarrassment, it is about victims and adding to their misery." When asked if he would like to volunteer for future programs, another man replies, "Volunteer? Very likely. Prostitutes have been humanized to me" (PAAFE, "John School," 2005).

The working group also found, however, that recidivism rates, which have always been low, may not give an accurate measure of the efficacy of such programs. The group notes, "Critics feel that the act of arrest is enough to deter most from re-offending and that john school is merely gratuitous if its purpose is, in fact, to deter offenders from using the street as a venue for obtaining the services of a prostitute" (Canada, *Report and Recommendations*). Regardless of these criticisms, the working group goes on to stress the importance of diversion programs and recommends that exit strategies for both sex workers and their customers continue to be evaluated and administered at the municipal level.

Predictably, the continued existence of john school programs in the intervening years has not resulted in the improvement or expansion of their curricula to educate participants on the ways that current laws marginalize and victimize sex workers. In order to make such changes, john schools would have to examine the ways that targeting paying clients, far from saving people from the dangers and sexual exploitation of sex work, instead makes sex workers more socially and professionally vulnerable by removing their means of support. Presumably, such additions to curricula would undermine the diversionary mandate of john school initiatives.

That said, these types of diversion programs tend to be better funded (often with government dollars) than outreach programs not explicitly opposed to prostitution. The public funding of such anti-prostitution initiatives is problematic, however, because, as Lowman observes,

> The rhetoric surrounding these developments nicely reveals the Canadian political doublespeak about prostitution, both in terms of the reason given for why we need "john school" and the curriculum itself....The purpose of the communicating law is to control the nuisances associated with street prostitution, not to prohibit prostitution itself. By extending the "education" beyond nuisance, "john school" imposes on its conscript clientele a moral position that the law does not contain. Its advocates conveniently forget that buying and selling sexual services are both legal in Canada. To be consistent with the law, the program should be called "nuisance school" and provide the same education about nuisance to prostitutes and clients alike (part of which might well be about where prostitutes and clients should meet in order to avoid creating a nuisance). By introducing epidemiological concerns, topics like drug-dealing, and the effects of prostitution on the prostitute and her

family, john school is a morality play on prostitution, not nuisance. ("Prostitution" 53–55)

Sociologist and co-investigator on STAR (the Sex Trade Advocacy and Research project), Jacqueline Lewis similarly condemns this aspect of john schools and other diversionary programs, which she analyzes through a restorative justice framework:

> The public moralizing/shaming/condemning aspect of prostitution [restorative justice/diversionary, or RJ-D] programs, resulting in part from such community conferencing, is meant to help clients and workers see the error of their ways, thereby reducing the demand-and-supply side of the industry and the harm to the community. However, due to the orientation of these programs—the lack of conferencing among workers, customers, and the community, on the one hand, and the blaming, shaming and moralizing that takes place within the conferences that do take place, on the other—it is difficult to see how they can bring about reparation and the reintegration of participants into the community, an essential component of RJ, or be anything more than an alternative form of punishment for violating the law. (290)

In addition to the legal and social hypocrisy that facilitate diversion initiatives, such programs also reinforce the dominant medical and sociological methodologies Pheterson critiques in The Prostitution Prism. Like these flawed methodologies, exit strategy outreach programs and the POPs with which they are too often affiliated "treat...'prostitute' as a fixed identity rather than as a contingent social status, thus assuming prostitution to be a female trait or destiny removed from the dynamic realities of group relations and political power" (Pheterson, Prism 10). For example, every sex worker who comes through the doors at CEASE/PAAFE is, theoretically, empowered only insofar as she works to change her prostitute identity—an identity she often has significant difficulty altering, regardless of the training and education she receives at the outreach centre. And the social conditions that inform her life and work, the broader relationship between her sex work and her community, are reduced to her own ability to orient herself in culture. She may accept help, but such assistance is offered with the understanding that she must change: she must work to refuse "sexual exploitation" and to integrate herself into mainstream society. In doing so, she must also acknowledge not only that sex work is not a normal, or acceptable way to make a living; she must "recognize" that the conditions that led her into sex work were unnatural and exceptional. She must acknowledge and recognize these presumed facts, regardless of prostitution's long history, a history which suggests that prostitution is one of the least exceptional or unnatural elements of civil life the world over.

Consequently, while CEASE/PAAFE's vision for "A community where there is hope, respect and transformation for individuals, families, and communities affected by sexual exploitation" is admirable indeed, their mission to "work through partnerships to create and pursue strategies to address sexual exploitation and the harms created by prostitution" includes a number of assumptions that effectively exclude many pro-sex-work social activists from these partnerships and from this caring community (PAAFE, "Welcome," 2005; CEASE, "About," 2012). Similarly, the John Howard Society's involvement in the development and administration of john schools across the country undermines their stated belief that "justice is best served through measures that resolve conflicts, repair harm, and restore peaceful relations in society" (John Howard Society of Canada, "About Us"). Groups like CEASE/PAAFE and the John Howard Society appear to read all sex work as exploitation, all choices to work in the sex industry as preceded by exceptional personal circumstances, any substance abuse problems sex workers may have as inherently connected to their work, and any satisfaction in sex work as particularly tragic false consciousness. Consequently, organizations like these, much like the community police who support their programs, unwittingly endorse the individualization of social issues as well as the increased policing and criminalization of socially marginalized populations and risk cutting themselves off from communities of non-survival sex workers and their allies who might otherwise augment and support their projects to assist and to raise awareness about at-risk populations. Some of the outreach programs discussed here do indeed provide important services for survival sex workers and other socially precarious persons. The growing need for such programs, however, reflects not the negative effects of sex work, particularly survival sex work, on urban neighbourhoods, but rather the erosion of the social safety net under neoliberal and neoconservative political systems in Canada.

ANTI-PROSTITUTION POLICING

> Prostitution regulations are always political and their enforcement is equally contradictory. That is because sex work is paradoxical as police must find a balance between enforcing what is a relatively minor offense in criminal terms...[and] appeasing/catering to powerful interest groups, residency associations, municipal and provincial governments, in a given city.
> —Dianne Grant, "Sexin' Work: The Politics of Prostitution Regulation"

Despite growing violence against sex workers in Canada, community policing continues to reinforce exclusive community-building and neighbourhood safety measures. For example, visions of the city proposed by Vancouver and Edmonton police services and the RCMP, with whom they partner, portray street-involved sex workers as "the problem" to be dealt with in coming years—this despite the fact that Vancouver and Edmonton are home to the biggest serial murders of sex workers in Canada to date. Perhaps responding to mounting public concern about appropriate community policing after the missing women case appeared in national headlines, the Vancouver Police Department (VPD) published a *Strategic Plan* for 2004 to 2008. The first step in this plan involved "Improving Community Safety," a goal the VPD planned to achieve by "1. Reducing property crime, 2. Reducing violence against the vulnerable, 3. Reducing violence caused by gangs and guns, 4. Improving traffic safety, 5. Reducing street disorder" (Vancouver Police Services). Here, market interests trump social goods and services; concern with the protection of private interests and the control of public thoroughfares prioritize traffic regulation and the reduction of property crime alongside initiatives aimed at protecting vulnerable people from violence. Notice, for example, how the final three initiatives target and criminalize a good portion of the vulnerable people the second initiative supposedly works to protect.

It is not particularly surprising that, despite the VPD's documented and by now notorious lack of concern over the disappearance of many very vulnerable women from the streets of the city, the document goes on to define vulnerable populations first as victims of domestic abuse. When sex workers are acknowledged as another vulnerable population, the VPD asserts that they will foster better liaisons and partnerships between police and sex worker associations so that prostitutes will be more likely to report assaults to police. However, part of this same protective plan calls for a crackdown on those who "live off the avails of prostitution" and advocates further development of the VPD's partnership with the John Howard Society's john school programs.

Sex workers and their advocates regularly highlight the ways that police crackdowns on johns, in concert with the solicitation and communicating laws (*Criminal Code* sections 195 and 213), decrease negotiation times between street workers and their customers. As a result, sex workers will often get into customer vehicles before prices and services have been agreed upon and without taking the time to "get a feel for" customers' character and intentions vis-à-vis violence and ability to pay (Lewis). In addition, sex workers have long objected to laws against living on the avails of prostitution (*Criminal Code* s.193) because such laws too often target their lovers, family members, and friends, instead of the abusive pimps[30] they are officially meant to disempower. Hence, even as the VPD sets out to increase communication and cooperation with sex worker associations, the other initiatives that accompany such a positive move hobble this plan. How are sex workers to trust that police want to protect and work with them to decrease their vulnerability when officers are simultaneously working to make their jobs more solitary and dangerous?

Modelled on the VPD/RCMP task force investigating the missing women cases in Vancouver, Project KARE is an Edmonton-based EPS (Edmonton Police Service)/RCMP "K" division task force formed in 2003 to investigate the kidnappings and murders of some fifteen sex workers in the Edmonton area. Much of KARE's mandate is designed to prevent EPS from receiving the kinds of criticisms levelled at Vancouver municipal and police officials regarding their initial responses to reports of missing women in the Downtown Eastside. Former Vancouver mayor Philip Owen infamously responded to these reports by remarking that he was not financing a "location service for hookers" (Phillips). Later, however, police established "Project Evenhanded," a location, or at least identification, service that does exactly that. Modelled on Project Evenhanded, a group of investigators—once referred to as KARE's "Insurgence Team"—works to "immerse themselves into the world of the Sex Trade Workers [sic]" (Project KARE, "Information: Proactive Initiative," 2012, 2006). In so doing, this team tries to become acquainted with, record physical descriptions of, and even collect DNA from as many street sex workers as possible in downtown Edmonton. (These investigators now work "throughout Alberta—as far north as Fort McMurray and as far south as Medicine Hat" ["Information: Proactive Initiative," 2012]). Without acknowledging the real possibility that, as Lowman argues, "Police cannot give an iron-clad guarantee that prostitutes' DNA will not be used against them" in court (qtd in G. Smith), KARE continues to describes this initiative—with which many prostitutes have cooperated—as "a proactive approach which provides us with much-needed information should one of" the sex workers "go missing" ("Information: Proactive Initiative," 2012).[31]

Project KARE's broader mandate requires that the unit "pursue strategies to minimize the risk of having additional HIGH RISK MISSING PERSONS (HRMP) murdered within the Provincial Capital Region" (Project KARE, "Information: Project Mandate," 2006, 2011).[32] However, KARE's HRMP registry and the "Safety Tips" they offer to at-risk populations illustrate only two of the many ways that police participation undermines such an initiative. The "missing persons" segment of the HRMP label reflects the focus of the Vancouver task force on the missing women's personhood instead of their status as sex workers. However, the words "high risk," in concert with a description of five murdered people as "sex trade workers," in past and present versions of the first sentence of KARE's homepage clearly indicates that sex workers are the HRMPs under consideration here. While all of the victims in Edmonton's current serial murder case were sex workers, the ways in which unqualified connections between street-involved sex work and murder negatively affect public interest appears to be a lesson KARE has not learned from the Vancouver case.

Since its inception, KARE's website has also included a list of "Safety Tips" for HRMPs that, regardless of the general language used, again clearly speak to sex workers. Having discussed, on other pages of their website, only the initiatives police are undertaking to investigate and arrest someone for the current HRMP murders, with these tips KARE implies that the protection of HRMPs is the responsibility of sex workers themselves:

- The most important tip is not to be involved in a high risk profession, lifestyle or activity such as prostitution or hitchhiking. These activities make you very vulnerable to becoming a victim.
- Use the buddy system. You can look after each other. Traveling or working together can lower your risk. If you must get in a vehicle, whether it is a stranger or not [sic], have your buddy document the license plate number, description of the car and the driver.
- Make sure someone knows where you are and who you are with at all times.
- Do not place yourself in vulnerable situations.
- Do not turn control of your personal safety over to anyone.
- Do not allow anyone to take you anywhere you are not familiar or comfortable. Someone should know where you are at all times.
- Be especially careful around people you do not know, but also be aware you can be victimized by someone you are familiar with. ("Information: Safety Tips" 2006–2012)

The foregrounding of victim responsibility over perpetrator profiles in instructions like these clearly illustrates sex workers' social and cultural isolation as well as the omnipresent threat of violence that accompanies their work.

Setting aside for the moment the condescendingly repetitive nature of these tips, reading the first item on this list, I find myself thinking that taxi-driving and working in late-night bars or service centres—not to mention police work and fire-fighting—are also high-risk professions or "lifestyles."[33] People involved in these jobs routinely make themselves "very vulnerable to becoming a victim," or must "turn control of their personal safety over" to another person. People involved in these professions also benefit from use of a "buddy system" and being "especially careful around people" they "do not know." These are professional connections KARE could usefully acknowledge here in order to address the whore stigma evident in the extreme violence to which victims to date have been subjected. In focusing on sex work as a high-risk occupation or lifestyle to be avoided, without also highlighting the ways that contemporary culture sets street sex workers up to become victims of extreme violence, KARE reproduces a firm, traditional, stigma-induced hierarchy between acceptable, socially sanctioned professional risk-taking, and prostitution-related dangers.

Nonetheless, KARE's safety tips are good rules of thumb to follow in many professions, including the street-involved sex trade, and sex worker organizations regularly recommend that all sex workers take these kinds of precautions. However, while KARE's site includes no links to sex worker-run organizations (of which there are many on the web), it is important to note that these groups regularly—and more respectfully—advise their members on how to deal with police as well as other perpetrators of assault, robbery, and violence.

Despite the positive associations called up by Project KARE's name, this task force takes an unimaginative and perhaps necessarily paternalistic approach. They advise HRMPs to reduce the risks they take in their work, and they offer to solve cold murder cases and to find and identify missing daughters, mothers, sisters, and friends. But their methods for doing so offer further violence to sex workers, murdered and living alike, in that they appear to allocate responsibility for violent assaults evenly between killers and victims. As such, Project KARE gives lip service to the prevention of violence against these vulnerable populations, but the task force ultimately serves the interests of victims' families after the fact: they offer to pursue kidnappers and murderers when registered women go missing, and to provide closure by identifying victims' remains.

Of course, as a police initiative, KARE cannot officially recommend that street sex workers consider working in teams from their own homes, apartments, or hotels. But would this not be the most valuable safety tip to offer? Neither can KARE suggest that sex workers take their time negotiating prices and services with clients so that they have a better chance to evaluate clients' intentions, because the communicating law that police are responsible to enforce (*Criminal Code* s.213.1) ensures such negotiations are conducted hastily or in relatively opaque code. However, an acknowledgement from such a high-profile police unit of the ways that current prostitution laws further victimize already vulnerable populations would go a long way toward lifting some of the whore stigma and social marginalization that, as so many who have studied the Vancouver case and other instances of violence against sex workers have argued, facilitates sex worker abjection.

In effect, both Project KARE and the VPD Strategic Plan constitute institutionalized forms of anti-prostitution work that both support and respond to anti-whore neighbourhood activism. In fact, anti-whore activists have important, influential, and very interested police and public audiences who remain, it seems, all too willing to blame sex workers for the violence enacted against them—by police, by johns, and by other private citizens who know that prostitutes, especially those on city streets, are an unprotected, socially isolated, and very vulnerable population. What remains especially disturbing in each of these policing strategies are the ways that such initiatives respond to public criticism by giving lip service to the improvement of relationships between police and organizations representing vulnerable people, while insisting that increased attention to status quo policing (in terms of faster and "cleaner" enforcement of the very laws that facilitate violence against these populations) constitutes an acceptable plan to prevent further harm.

SURVIVING GLOBAL CAPITALISM

Contemporary Canadian urban regimes criminalize and socially marginalize sex workers, especially those who work urban streets or in the survival sex industry. Simultaneously echoing and reinforcing such socio-political agendas, mainstream news media and the public and private anti-prostitution initiatives so often supported in these venues represent and reify dominant contemporary understandings of citizenship and belonging, of who matters and who does not. Sensational news stories about metropolitan crime waves, about the supposedly inherent dangers of street prostitution for sex worker and non-sex worker neighbourhood residents alike, and about the criminal and/or pitiable nature of street-involved sex workers provide little in the way of analysis of legislative or socio-economic factors contributing to, for example, the high visibility of prostitution at this time in Canadian history, or the growing numbers of women and youth in the survival sex industry. Such popular portrayals play a major role in shoring up support for more urban policing, for the resulting decrease in freedom of movement, and the for the devaluing of citizens who work or live on urban streets.

Yet, as theorist Zygmunt Bauman argues, "Doing something, or being seen to do something, about fighting crime threatening personal safety" is perhaps the best a government may be seen to do to assuage the less visible, and less easily discernable anxiety-provoking forces global capital brings to bear within nations (*Globalization* 118). In his view, contemporary concerns with public safety, "more often than not trimmed down to the single-issue worry about the safety of the body and personal possessions, are 'overloaded,' by being charged with anxieties generated by other, crucial dimensions of present-day existence—insecurity and uncertainty" (*Globalization* 5). As discussed in the introductory sections of this book, the pressures of global neoliberal economics are reflected in current governmental downsizing, the privatization of once public space, and cost-cutting that results in the elimination of social programs despite the high unemployment rates that help transnational corporations to keep labour costs down. Resulting widespread uncertainty, in public and private realms of employment, for example, and the social anxieties provoked by the loss of a social safety net coupled with real fears of downward social mobility, "tend to rebound as perceptions of threats to public safety—first to the body, and then to property, the body-space extension" (Bauman, *Globalization* 117).

Bauman offers a useful framework for analyzing the material presented in this chapter concerning contemporary Canadian efforts by police, the governments who fund them, and the private citizen initiatives with which they are affiliated to control and secure city streets. Indeed, my research strongly supports Bauman's argument that, in current contexts, it is a universally acknowledged foregone conclusion that national governments must cede control of their territories to the forces of globalized capitalism to survive:

> In the world of global finances, state governments are allotted the role of little else than oversized police precincts; the quantity and quality of the policemen on the beat, sweeping the streets clean of beggars, pesterers and pilferers, and the tightness of jail walls loom large among the factors of investors' confidence, and so among the items calculated when the decisions to invest or de-invest are made. To excel in the job of precinct policeman is the best (perhaps the only) thing state governments may do to cajole nomadic capital into investing in its subjects' welfare; and so the shortest roads to the economic prosperity of the land, and so hopefully to the "feel good" sentiments of the electors, lead through the public display of the policing skill and prowess of the state.

The care of the "orderly state," once a complex and convo-
luted task, reflecting the multiple ambitions and wide multi-faceted
sovereignty of the state, tends as a result to narrow to the task of
fighting crime. (*Globalization* 120)

The main function of this growing prison system—what Parenti terms
the "Prison Industrial Complex"—is, according to Bauman, to isolate threatening persons from the rest of society. In addition, as Bauman, Davis, Parenti,
Lowman, and others note, definitions of criminality seem constantly to be
expanding so that more and more persons on the bottom end of racialized,
gendered, classed, and other systemic hierarchies are arrested and imprisoned. Critics discuss contemporary prisons as fortresses designed to house
modern-day low-waged or slave labour (Parenti), as increasingly privatized
holding houses for the proverbial great unwashed: those masses of the increasingly criminalized, racialized, and otherwise marginalized populations (A.
Smith). Alternatively, we may see them as metaphoric coffins offering a form
of living death to those who do not succeed as required within contemporary
socio-economic contexts (Bauman, *Globalization*). But what of those whose
required isolation results in their "relocation" to actual cemeteries, or to even
less visible spaces or states of being?

Are there parallels to be drawn between the coffin-like rooms inhabited
by inmates of Pelican Bay prison in California (Parenti 208–09) and the graves to
which the murdered women of Vancouver and Edmonton have gone? Or between
the revolving door prison systems that keep marginalized populations—and
thus low- and no-waged labour—inside prisons, and the increasingly criminalized existences of inner-city street-involved sex workers in Canada? Certainly the
systems developed by the VPD and Project KARE to monitor street sex work and
to identify the bodies of murdered women mimic, to a certain extent, the record-
keeping of an efficient prison system. In prison, however, despite pervasive
stories of prisoner-on-prisoner or guard-on-prisoner assault, rape, and murder,
inmates are offered certain protections: an imprisoning nation-state reserves
the right to control the fates of its imprisoned, and to restrict access, violent or
otherwise, to prisoners' bodies to a select few state representatives.

Sex workers are occasionally imprisoned for prostitution-related offences
in Canada. But they are usually fined first, given "no go zone" restrictions, or

physically relocated—either by police or private citizens—to other areas of the city, areas that are at worst, darker, less populated, and more dangerous, and at best, less familiar neighbourhoods in which to work. What does it mean that private citizens as well as police are involved in the policing and relocating of street-involved sex workers in urban neighbourhoods? At best, as discussed above, it means that street-involved sex workers are not recognized as legitimate members of urban communities, that stigma-inflected social and legislative policy continues to define street-involved sex workers as outsiders to "ideal" urban communities. At worst, it means that by their very participation in the street sex trade, sex workers forfeit both their civil and human rights. They are not free to traverse public thoroughfares, or to have a voice in or the protections offered by civil society. As the cases of Vancouver and Edmonton's murdered women poignantly indicate, private citizens may subject these disenfranchised persons to whatever measures of control, or unmeasured violence, they wish. Those who resort to violence, who usurp the nation-state's once unique or sovereign right to police and take deadly action against its (transgressive) citizens, may do so with increasing impunity—impunity facilitated by the blaming, on the part of police and public officials, of sex-worker victims for their own kidnappings and murders.

Sensational news stories about metropolitan crime waves, about the supposedly inherent harms of street prostitution for urban neighbourhoods, and about the abject "criminal" existences of street-involved sex workers indeed provide little insight into the socio-political and global economic factors contributing to growing numbers of women and youth in the survival sex industry, or to the high visibility and de facto criminalization of prostitution at this time in Canadian history. Such popular portrayals function to encourage public support for politicians who promise more urban policing to protect the citizenry from the threatening realities of modern life. The resulting limitations on sex workers' freedom of movement, as well as the devaluing of those persons who work and/ or live on urban streets, indicates that a particularly dangerous order is being imposed on some of the most disenfranchised populations in Canada. Given the many connections between the citizens treated as legitimate and these so-called others (connections discussed in the concluding paragraphs of the previous chapter), such orderliness signifies a general and alarming disavowal on the part of the Canadian liberal democratic nation-state of its responsibilities to uphold and protect the social, civic, and economic freedoms—as well as the basic human rights—of all of its citizens.

Such abdication of governmental responsibility must be resisted and reversed. Exposure and critique of the colonialism and necropolitics underscoring the serial kidnap and murder of sex workers across the country constitute important incarnations of such resistance. Current cultural and media bias, however, allows sex worker activists and advocates few opportunities to resist their own sociocultural erasure and to re-implicate themselves, their lives, and their work, into (legitimate) urban contexts. Nonetheless, there is a growing local, national, and international sex workers' rights movement that has begun this necessary project. Members of this movement acknowledge that urban class proximity and widespread social dissatisfaction in the face of contemporary culture's simultaneous production and fear (expressed through criminalization and brutal policing) of a growing underclass have the potential to produce solidarity as well as exclusivity—though such solidarity is too often established over the bodies of the poor and disenfranchised.

Routinely required to employ less traditional methods of disseminating this message and establishing such solidarity, sex-worker activists in industrialized countries like Canada often turn to the Internet. In doing so, they re-represent themselves and their work, complicating, undermining, and speaking back to their abject representations in dominant cultural forums. To date, a number of politically engaged sex workers and their advocates administer an array of publicly accessible, user-friendly, educational, and activist websites, forums, and sex work-related media archives. The next chapter analyzes the effectiveness of both the medium and the messages of some key forms of Canadian sex worker online activism.

3

TECHNOLOGIES OF RESISTANCE
CANADIAN SEX WORKER ACTIVISM ONLINE

For four decades, activist sex workers have identified prostitution as a legitimate work relation, and prostitutes as workers deserving of occupational control and the same rights, respect, and protections extended to other citizens in Canada and beyond.
—Becki Ross, "Sex and (Evacuation from) the City"

As noted in the previous chapter, sex workers rarely appear in mainstream news outside the contexts of violence, and what representations dominant media agencies offer routinely employ a set of stock images to accompany archetypal tropes and repetitive narrative forms. Yet as Becki Ross's fascinating research into Vancouver-based sex worker activism since World War II illustrates, these marginalized activists and their allies have much to teach the mainstream. Given the extreme violence to which past refusals to respect and honour the basic humanity of sex workers has led, it is high time, I would argue, for Canada to listen, learn, and change.

In order to examine sex workers' self-representations and the lessons they offer, in this chapter I study their activism on the Internet, one of the few free public spaces left to sex worker communities in Canada. Here I analyze the ways that groups like SWAV (the Sex Workers Alliance of Vancouver, which disbanded in 2005),[1] the currently active SPOC (Toronto-based Sex Professionals of Canada), and Stella of Montreal work to reclaim urban space, insisting on positive connections between themselves, their sex work, and their respective cityscapes. This chapter focuses on these three sex worker activist groups in particular because their web presences include a variety of photographs of group members and events that provide powerful rebuttals to the prejudicial popular representations of prostitutes and prostitution discussed in previous chapters.

This chapter also considers ways that web technologies simultaneously expand and limit the access of sex worker activists to political, cultural, and moral capital. Sex worker online activism is prolific, rich, and interactive. However, while this activism appears to facilitate solidarity in the pro-sex-work movement and communicates important information to sex workers who might otherwise have no access to it, such technopolitical communication caters to a self-selected audience. It is thus necessary to consider the substantially different levels of political power to which pro- and anti-prostitution activists have access, as exemplified by the SSLR proceedings and the successful Ontario-based constitutional challenge to Canada's prostitution laws. What are the consequences of this power imbalance? In relation to the current numbers of serial kidnap and murder cases involving sex workers in cities across Canada, violence that sex worker activists and other advocates convincingly link to a contemporary discourse of disposability regarding street prostitution, this unequal access to power is particularly alarming. And the ways we address the question of who matters (and who does not) in Canada's future global cities inevitably reflect the increasingly complex influences of technology and capital on dominant cultural definitions of the human and the humane.

COMPUTER-MEDIATED COMMUNICATION AND SUBALTERN COUNTERCULTURES

The dominance of anti-prostitution groups in the broader culture and in mainstream media forces sex-worker advocacy into more innovative, or at least less traditional means of garnering support and communicating with the wider public than anti-sex-work groups need employ.[2] Using the Internet to achieve these ends, sex worker activists join an emerging tradition of grassroots activists harnessing the increasingly interactive and collaborative "Web 2.0"[3] to foster community and to organize a variety of on- and offline public interventions aimed at promoting and protecting human rights.[4] Many scholars highlight the ways that the Internet's provision of low-cost, high-efficiency, collaborative access to information effectively encourages citizen activism. Others also point to the potential of digital technologies to unite sub- and countercultural individuals whose common political interests might not otherwise be connected due to geographical or other communicative restrictions. As Richard Kahn and Douglas Kellner explain, "online activist subcultures have materialized as a vital new space of politics and culture in which a wide diversity of individuals and groups have used emergent technologies in order to help to produce new social relations and forms of political possibility" (94).

However, such endorsements of computer-mediated communication, or CMC, as a countercultural tool are regularly qualified today by warnings that, for example, "going online does not by itself subvert the typical, state-sanctioned technocratic modes of authority and governance that have disenfranchised individuals from input into political decisions" (Galusky 193). Arguing that the Internet reproduces hegemonic neoliberal relations of power, Vernadette V. Gonzalez and Robyn Magalit Rodriguez cautioned in 2003 that "the cyber-frontier as 'democratic' becomes important for us to critique, especially when the Internet is being celebrated as the new space for transnational solidarity and struggle by some and 'commercial democracy' by others" (379). Kahn and Kellner likewise observe that the Internet is "a contested terrain, used by Left, Right, and Center of both dominant cultures and subcultures in order to promote their own agendas and interests" (94).

Furthermore, online activism cannot be understood in isolation. As Michael D. Ayers noted in 2003, "an online social movement must have some level of activism in the 'real' world if the changes it seeks are to go beyond the realm of the Internet itself" (162). Conversely, Kahn and Kellner, writing in 2004, predict—rightfully, as it turns out—that future activism will inevitably draw on CMC: "The political battles of the future may well be fought in the streets, factories, parliaments, and other sites of past struggle, but politics is already mediated by broadcast, computer, and information technologies and will be so increasingly in the future" (94). In his 2009 analysis of online sub- and countercultural activism in China, Guobin Yang similarly affirms that online community formation and political organization "are not sufficient for democratization, but at the same time they are essential aspects of any process leading to it" (36).

Partially eschewing understandings of CMC that reinscribe binaries between on- and offline worlds, Wael Salah Fahmi, in his 2009 article, "Bloggers' Street Movement and the Right to the City: Reclaiming Cairo's Real and Virtual 'Spaces of Freedom,'" identifies "new geographies of protest," or "spaces of resistance," located in what he describes as "hybrid physical and virtual worlds" (90). Fahmi notes that "media activism no longer means just making and editing images/texts, or viewing video or audio clips; it also uses the Internet as a work space, social centre and project workshop so that virtual and physical spaces are experienced almost as a single space of communication" (90). Ongoing Canadian sex worker activism is beginning to occupy such a hybrid space, but many groups still appear to rely primarily on the more traditional website rather than blogs and other forms of new social media to communicate with their members. It is beyond the scope of this project to speculate on the reasons for this lag in contemporary Canadian contexts (though I would guess that underfunding and an exceptionally busy, even overextended, and largely volunteer group membership constitute at least part of the reason).

I note, however, that sex worker activist web self-representation and communication has begun to change. At the time of writing, a comprehensive blog entitled *Trade Secrets: Health and Safety in the Sex Industry* operates on the weblogging platform Blogger; the BC Coalition of Experiential Communities and Vancouver's PEERS Resource Centre retain presences on weblogging platforms Wordpress and Blogger respectively; Vancouver's PEERS and PACE Society, Winnipeg's Sage House, Toronto's SPOC and SWAT, and Quebec's Alliance Féministe Solidaire Pour les Droits des Travailleuses/rs du Sexe have recently established Facebook groups;[5] and a number of groups have established Twitter accounts. In its current evolving incarnation, online sex worker activism would seem, at least to an extent, to facilitate potentially revolutionary relationships and cultural possibilities. Given the numerous, longstanding initiatives by inner-city community centres, drop-in/outreach centres, and libraries to counter computer illiteracy and limited access issues for the most disenfranchised populations, these relationships and possibilities increasingly reflect the concerns of sex workers from all strata of the industry.

Within the contested online terrain, as a result, sex worker activists have come to constitute what social theorist Nancy Fraser terms a "subaltern counter-public." According to Fraser, counter-publics are "parallel discursive arenas where members of subordinated groups invent and circulate counter-discourses, which in turn permit them to formulate oppositional interpretations of their identities, interests, and needs'" (81). Fraser further notes that, "in stratified societies, subaltern counter-publics have a dual character. On the one hand, they function as spaces of withdrawal and regroupment; on the other hand, they also function as bases and training grounds for agitational activities directed toward wider publics. It is precisely in the dialectic of these two functions that their emancipatory potential resides. This dialectic enables subaltern counter-publics partially to offset...the unjust participatory privileges enjoyed by members of dominant social groups in stratified societies" (82). As the SWAV, SPOC, and Stella websites make clear, the Internet constitutes an undeniably excellent (and relatively safe) sphere for subaltern counter-publics like Canada's sex worker activists to regroup and develop agitational political activities.

Indeed, several scholars argue that the web is a particularly effective meeting space for sex workers. For instance, in their 2005 analysis, "The Mobilization of Grassroots Activities via the Internet," Noriko Hara and Zilia Estrada explain,

> The internet especially capitalizes on the following resources: knowledge, interpersonal interactions, identity support, and the building of credibility and legitimacy. Knowledge can easily be disseminated world-wide via websites and e-mail mailing lists. Solidarity can be generated and enhanced through interpersonal interactions, as like-minded people find each other via online networks. At the individual level, the internet can be a medium through which identity support is provided through such things as validation of personal views (through discussion forums and chat rooms), as well as through the provision of identity and group symbols (i.e., group iconography for personal display). Publicity, outreach, and networking can take place through referrals, linking

between websites, and promotion through the website or other media. For marginalized groups, the internet can provide opportunities to legitimize their existence, and increase credibility, visibility, and marketability. This "legitimating" resource can be seen in the ways that hate groups have used the internet to establish an aura of legitimacy. The strategies for establishing legitimacy online are various and cheaper than through other mass media. (504)

Kirsten Pullen, in the concluding chapter of her 2003 book *Actresses and Whores*, argues more specifically that Internet technologies foreground "new strategies for mitigating the whore stigma, and new ways to occupy the whore position" (174). Examining Nancy Quan's sex worker serial on the US-based *Salon.com* as well as WAN (The Whore Activist Network), Pullen notes that websites by and about sex workers allow for "more concrete responses to traditional notions of prostitution" (172). Such concrete responses on Canadian sex worker activist sites—many of which link to, draw resources from, and quote one another—indeed contrast remarkably with the repetitive, stereotyped stories, popular images, and stigma-inflected political dialogues about sex work typical of contemporary neighbourhood politics and city policing. In particular, SWAV, SPOC, and Stella's hybrid on-offline political advocacy significantly portrays sex workers as concerned citizens and works to establish them as legitimate members of urban communities.

Hegemonic representations of and responses to sex work continue to limit the sphere of influence available to sex worker activists in, for example, dominant news media. As social theorists William Carroll and Robert Hackett caution, the overreliance of a subaltern counter-public group on Internet technologies can effectively limit the wider cultural influence of the group. "On one hand," they observe, "efforts to build and sustain a specific counter-public—to enrich the communicative practices within a subaltern group—make important contributions to communicative democracy by enabling that counter-public to find its political voice. On the other hand, counter-publics must address wider publics, and their ability to do so requires practices that also fall within the ambit of what we have termed democratic media activism [DMA].

It is worth noting, however, that DMA seems especially prone to 'getting stuck' at the first stage—the building of counter-publics" (98). Nevertheless, sex worker activists' hybrid (on-offline) self-representation, in addition to the efforts of sex worker activist groups to support their own and to establish on- and offline networks with academic researchers, police, lawyers, doctors, other allies, and the wider public, has had results; their influence in the recent past has begun to be felt outside their particular subaltern counter-political groups in Canada. This expanded scope of influence is evident in the September 2010 ruling by Ontario Superior Court Justice Susan Himel in favour of three SPOC plaintiffs, represented by Toronto lawyer Alan Young, who challenged existing prostitution laws under the *Canadian Charter of Rights and Freedoms*. Despite largely unsuccessful efforts, most notably on the part of the federal Conservative government as well as the Attorney General of Ontario, to appeal this decision,[6] this official acknowledgement that certain prostitution laws in the *Criminal Code* infringe on the basic human rights of sex workers is an important victory in SPOC's ongoing struggle to decriminalize sex work in Canada.

Online sex worker activism in Canada includes an array of websites—the traditional website format is one that organizations still appear to use most regularly—produced and maintained by organizations such as the web-based CSIS (Commercial Sex Information Service); Vancouver's PACE Society, PEERS Resource Centre, WISH (Women's Information Safe House) and SWAV; Toronto's SPOC and Maggie's; Hamilton's Big Susie's; Montreal's Stella and Spectre de Rue; Montreal-based STAR (Sex Trade Advocacy and Research) and Coalition for the Rights of Sex Workers/La Coalition Pour les Droits des Travailleuses et Travailleurs du Sexe; Halifax's Stepping Stone; and others. Initiatives such as drop-in centres, Bad Date Lists,[7] legal advice, tips for dealing with police, and news and research archives demonstrate the commitment of these and other similarly mandated agencies past and present to assisting urban sex workers. However, SWAV, SPOC, and Stella's choices to include photographic records of group members that go back a number of years,[8] the political events they organize and attend, and the cityscapes in which these events take place set them apart from the others.

These publicized images are important because, despite the essential legality of the exchange of sexual services for money in Canada, whore stigma and prostitution-related laws that criminalize all but the actual exchange make it relatively risky (even dangerous, in some cases)—and still quite remarkable—for people to "come out" as sex workers to unknown audiences. In addition, because anti-prostitution initiatives and policing in city neighbourhoods effectively make all city spaces "no go zones" for sex workers, it remains similarly risky—and thus similarly remarkable—for sex workers to locate and discuss their strolls publicly and to organize and publicize political events in busy urban neighbourhoods. Thus, while all of the organizations listed above have web presences that offer important, even invaluable services to sex workers across the country, SWAV, SPOC, and Stella stand out as longtime risk-takers, as organizations whose members' visibility on their websites and in the community-based initiatives they record there works in distinctive and important ways to combat whore stigma by undermining stereotyped images of sex workers and sex work.

In doing so, these groups problematize the Lone Streetwalker and Missing Woman archetypes in potentially revolutionary ways. Advocating for street-involved and other sex workers as integrated members of the communities from which they too often disappear and in which they consistently suffer robberies and assaults, SWAV, SPOC, and Stella's vision of urban community may provide what critics of technology describe as the (virtual, or online) starting point for an emergent politics of coalition and cohesion that exceeds the restrictions of postmodern identity politics.[9] In this way, online sex worker activism echoes and endorses what cultural critic Paul Gilroy terms "conviviality." While Gilroy discusses conviviality specifically within the contexts of postcolonialism, race politics, and the failures of multiculturalism, his use of the term to describe "the processes of cohabitation and interaction that have made multiculture an ordinary feature of social life" in cities around the world applies in this instance as well (xv). "Conviviality," as Gilroy defines it, "introduces a measure of distance from the term 'identity,' which has proved to be such an ambiguous resource in the analysis of race, ethnicity, and politics. The radical openness that brings conviviality alive makes a nonsense of closed, fixed, and reified identity and turns attention toward the always unpredictable mechanisms of identification" (xv). By keeping sex-worker and non-sex-worker identities in sight, but refusing popular divisions of communities along these lines, SWAV, SPOC, and Stella clearly welcome conviviality's radical openness and the potential for positive renegotiation of community interrelationship such openness provides.

March 18, 2005

Hello,

There is something important in all this SWAV disbanding publicity
which I'm embarassed to admit I forgot to say. We have talked in our
discussions recently about the high cost of being a public figure —
often personal costs which include barriers to advancement in other
aspects of our lives. The most obvious example is career change. It's
no easy task trying to figure out what the hell to do after a career in
prostitution. I have known personally several people who have found it
impossible.

But we have never discussed the other side of this equation — the high
cost of anonymity. When you are anonymous you forfeit having your
own voice. Over SWAV's decade of history there have been several
members who have always kept their support quiet. These members
have been unwavering in their support, with their trust, dedication,
labour, insightful advice and financial commitment. And never have
they ever received any public acknowledgment or gratitude. It is
because of these members — helping those of us who have been
public figures to be the best that we can be — that SWAV had grown
into such a productive and influential organization.

I just want to say with all my heart a very, very big THANK YOU. You
know who you are.

> *"Without you I'm nothing."*
> — Sandra Bernhardt

With eternal gratitude.
— Andy Sorfleet

sex workers alliance of vancouver ¶ http://www.walnet.org/swav/

Created: July 13, 1995
Last modified: March 18, 2005

Sex Workers Alliance of Vancouver
Box 3075, Vancouver, BC V6B 3X6
Tel: +1 (604) 488-0710
Email: swav@walnet.org

FIGURE 3.1

Andy Sorfleet's 2005 letter to supporters, on SWAV's website.

Used by permission.

THE SEX WORKERS ALLIANCE OF VANCOUVER

Despite SWAV's decision to disband in 2005,[10] the group's homepage remains an important testament to countercultural regroupment and a historical record of political agitation. Significantly, aspects of the site also recall Caroll and Hackett's concerns about countercultural activists' reliance on CMC. For example, the Bernhardt and Sorfleet quotations accompanying the "Whore Lover" banner in Figure 3.1—one of SWAV's many great campaigns to "re-brand" prostitution— conclude a letter to the alliance's online supporters from Andy Sorfleet, administrator of the SWAV website. This letter appeared for only a short time after SWAV's March 2005 announcement that they were disbanding so that leaders could pursue other political interests. The letter speaks to many of the strengths and weaknesses of online and other public forms of sex worker activism. For the letter's full text, see Figure 3.1.

In discussing so candidly the price of publicity and anonymity, Sorfleet foregrounds the ways that online activism both combats and endorses whore stigma. On the one hand, SWAV's site fosters community by keeping those members who wish to remain anonymous or out of the public eye informed about the group's political activities and the uses to which SWAV has put their donations. On the other hand, cultural stigma continues to reduce member turnout at the public events the alliance promotes on their site. As a result, those few members who are comfortable being "out" as sex workers lose the protective anonymity of being surrounded by a larger group at public events, even as they speak for and about a large and diverse population. In addition, while online and email discussions keep spokespeople informed, such reliance on private, virtual connections significantly limits the impact of the group's public events, as sparse attendance puts forward a quieter (and thus less impressive) group image and potentially less influential public message.

The overrepresentation of Sorfleet's political views and engagements on the site is perhaps another potentially negative effect of whore stigma and the group's reliance on CMC. In addition to administering the SWAV website and writing many of the reports included therein, Sorfleet contributes to or appears in most of the photographs on the site. Other members' photos and articles appear as well, but Sorfleet's overwhelming presence here may give us pause. Despite his letter crediting SWAV's many unnamed supporters, we may wonder if this is or was effectively a one-man show. Does whore stigma keep so many supporters "lurking"[11] in the activist realm? In the end, given the accessibility of the technology, and the usefulness for sex workers of much of the information provided here, does this question matter?

SWAV's homepage consists of a few strategically placed graphics, links to news items of interest to SWAV readers, and a categorized list of SWAV's many initiatives—like Bad Date/Client Lists and the group's much-lauded *Trials of the Sex Trade*—to make sex workers' lives and work better. Many of the links on the homepage lead to reports and records that are sometimes cheeky or humorous, but always extensive and detailed, of the organization's contributions to municipal, national, and international political activism and research. For example, Sorfleet, as coordinator and representative of SWAV, has been involved in Social Sciences and Humanities Research Council of Canada-funded research with SWAT, Maggie's, and Stella. In addition, SWAV is one of the agencies responsible for producing Dan Allman's 1999 book about male sex trade workers, *M is for Mutual, A is for Acts*. As well, the group worked with Maggie's to develop and write *Trials of the Sex Trade* (publicly accessible online), an illustrated guide to the Canadian legal system for sex trade workers who have been arrested and/or charged with prostitution-related offences, and SWAV was the first agency to get *Trials* into print.

In addition to these more publicly and politically focused initiatives, the SWAV site records a number of alliance initiatives that build group solidarity and morale. The photographs on SWAV's website provide important visual records and stories for and about sex workers in Canada. Through this means, SWAV effectively insinuates sex workers into the historical and everyday fabric of Canada. For example, Figure 3.2 is the first—and least racy—of the photographs (taken by Bill Powers) the visitor encounters after clicking on the "Birthday Suit Salute" link on the SWAV homepage. "Andy Sorfleet bares all for Canada's birthday celebration," a caption at the top of this page reads. Sorfleet's patriotic hat, his bare torso, and the "whore love" sticker he holds includes those whose sexualized bare bodies constitute their means of making a living into mainstream Canadian patriotism. This picture suggests that sex workers love their country, too. Significantly, Sorfleet's appearing nude *for* his country and the whore love graphic he holds while inviting "Canada's" gaze encourages the country to recognize this cheeky (pun intended) but friendly patriotic gesture, and to return whores' affections.

FIGURE 3.2

"Andy Sorfleet bares all for Canada's birthday celebration": SWAV's Birthday Suit Salute.
Photo by Bill Powers, used by permission.

Given the general Canadian public's overall intolerance for public nudity, however, let alone pornographic naked poses, this public may not be Sorfleet's primary audience for these pictures. SWAV's graphics, photos and drawings alike, consistently eschew prudishness, regularly featuring naked or near-naked people posing seductively or unabashedly engaging in a variety of sexual activities. In this way, the organization unapologetically caters to a very specific— perhaps even exclusive—audience, even as representations like the Birthday Suit Salute assert the legitimacy of this select group's citizenship in Canada.

SWAV also records and shares what may be termed "whore history" from in and around Vancouver. For example, it entitles the link leading to pictures like the one in Figure 3.3, "Historical sites in Vancouver." This is one of a group of photographs of Seymour Street's former Penthouse, the city's most notorious brothel site, which closed in 1975 after its owners were charged with living on the avails of prostitution. Rightly marking this period as a significant turning point in Vancouver whores' history, the caption above this photograph reads, "This famous bust is said to have been the cause of a large increase in street prostitution. Seymour Street today is Vancouver's 'high track' [or stroll] where Vancouver's prettiest and priciest work."

"The Penthouse at Dusk, 1019 Seymour," one of SWAV's "Historical sites in Vancouver."
Photo by Andy Sorfleet, used by permission.

The Penthouse bust remains one for the history books in Vancouver, whether from the perspective of sex workers or police in the area. Police crackdowns on brothel-based prostitution that followed the further retrenchment and enforcement of the bawdy house laws[12] in cities across Canada in the 1970s and 1980s were facilitated by increased government funding that allowed agencies like the VPD to pursue a six-month criminal investigation into Penthouse owners' business practices before the bust. However, as the caption noted above suggests, the closing of brothels changed but did not eliminate urban prostitution. Sex workers continue to make their presence known along Seymour Street; now, however, they work outside where their work is both more visible and more dangerous than before.[13] It is the visibility and perseverance of this population that the remaining photos highlight. In these photos, on this website, and perhaps even in the real city, the former Penthouse space belongs to and is characterized by its sex worker population as much as anyone or anything else.

Further staking whores' continuing claim on this area, the text introducing Figure 3.4 describes a paint-bombed advertisement for a local radio station in the parking lot behind the former Penthouse. (The image appears to feature a reclining nude man whose genitals are covered by a phallic object and whose

FIGURE 3.4

Paint-bombed advertisement for local radio station: "The Penthouse, parking lot beside,"
one of SWAV's "Historical sites in Vancouver."

Photo by Andy Sorfleet, used by permission.

chest is covered in red nail polish or paint. He reclines under the caption, "Do
I look like a hooker to you?") The defacement of this signage is explained as "the
response from the girls to a smart ass's idea of a funny rotating billboard in the
summer of 1999." Curated images like these claim this urban space as one of
many sex work-related historical sites in Vancouver. In this paint-bombing, "the
girls," or sex workers in this neighbourhood, actively resist efforts to reframe or
revision their cityscape. Including the photo on the website and referring to the
billboard's creator as a "smartass," SWAV clearly takes the side of the people
it sets out to represent, simultaneously including its online readers in this
resistance and its representative reframing. The police who closed the Penthouse
are not the victors in this historical account. Rather, they appear as the villains of
this piece, villains whose interests are thwarted by SWAV's memorialization and
sex workers' continued occupation of this urban space.

Other photos on the website similarly "flesh out" local history, further
proving sex worker and non-sex workers' joint ownership of particular Vancouver
buildings and streets. Figure 3.5 shows Mescaleros, another of SWAV's historical
sites, a Vancouver restaurant that, SWAV's writer tells us, was a finishing school,

FIGURE 3.5

"Mescaleros, 1215 Bidwell at Davie," one of SWAV's "Historical sites in Vancouver."
Photo by Andy Sorfleet, used by permission.

hotel, and prohibition-era brothel. Apparently, the girls from the finishing school "serviced" hotel guests on evenings and weekends. The source of this information—a waiter at the restaurant who heard of news clippings found in the building during renovation—makes this history less reliable than that of the Penthouse. However, the legendary quality of the story is important nonetheless. As noted in Chapter 1, both Nigerian poet and novelist Ben Okri and Canadian Aboriginal novelist and literary critic Thomas King argue that groups develop into close-knit communities through the individual histories they learn from and of one another as well as the communal stories they share. In the face of mainstream insistence that prostitutes remain placeless, voiceless, and alone in our culture as in our cities, SWAV records different stories for sex workers, providing whores with a shared history, a virtually and geographically grounded community, and a positive understanding of their place in contemporary society.

In the SWAV photos included here, and in others like them on the group's site, SWAV effectively—if only virtually—creates a positive geographical and shared history of whores' continued presence, against a mainstream culture that largely portrays their lives and their histories as public travesties and tragedies, and tries to move them out of Canada's cities altogether. In addition, SWAV's photos, in concert with the group's online archive of projects, research and publications, and pamphlet, sticker, and poster-based neighbourhood campaigns (many of the materials for which remain available to download, free, through the website) work to legitimize sex workers and their experiences, and to critique the moral illegitimacy of prostitution laws that would understand sex workers as outsiders, even in the communities in which they live, or work, or both.

SWAV's website, as a whole, also provides somewhat of a record of the organization's ten years of political action, research, and advocacy for the decriminalization of sex work. The site and its now-defunct offspring, CSIS (the Commercial Sex Information Service), thus firmly establish whore history, whore politics, "whore love," and a raising of consciousness regarding whore community in a public yet safe realm. And the website of the Sex Workers Alliance of Vancouver at one time showed up alongside other sex-industry sites in any basic Internet search—a small form of extra exposure that may even continue today to expand the organization's re-branding of prostitution slightly beyond its subaltern realm.

Next to the Canadian-focused CSIS (also administered by Andy Sorfleet; last update June 29, 2009), SPOC, and Stella, the SWAV site includes some of the most extensive public records available of urban Canadian pro- and anti-prostitution campaigns over the last three decades. Notably, the site remains in good standing, suggesting Sorfleet's (or another administrator's) dedication to this activist effort, even after the alliance's dissolution. In addition, as a complete—and completed—digital archive, SWAV's website constitutes an intriguing and critically useful case study with which to compare the evolving web presences and archives of sex worker activist groups in existence today.

THE SEX PROFESSIONALS OF CANADA

Unlike SWAV's complete(d) online record, SPOC's site provides regularly updated records of a vibrant association of sex worker activists. Founded in 1983 as CORP, or the Canadian Organization for the Rights of Prostitutes, to challenge Canadian prostitution laws,[14] the Toronto-based SPOC initially established a web presence in order to more widely disseminate Bad Date/Client information to sex industry workers.[15] This initiative coincided with the organization's re-branding of itself as a *professional* association.[16] While SPOC continues CORP's (and SWAV's) work advocating comprehensive decriminalization of prostitution in Canada, and even as they continue to provide services for sex workers that combat current legislative and cultural realities, their current name and site envision a post-decriminalization society. The type of cyberactivism by which they work toward this future is well described by Kahn and Kellner: "In opposition to the capitalist strategy of globalization-from-above, subcultures of cyberactivists have been attempting to carry out globalization-from-below, developing networks of solidarity and propagating oppositional ideas and movements" (89). Visually recalling the social labour and Black Power movements, and simultaneously reflecting their own unapologetic political starting point, SPOC's logo—a black-and-white image of a woman with long dark hair who wears a black bustier and opera gloves, and holds her right arm straight above her head, her fist clenched—signals the organization's dedication to just the sort of cyberactivism Kahn and Kellner identify: "propagating oppositional ideas" and pursuing convivial "networks of solidarity." The Canadian Organization for the Rights of Prostitutes cannot necessarily approach the courts or government from the same institutionally legitimate position as, for example, the Canadian Medical Association. Perhaps the Sex Professionals of Canada, an association whose title asserts rather than demands its members' legitimacy and does not include the culturally loaded term *prostitute*, is better able to do so.

At the time of writing, SPOC's homepage includes information about their constitutional challenge, as well as a mission statement emphasizing their dedication to decriminalization, and to the fostering of sex worker communities. Along the left side of the homepage is a list of navigation buttons, including "Meeting Information," "Upcoming Events," "Past Events," "SPOC in the News," "Be A Good Date," "Bad Client List," "Undesirable Clients," "Resources," "Court Decisions," "SPOC's Shop," "Links," and "Contact Us." Clicking on "SPOC in the News" takes visitors to a links page entitled "Sex Professional of Canada in the News." The page includes a photo (discussed below) and three lists of hyperlinks under the headings "Audio," "Video," and "Print Media." Each of the hyperlinks on this page is functional and leads to extensive records of local and national news appearances and interviews by SPOC members, many of which indicate that SPOC's constitutional challenge draws support from and has extended relationships with an impressive array of allies with varying degrees of power and public influence (not the least of whom is Osgoode Hall law professor Alan Young, SPOC's lawyer).

The photograph SPOC includes on this page acknowledges one of the organization's more longstanding political alliances. In this image, two SPOC members stand on an urban street in the summer, holding signs that read "Sex Workers and Dykes Unite in The Fight For Our Rights" and "Keep Your Laws Off My Body / Support Your Local Prostitutes / End Violence Against Women." The caption below this image reads, "Valerie & Patricia at Dyke March. June 22, 2007, Toronto," thus drawing attention to the historical connections between politicized lesbians and sex workers that have been highlighted by both sex worker activists and academic critics; these include Jill Nagle and Eve Pendleton, to name only two of many. These relationships were initially established between some lesbians and sex workers in the early days of the lesbian feminist movement of the late 1960s and 1970s, and were further cemented in the 1980s and 1990s. In her introduction to the collection *Whores and Other Feminists* (1997), Nagle positions sex worker and lesbian feminism alongside one another, noting that the "pariah status" of both the sex worker and lesbian identities in contemporary dominant North American culture are formed in relation to binaries such as "lesbian/heterosexual, and good girl/bad girl" (5). Under the subheading "Compulsory Virtue and Harlot Existence," Nagle draws parallels to the late Adrienne Rich's assertion in "Compulsory Virtue and Lesbian Existence" (1986) that the lesbian/heterosexual binary underlies the choices of all women "since it forces even heterosexual women to be forever vigilant lest their membership in the 'good' category be challenged, as in, 'I could never wear/say/do that; someone might think I'm a dyke!'" (4–5). Noting that compulsory virtue also "informs and constricts women's every move, i.e., 'I could never wear/say/do that, someone might think I'm a whore!,'" Nagle argues that "heterosexual privilege generally functions as a subset of 'good girl' privilege, while lesbianism and prostitution are subsets of 'bad girl' categories" (6).

Pendleton's analysis of the cultural connections and political alliances between lesbians and sex workers as stigmatized members of sub- or countercultures goes even further, for she insists that, "since both lesbianism and sex work destabilize heteronormativity, linking the two practices is a critical political and theoretical move" (74). Pendleton also notes that early lesbian feminism, "which attacked heterosexuality as a social system that maintained the subordination of women," has much to offer contemporary queer and sex worker cultural critiques (73). So, too, has the study of "lesbians who work in the sex industry....Numerous historians and cultural critics have begun to document the rich history of lesbian sex workers; their work often highlights the stigmatized social spaces historically shared by whores and lesbians" (74). Both Nagle and Pendleton, then, argue that lesbians and sex workers are similarly stigmatized (and thus allied to one another) not only because of embodied relationships between the groups, but also because they may be understood as collectively resisting patriarchal control of women's sexuality—lesbians by engaging in sexual activity that does not cater to or depend on male sexual desire, and sex workers by refusing to subject themselves to male sexual desire without exacting fees for services rendered. Lesbian, gay, and queer activists' continued efforts to destabilize the "heterosexual economy" (Pendleton 73) by proliferating sexual deviances—or by foregrounding and normalizing a diversity of sexualities that subsequently undermined the centrality and normalcy of "straightness"—in the 1980s and 1990s further cemented political links between sex workers and these communities.

Another way in which this photographic evidence of SPOC's attendance at the 2007 Dyke March (an annual event at Toronto's week-long Gay Pride Festival) offers a visual nod to the organization's ongoing countercultural connections to politicized lesbian groups is its inclusion of Valerie Scott, a blonde woman standing to the viewer's left. Scott, current legal coordinator (also former SPOC—and CORP—executive director), is at least a thirty-year veteran in the sex industry and has been involved in Canadian sex worker activism since the mid-1980s. Herself involved in a long-term relationship with a man, she has given a number of interviews in which she discusses her political and professional involvement with lesbian and gay communities over the years (Klinck; Brock and Scott 15). The photo thus signifies historically and in the present; in so doing, it becomes an important and politically savvy reference in this online forum.

The combined use of the terms "whore" and "dyke" in Scott's Dyke March sign speaks to the depth and longevity of alliances between sex worker and lesbian communities. *Whore* and *hooker*, like *dyke*, are powerful words still too often applied as negative mainstream labels for those who work in the sex industry. Like some lesbian communities who have reclaimed *dyke* and applied the label to themselves as a marker of identity and pride, sex workers have begun to reclaim *whore* and *hooker*. Generally, however, respectful outsiders to these communities use the less politically charged terms *sex worker* and *lesbian*. That sex workers and lesbians may refer to one another as whores and dykes simultaneously points to overlap between the groups and to the insider status allied members of each group possess in the other. The right to use such powerful reclaimed linguistic signifiers is not one that is earned quickly or easily.

Other sections of SPOC's website offer further evidence of an organization that, like SWAV, creates and maintains—through archived news, in this case—a regularly updated cache of information about persons who have threatened, robbed, or been violent with Canadian sex industry workers. The site also includes photographs of (some) SPOC members and details of the political events they organize and promote. Clicking on the "Past Events" navigation button takes visitors to a page entitled "Past events and political actions." At the time of writing, this page lists, in chronological order beginning with the most recent (June 8, 2012) and dating back to December 2004, a series of titles of events, with the date each event took place in parentheses after the title. Each title is a functioning link to further information about the event referenced. Moreover, reading through this list offers site visitors an indication of SPOC's vision as an organization, as well as the strategic planning underlying the initiatives undertaken by this very focused organization over the past eight years and more.

SPOC members advocate decriminalization of prostitution and explain why this would benefit their members and the wider Canadian public by granting basic legal rights to disenfranchised citizens. In pursuit of this goal, SPOC regularly demonstrates their dedication—on- and offline—not only to reaching as many sex workers as possible, but also to presenting to the public a more complex, nuanced, responsible, and attractive image of sex professionals than mainstream representations generally provide. Most links on the "Past Events" page from recent years in particular (2009 to the present) lead to information—sometimes including posters and media releases—about university student- or faculty-organized talks and panel discussions on campuses across southern Ontario examining Canada's prostitution-related laws. SPOC spokespersons Valerie Scott and Amy Lebovitch often "headline" or are key participants in these events—a fact that is not particularly surprising since news of SPOC's constitutional challenge made headlines in 2007 and garnered further academic and public interest in the years that followed.

Clicking through the event hyperlinks for recent years, it becomes apparent that professional-looking colour headshots like the ones included in the "Sex on Trial" poster of Valerie Scott and Terri Jean Bedford (two of the three plaintiffs in SPOC's constitutional challenge) are de riguer in promotional material for these events. Images of SPOC's lawyer, Alan Young, appear less often in these forums—but more often in news features. By including an array of posters such as "Sex on Trial" on their site, once again SPOC carefully foregrounds their political alliances, this time within institutionalized networks of power.

From 2004 until 2007, and increasingly in the months following the launch of their constitutional challenge in June 2007, according to SPOC's web records, the group's "Past events and political actions" took the form of a series of fundraisers and public awareness campaigns. For example, SPOC records a "Holiday Pimp Chocolate" campaign undertaken in December 2005. This campaign was designed to illustrate the extent to which sex workers are socially marginalized and isolated by prostitution laws in Canada. Specifically, the campaign highlighted the ways that sex workers' personal relationships are negatively affected by Section 212 (j) of the *Criminal Code*. Under this law, "Every one [sic] who lives wholly or in part on the avails of prostitution of another person is guilty of an indictable offense and is liable to imprisonment not exceeding ten years." For this campaign, SPOC sent chocolate coins as gifts to all 308 members of Parliament, explaining in the accompanying letters, "Under our current laws, receiving this holiday gift...from the prostitutes of Sex Professional of Canada makes you a pimp" ("Holiday Pimp Chocolate").

In terms of strategic visual and political self-representation for this group, however, SPOC's March 3, 2005 rally held at Toronto City Hall is perhaps most remarkable. From the "Past Events" page, visitors who click on the link entitled, "'Traffic Stopping Hookers'–International Day to End Violence against Sex Workers," are taken (at the time of writing) to a page that includes photographs from and a promotional write-up and poster for this event. "Join Traffic Stopping Hookers to Educate and Celebrate!" the poster proclaims (see Figure 3.6). The announcement to the left of the poster-graphic on the site (a slightly modified version of which appears as a press release posted on the Ontario Coalition Against Poverty [OCAP] website on February 25, 2005) explains the impetus for such an event:

Currently the only time we're visible is when a sex worker has been killed; only then do we have a name, a family, a history. We are changing that! Prostitutes are refusing silence & invisibility.

Prostitutes, other sex workers and our allies are welcome & encouraged to join us stop[ping] traffic. Wear your most sexy traffic stopping outfit and help turn up the heat on the federal government.

Sex workers will be speaking about work in progress to reform Canadian laws.

Addressing in this way the same problems with mainstream sex worker memorialization that critic Amber Dean addresses,[17] SPOC's event insists that prostitutes "have a name, a family, a history" at all times, even when they are working.

The poster for the event further asserts that those who work in the sex industry shame neither themselves nor their families by "coming out" at public, daytime events. By enthusiastically inviting their members to capitalize so publicly on their physical and fashionable assets at this daytime rally, SPOC both acknowledges and undermines such traditional representations of themselves as the Lone Streetwalker or the Missing Woman, in which the sex worker is represented as perpetually working. This representation of the event also highlights the violence so commonly suffered by SPOC's members and others in the industry, and works to counteract trends that place sex workers in the news only when one—or many of them—die. Surely stopping traffic with their living, provocatively dressed bodies to create dialogue about the decriminalization of sex work provided Canadian news sources with some more positive stock images for prostitution-related reports.

A selection of images from this rally, now included under this poster, once appeared on SPOC's homepage and on a former page entitled "Decriminalization vs. Legalization." These images, by independent photojournalist John Bonnar,[18] are black-and-white shots of SPOC members and supporters at this event. Like SWAV's many online photos, one image in particular puts happy, healthy-looking faces on sex workers in this cityscape and points to their identity as more than

Poster advertising SPOC's 2005 rally at Toronto City Hall, "Traffic Stopping Hookers." Used by permission.

simply sex professionals in their neighbourhoods. This group picture, for which the women appear to be posing with their arms around one another, is a variation of a shot by another photographer that appears in local alternative *Eye Weekly*'s coverage of the rally; however, the photo no longer appears on the SPOC site. The removal of images that include the recognizable faces of sex workers is common practice on sex worker activist websites. Nevertheless, I discuss the image here because it appeared in other public records, including the above-noted OCAP site, and because, frankly, it is one of my favourite SPOC pictures, and I regret its removal. It communicates such warmth of feeling between the five SPOC demonstrators it captures. So many of the images of sex workers that circulate in public media forums show us solitary women either in serious conversation with journalists about murder and marginalization, or working on a street in the dark, as though sex work is all they ever do or think about. Photos like this one, with daylight highlighting the women's smiling faces and the recognizable urban backdrop, insist on sex workers' normalcy, their humanity, and their relationship to and legitimate membership within the larger urban community.

At the very least, if made available publicly, these and other similar images could offer mainstream news reports an alternative angle on and a cache of alternative images of some of the women involved in sex work in the Greater Toronto and Hamilton areas. If these women, for lack of laws to protect them, should disappear, then perhaps these photos of laughing, smiling people, well-dressed and standing with their arms around each other in the winter sun in front of Old City Hall would inspire the public to care. Could these women actually be enjoying themselves? Could they be happy? Even as they demonstrate against anti-prostitution legislation, working to highlight and prevent violence against sex workers in cities across Canada, these people laugh together. Both the laughter and the gravity of this event reflect the fact that sex workers, like other citizens, are multi-faceted human beings. These people, like their neighbours and friends in the city, have personal as well as professional ties to the many intersecting communities of the metropolis.

In fact, by foregrounding rally participants and blurring the city streets on which they stand, these photographs reverse the trend in more mainstream photojournalism to treat modern city streets and street-involved sex workers as interchangeable. Such images suggest that sex workers are literally *part* of dismal cityscapes; their darkened, blurred faces and bodies are employed to facilitate character studies of socio-economically depressed urban neighbourhoods. Through this and other public awareness campaigns, however, SPOC demonstrates their dedication to presenting to the general public a more complex, nuanced, responsible, and conventionally attractive image of sex professionals than we generally see. They assert sex workers' willingness to participate in civil society, and they demand for sex workers the same rights, protections, and privileges afforded other Canadian citizens.

The "Keep Your Laws Off My Body" poster is also featured in another of Bonnar's images (Figure 3.7). This photo, which features some of the signs carried by SPOC members during their March 2005 rally, first appeared in the SPOC web record of the rally in 2005; it appeared again in 2008 on the "Legalization vs. Decriminalization" page that was subsequently removed. In addition, it once appeared in the photo album entitled "Me and My Insane Friends" on W.H.O.R.E., now-defunct website of the late indie sex worker activist and law student Wendy Babcock.[19] This photo will, I hope, appear on SPOC's site again in the future; it effects an important insinuation of the virtual community into the rally's political contexts, both during and after the event. The interrogative sign on the viewer's left reads, "How Can We Protect Ourselves from Rapists

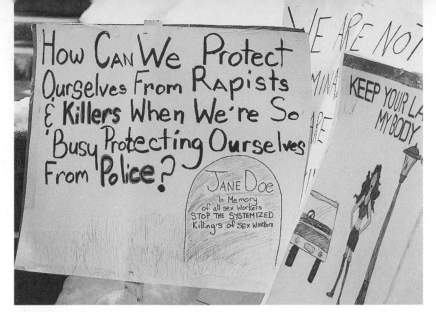

FIGURE 3.7

Signs carried by SPOC members during 2005 rally.

Photo by John Bonnar, used by permission.

& Killers When We're So Busy Protecting Ourselves From Police?." This does much more than acknowledge a particular community existing in March 2005; it continues in the present to foreground sex worker concerns about institutionally endorsed violence and to hail its readers into a politically concerned subaltern group, a group linked by the collective pronoun "we" on the sign itself.

The message on the sign on the right, the one that reads "Keep Your Laws Off My Body," may also be seen in one of the photos currently included in SPOC's digital records of this event: it appears on a different sign, carried by another rally attendee, featured in the top left photo on SPOC's "Past Events" page. There, the message further endorses decriminalization, using anti-sexual harassment rhetoric to connect sex work legislation with violence against prostitutes. Next to the other signs here, in Figure 3.7, this message evokes a community of sex workers who work together and support each other. At the same time, the sign both excludes a wider public that would support such laws and demands of that public that it refrain from legislating against those who deserve to be protected by, not excluded from, their communities. The poster's other message, mostly visible in Bonnar's photograph, reads, "Support Your Local Prostitutes." This too insinuates sex workers-as-community-members into the very neighbourhoods whose laws affect their bodies, and reflects the divided yet unified way that we understand urban geography (i.e., the city, and its distinct urban neighbourhoods). In addition, the word "local" points toward the myriad of ways in which sex work necessarily involves other community members—as consumers, as witnesses, as daycare-givers for sex workers' children, and as participants in personal, neighbourhood, and legislative initiatives that facilitate violence against sex workers. This photo, then, joins other photos currently included in SPOC's online record to collectively indicate an array of voices to whom others— local media, perhaps?—appear to be listening.

Reports and photographs from the rally suggest that the event was sparsely attended. Like SWAV's administrators, SPOC leaders recognize that such dismal turnout at public events is, to a certain extent, one of the many negative effects of whore stigma and anti-prostitution laws in Canada. Nevertheless, while public community-building and consciousness-raising initiatives undertaken by sex worker activists enjoy limited immediate success, online photos from SPOC's rally enable a growing virtual community to experience the hope and pride that come with the recognition that others care enough to fight for their protection and rights, and to consider joining such initiatives in the future.

The "Past events and political actions" page also records that on June 10, 2007, SPOC held their first "Red Light Night at Goodhandy's,"[20] an event they describe as "a social night for sex workers and their friends." Of the four Red Light Nights included in SPOC's web records, the group provides an event report only for the June 10 night. As both the June 10, 2007 report and the accompanying posters for this evening and the four subsequent events with the same title make clear, however, the Red Light Nights were also fundraisers for SPOC's constitutional challenge. Hosted by Mandy Goodhandy, a local personality SPOC describes as a "she-male sexpot," the June 10, 2007, special guests—listed with accompanying photos on the event poster—included Vancouver East NDP Member of Parliament Libby Davies, and Toronto-based can-can burlesque troupe The Saucy Tarts. The accompanying report introduces SPOC and provides some basic information about their constitutional challenge. It also briefly introduces and thanks each of the evening's special guests, thanking The Saucy Tarts for "turning the room into a Dawson city saloon," noting Mandy Goodhandy's talents as hostess, and expressing appreciation for SPOC lawyer

Alan Young, who also spoke at the event. A quotation from Davies asserts, "We must keep the pressure on all levels of government to make changes to protect the rights and safety of individuals working in the sex trade." SPOC notes that Young, "together with several other lawyers and law student volunteers, are providing their services pro bono in support of this case" ("Red Light Night"). Young is quoted as saying, "The law must protect the vulnerable and not expose Canadians to the risk of preventable violence. Ultimately, this fight is destined to go all the way to the Supreme Court, and without additional funds the modest amount of disbursement funding provided by Legal Aid will run out quickly" ("Red Light Night"). This convivial mixture of institutionally powerful figures and well-known personalities from within Toronto's sexual subculture coming together to finance and support a case headed for Canada's Supreme Court offers event attendees and SPOC site visitors clear evidence of the group's increasing power base and underlines the cultural significance of their legal challenge.

Moreover, alongside the "Holiday Pimp Chocolate" campaign and the "Traffic Stopping Hookers" rally, the Red Light Night records demonstrate SPOC's continuing focus on their goal of changing legislation to decriminalize prostitution. Such promotion and celebration of these simultaneously practical and playful endeavours celebrate the diversity of voices and talents of SPOC members and their allies. SPOC thus maintains a sense of play in a political movement that is, as SPOC's rally promotional material rightly notes, often publicly accessible only in the very serious contexts of extreme violence suffered by one or more of its members.

SPOC's website also has a regularly updated page accessible via the "Editorials by SPOC" navigation button. This page includes a series of written pieces by group members responding to local and national news reports or to other events that affect sex workers. Authors' names and dates of posting are included with all but one of these editorials. The following excerpt is from the only undated editorial, entitled "Why a Public Bad Client List?" At the time of writing, this message is the last item on the editorial page and appears to be a collective statement from SPOC to site visitors:

There has been some discussion around the GTA [Greater Toronto Area] recently about the content of the Bad Date List on this site.

Some sex pro's, (from other sites) are concerned that by posting identifying info about bad dates so publicly, the guys may then change their M.O.'s, such as Internet handles, switch hotels they stay at, or use different phone numbers, etc.

On every other site we have been to in order to access bad date info, you must be a member of the site, with a password, confirmation e-mail, and [you] usually have to prove you are a sex pro.

On this site, all you need to have access to any part of the site is a computer and Internet access....In fact, this info should be available to anyone who may have any kind of relationship with these men....Our goal is to protect as many sex pro's as possible. Bad date info is not about ownership of the people collecting it and no one should have to join a club in order to gain access to info about violent and potentially dangerous men. ("Editorials by SPOC")

While anti-violence neighbourhood outreach programs directly affiliated with police express concerns about harm reduction in and for communities, few offer lists of those known to rob, rape, and otherwise assault sex workers. SPOC's Bad Client List thus offers valuable outreach and increased safety to sex workers in their home and working communities.

In addition, while SPOC's stated goals centre on meeting the needs of sex workers, this assertion that SPOC's Bad Client information is available for "*anyone* who may have *any* kind of relationship with these men" (emphasis added) illustrates the organization's willingness to do what police so often will not: refuse to discriminate against potentially vulnerable people, regardless of profession or personal affiliations. As well, this editorial consciously rejects the most negative, exclusive, and insular aspects of identity politics. Indeed, with these words, SPOC instead expresses their intent to foster a convivial, or inclusive, online forum. The group's acknowledgement that violent men also prey on non-sex worker citizens illustrates one of the many ways that sex worker and non-sex worker persons are necessarily connected. In thus making "nonsense of closed, fixed, and reified" identities and turning "attention toward the always unpredictable mechanisms of identification" (Gilroy xv), SPOC emphasizes similarities between their subaltern counterculture and the wider community. The organization's assertion that professional affiliations or lack thereof need not be a barrier to information that may keep people safe reflects what critic Paul Gilroy describes as the radical openness of conviviality. Significantly, what is most radical in this instance is the implication that such openness could enable wide-scale reduction in violence against sex workers and other citizens.

Furthermore, by including as much information as possible about Bad Dates/Clients,[21] SPOC simultaneously finds ways to work within laws that arguably protect violent criminals and criminalize their victims and to offer a growing archive of examples supporting their contention that certain kinds of laws must be eliminated because they result in violence against sex workers. SPOC's Bad Client List begins with a bold-text statement noting that "bad and undesirable clients are the exception, not the rule. They represent a tiny percentage. The vast majority of clients are kind and good men. They are fathers, husbands, brothers, sons, etc. and are nothing like the men listed here" (July 2012). Suggesting, however obliquely, that the actions of bad clients have negative repercussions for sex workers and their clients, whom they identify as normative members of mainstream communities, SPOC again highlights shared concerns between their subaltern counterculture and the wider community.

STELLA

SPOC endorses Stella's work both via their "Links" page and on their Bad Client List. "Stella's, a sex workers advocacy agency based in Montreal, has excellent Montreal area bad date information," SPOC's "Bad Client" page reads. "They can be reached at 1-514-285-1599 or 1-514-285-8889 (they accept collect calls from women in prison) / stellappp@videotron.ca / www.chezstella.org." Unlike SPOC, Stella does not make their "Bad Tricks and Assaulters List" publicly available online. Unlike SPOC's more convivial approach to issues of protection and safety, Stella's approach both indicates the importance of fostering ties between sex workers and the larger community and delineates strict boundaries between sex worker and non-sex worker citizens. For example, Stella's "Bad Tricks and Assaulters List" is included in a larger monthly bulletin of Stella-hosted events and information for sex workers. This bulletin appears to be available either in print or via a digital listserv. Clicking "By and For Sex Workers" on the drop-down menu attached to the "Things to Know and Advice" button in Stella's navigation bar takes visitors to a page of the same title. The blurb at the top of this page reads as follows:

> At Stella, we produce a ton of tools conceived by and for sex workers. Some of these tools are also meant for the general public. Offered free for people who work in the sex-trades, Stella's creations each possess their own objectives. If you are a sex-worker and would like to share your expertise through one of our tools, don't hesitate to let us know. And if you would like to get a copy of the following guides, **contact us**. ("Things to Know and Advice: By and For Sex Workers," emphasis in original indicates hyperlink)

Stella thus avoids the criticism SPOC has garnered as a result of their publicly accessible online "Bad Client List" *and* indicates the exclusivity of their sex worker community. Conceivably, a person desiring access to the list without having to pay for it would somehow have to prove their eligibility. Moreover, unlike SPOC, Stella appears to assert a level of ownership over the information they collect about violent persons in their city. Whatever their reasons for doing so, the effect is the establishment of insider/outsider status in relation to Stella's online and offline communities, a model that would seem to cater most directly to women who are willing to "come out" as sex workers and to shut down rather than encourage solidarity with non-sex worker anti-violence groups.

Differing approaches to bad date lists aside, however, Stella's website demonstrates SPOC/Stella solidarity in multiple ways. For instance, Stella's site incorporates numerous references to SPOC, including a hyperlink to SPOC's website on their "Sex Work: A Movement/un mouvement international" links page, as well as a segment from and hyperlink to SPOC's September 28, 2010 press release expressing their pleasure over Justice Susan Himel's decision in their favour in their constitutional challenge. Stella's homepage also currently includes a statement from Concordia University's Simone de Beauvoir Institute expressing support for Justice Himel's decision, as well as a number of items (noted below) indicating Stella's political interest in the decriminalization of sex work in Canada.

First formed in 1995, Stella launched their bilingual website soon after. Today, Stella has a higher public profile and more extensive ties to the communities of social and medical service providers, journalists, and researchers in their home city and around the world than either SPOC or SWAV has had. The "About Stella" navigation button on their site once led to the following list of their objectives as an organization:

- to provide support and information to sex-workers so that they may **live in safety and with dignity**;
- to sensitize and educate the public about sex work and the realities faced by sex workers;
- to fight discrimination against sex workers;
- to promote the **decriminalisation** of sex work.
  (emphasis in original indicates hyperlink)

Like SWAV and SPOC, Stella works to achieve these goals through community- and web-based public consciousness-raising, sub- and countercultural community formation, and through the distribution of their "Bad Tricks and Assaulters List." Stella also offers a variety of support services for current and former sex workers, services that include support groups for survivors of violence and women living with HIV, employment counselling and training, biweekly medical clinics, and legal advice and assistance for women involved with the justice system. Unlike SWAV and SPOC, however, Stella receives government funding, and consists of volunteers as well as a number of paid, full-time staff. Both the benefits and the disadvantages of such funding are immediately apparent upon entering their website.

At chezstella.org, Stella's simple two-link entry page, visitors choose either the French or English version of the site by clicking on a link that reads (in the language of their choice): "By and For Sex Workers. The information presented on this website is not intended to influence anyone to commit an illegal act. This website is a tool offered to sex workers so they may improve the quality of their lives and their working conditions." Even as sex workers assert their ownership of Stella and their control over the site's content and initiatives, however, the disclaimer about "illegal activity"—clearly intended to free Stella from any criminal liability and to avoid any politico-legal quagmires resulting from use of government funds to undermine federal laws—simultaneously reminds readers of the traditional juridical association of sex work with criminality in Canada. In addition, preceding a statement about improving the quality of sex workers' lives and work, the disclaimer adds more than a hint of historical hegemonic moral judgement to an initiative that otherwise does not assume that a change in profession inevitably improves sex workers' lives.

At each of my bimonthly visits to Stella's website since May 2005, I have entered the site via the increasingly extensive homepage. The relatively user-friendly design of the site has not varied significantly in the past seven years, though an increasing number of hyperlinks have been added (phrases in bold pink typeface are functional links), and the mediums through which some information is communicated (digital video, for example, or links to relevant resources such as blogs) have evolved as new technologies have become more widely available. The black-and-white navigation buttons across the top of each page below the logo and subtitle, "Making Space for Working Women," have changed very little over the years: "About Stella," "Things to Know and Advice," "Press Releases," "Special Events," "ConStellation," "Sex Work," "Contact Us," and "Map." A growing number of drop-down menus have been added to each button over the years, however; and corresponding resources for, by, and about sex workers, as well as the records of Stella's and other local, national, and transnational sex worker groups' activist initiatives, have grown significantly during this period.

At this point of entry to the Stella site, the pros and cons of government funding once again become apparent. The dark-haired, white-skinned female figure who appears to be dancing or posing sensuously in eveningwear in Stella's logo is significantly less politically charged than the lingerie-clad woman who raises her fist in SPOC's logo.[22] However, the raised fist of the blonde woman in the left-centre foreground of the colour photo placed in the sidebar (directly below Stella's logo and the "About Stella," and "Things to Know and Advice" navigation buttons) provides a more overtly politicized counterpoint to the logo. Moreover, the site header, "Making Space for Working Women" suggests more generalized political alliances than are directly evident in the website. The banner carried by the blonde woman with the raised fist and her two companions more directly indicates Stella's organizational politics and focus. The visible portion of the banner appears to read, "TO FIGHT HIV, SEX WORKERS NEED HUMAN RIGHTS." The remainder of the message on the banner is not entirely discernable in this photograph, but a quick click of the "Special Events" navigation button helps to complete the statement. The banner slogan reads, in both English and French, "TO FIGHT HIV, SEX WORKERS NEED HUMAN RIGHTS AND WORKERS' RIGHTS." The central image on the banner appears between the French and English messages; it is a silhouette of a female form wearing a red HIV/AIDS ribbon around her shoulders and torso—an image that appears, again, on the bright turquoise T-shirts of the people marching together here, and in the left sidebar of the "Toronto 2006" information pages. This image connects this photograph to others taken at the 16th International AIDS Conference, held in Toronto, Ontario, in August 2006, in which Stella participated.

While the conference and Stella's accompanying images addressed whore stigma by advocating for sex workers' rights not to be infected with HIV (or any other sexually transmitted infection) by the persons who buy sex from them, the association of politicized sex workers with HIV at this particular point on the group's website risks reinforcing hegemonic stigma-laden representations of sex workers as public contaminants, or vectors of disease in and of themselves. Moreover, at each of my bimonthly visits to the site over the past six years, among the first Stella initiatives for which information is provided on this page are free medical clinics. Though clinic information once appeared on the homepage, a bullet-point announcement now indicates biweekly medical clinic dates and times followed by the words "Medical Clinic" in bold pink text. "Medical Clinic" now functions as a hyperlink that takes visitors to an information page. On this page, visitors learn that clinics take place at Stella's drop-in centre and offer gynecological exams, as well as testing for, treatment of, vaccination against, and education about Hepatitis A and B, and other sexually transmitted infections (STIs).

Services like these are, of course, important for all sexually active women. And such services at Stella-hosted clinics conceivably help sex workers to avoid both the uncomfortable and often tragic effects of living with STIs or other health problems, as well as the many different incarnations of whore stigma so many report experiencing in other clinics and hospitals.[23] However, while Stella-sponsored clinics indicate that sex workers are taking their health seriously, working to refute traditional linkages between sex work and sexual diseases, for uninitiated visitors to the site, the placement of medical clinic information near the top of the homepage, in concert with the above-noted photograph (not to mention the notation in the first line of text under this photo in the left sidebar that reads "Health and Social Services Network Excellence Award" as well as the logos for the Canadian HIV/AIDS Legal Network, and the Canadian AIDS Society), threatens to underline inaccurate traditional connections between sex work, sex workers, and disease.

Medical research that charges sex workers with the spread of sexually transmitted diseases like HIV/AIDS and infections like Hepatitis has long been contested and its biases examined in scientific, sociological, and theoretical inquiries.[24] Moreover, sex workers and their allies in and outside of research institutions have long insisted that sex workers are *more* likely than non-sex workers to use condoms and other precautionary measures against STIs. Nonetheless, bias continues to inform medical studies that in turn inform the practices of doctors and medical associations, like the Canadian Medical Association, with whom the Canadian government consults when writing *and funding* public policies relating to sexuality and health. It is disappointing (not to mention disturbingly reminiscent of the notorious Contagious Diseases Acts in mid-Victorian England[25]) that government funding appears most often to be granted to those groups whose programs for sex workers focus on disease prevention and vaccination.[26]

Such hegemonic cultural and governmental realities notwithstanding, the extensive non-disease-related records posted under the clinic information on Stella's homepage and on other pages throughout the site indicate that the organization makes their relationship with government work for, not against, them. Stella's homepage includes items such as the following:

- information about Stella-sponsored legal and medical clinics
- invitations to a picnic in a local park and a fundraising dance for Stella at a local club
- an invitation to Stella members for a workshop entitled "Testimony as Personal, Educational, and Political Strategy: Yes or No?"
- contact information and an enthusiastic invitation for other sex workers to get involved at Stella

- an invitation to join and/or volunteer for upcoming initiatives such as
  - Stella-run support groups for survivors of violence, for women living with HIV, and for those recently diagnosed with HIV;
  - local information services and Stella-endorsed studies;
  - "Stella Deboute!," a project for which Stella is collecting stories "so that we can educate the public on how the laws make our work more dangerous and complicated";
  - "Rethinking Management in the Adult Sex Industry," an academic study Stella and its partners have endorsed; and
  - a number of sex work-related upcoming events in Canada and the United States.
- a call for potential participants in a class action law suit regarding illegal strip searches in Quebec prisons
- a linked report with the title "The Global Commission on HIV and the Law Recommends End to Laws Against Sex Workers"
- a link to the Native Youth Sexual Health Network under a heading entitled "Indigenous Peoples in the Sex Trade—Speaking for Ourselves"
- publication announcements (and links) for recently published sex work-related pieces by academics and journalists from Canada and around the world (Currently, most of these publications deal with sex work and the law, with a particular interest in the benefits of decriminalization of sex work.)
- embedded digital videos produced by and for national and international sex workers (Currently, most of these videos deal with sex work and the law, with a particular interest in the benefits of decriminalization of sex work.)

Notice that this list includes no rhetoric about disease control. This exclusion—noteworthy given the language and images included at the top of this page—instead reflects Stella's singular aim to promote safety and dignity for sex workers. Moreover, the list highlights Stella's alliances with local and national academic researchers and feminists, as well as an impressive—some have called it "heroic" (Willman and Levy 2)—network of international sex work-related social supports, political initiatives, and academic research. Indeed, Stella's website offers invaluable and extensive records of the diverse initiatives the organization has undertaken in the last decade-and-a-half.

Another excellent example of Stella's commitment to locally embedded community formation and activism is *ConStellation*. Clicking on the "ConStellation" navigation button on the Stella site leads to a brief introduction and links page for a small archive of special issues of *ConStellation*, described here as "a unique magazine whose content, illustrations, and design are provided almost entirely by sex-workers. Published on average twice a year from 1996 to 2005, *ConStellation* is an uncensored forum for sex-workers so that we can share our opinions and our knowledge." The page concludes with a statement that *ConStellation*, like Stella's bulletin, is available to sex workers free of charge. Non-sex workers pay a small fee/donation per issue. Such access guidelines perhaps explain why the magazine's online archive is incomplete: some issues appear to be reproduced here in their entirety, in French and English with accompanying images. Others appear only in French with little to no accompanying images. Some links open a single digital scan of an issue's cover. Nonetheless, even the briefest perusal of the archive in its current incarnation offers evidence of a rich and varied artistic, comedic, political, legal, and practical publication of interest—and use—to sex workers and their allies.

From the standpoint of a researcher like myself who is interested in sex worker self-representation through photographs as well as text, the *ConStellation*'s March 2005 *Prison Special* constitutes one of the most compelling records in Stella's online archives. Once part of a promotion on Stella's homepage for this issue of the magazine, Figure 3.8 now appears on a page entitled "Éditorial du *ConStellation* 'spécial prison.'" (This particular issue currently appears only in French online.) The text of this editorial notes that the legal repression of sex workers is a worldwide phenomenon, while quickly locating and contextualizing this issue for contemporary Montreal readers. Stating that in Montreal, numbers of solicitation arrests have grown from 38 in 2001 to 715 arrests in only the first nine months of 2004, the editors explain that urban gentrification projects, anti-trafficking initiatives, and moralistic social rehabilitation programs ensure that street-involved sex workers bear the brunt of this local oppression and are thus overrepresented not only in incarcerated populations, but also in other areas of the justice system.

FIGURE 3.8

Image used to promote Stella's 2005 *Prison Special* issue of *ConStellation*.
Used by permission.

Included with the editorial is this image, all in dark pink, featuring several women wearing crests reminiscent of Superman and Supergirl, capes, and aggressively sexual attire. They stand in front of bent prison bars; two of them have fists raised. The attire, the bent prison bars, and the women's direct gaze toward the viewer—in concert with the magazine's title across the top of the image—highlight Stella's concern with getting sex workers out of prison. The editorial offers no direct discussion of this image. But the women's cheeky masquerade as incarcerated sex workers suggests both Stella's current foregrounding of the plight of women jailed for prostitution-related offences and the powerful potential of the solidarity the association works to foster. The bent prison bars and the provocative Supergirl masquerade indicate that capitalizing on one's personal assets—if one enjoys the camaraderie and support of others who do the same—can effect significant changes in one's social position. After all, these women are dressed to titillate; they are dressed for sex play, and they are dressed for heroic public service; they are no more criminals than the lingerie models, superheroes, or masquerade party attendees they resemble.

Like many of the bawdy graphics and racier photos on the SWAV site, this image foregrounds without shame or apology the sexual nature of Stella's members' professions. Like some of SWAV's pictures, as well, this photo offers a nod to popular representations of sex workers—how many movies or television police dramas, for example, include scenes featuring sex workers grouped together in prison holding cells?—while the bent bars and costumes clearly signal workers' potential political agency-via-solidarity. In addition, this saucy image is juxtaposed against records—here in this editorial, and in Stella's site more generally—of significant textual production, political initiatives, positive community involvement, academic research, and arguments against the criminalization of prostitution.

In effect, then, this image, and others like it throughout ConStellation's Prison Special, reclaims the hegemonic image of the incarcerated prostitute, insisting that it be read through a more powerful, playful, and distinctly less tragic lens. Stella's primary (or non-paying) audience for these photos have sex— or sex play—for money; they play with, titillate, and perform sexual services for a significant segment of the general population. As a result of this re-branding of sex work and workers, these people become heroes instead of criminals.

Like SWAV's and SPOC's photos, this image portrays sex workers not as faceless forms on darkened city streets, but as smiling, healthy people— photographic subjects who are aware of and involved in the process of recording their images. It is interesting, then, to juxtapose this picture with the actual cover of the Prison Special (Figure 3.9), a cover that seems to mimic and rework the reward poster for Vancouver's Missing Women. As discussed in previous chapters, all of the official Vancouver posters feature a grid of single-subject, mug shot-like photos of the missing women. The use of this layout and these types of photos—including some actual mug shots—seems inevitably to point toward subjects' arrest records. This fact, in concert with the poster format, effectively labels the missing women as criminals.

Given the notoriety of the Vancouver case, the national and international attention it continues to garner, the location of a wall-size mural painted in tribute to the Missing Women of Vancouver in downtown Montreal, and Stella's

FIGURE 3.9

Cover of Stella's 2005 *Prison Special* issue of *ConStellation*.

Used by permission.

participation in the SSLR hearings inspired by the Vancouver case, it would seem logical to assume that Stella's editors are aware of the Vancouver Missing Women poster. The editors thus evoke the seriousness of this tragic case for the cover of ConStellation's *Prison Special*, an image that currently appears on the Table of Contents page (also a list of hyperlinks) accessible at the time of writing by clicking the "Prison Special" hyperlink on the "ConStellation" page. This cover image also appears in the sidebar of every page in the online version of this issue (all of which are currently linked to the "Sommaire/Contents" list).

As previously noted, the photos on this cover resemble criminal mug shots, showing only the head and shoulders of subjects who pose under stark light against a white background. This is where the resemblance ends, however; these images show a series of well-groomed men and women of varying racial ethnicities, all of whom appear to be singing, speaking, or mugging for the camera in some way.[27] One picture (second from the right in the second-last row) shows a woman holding a child whose skin tone and hair colour are significantly lighter than her own. Given the sentence that emerges from the lettering that runs above each line of photographs, are we to assume that this is her child? The child of an incarcerated woman? The single declarative sentence running above the rows offers only the vaguest of clues. Yet this text unites these and all other subjects in these pictures, even as the series of single-person photos suggests a plurality of perspectives on the issues discussed between the covers of this magazine. "On ne veut plus nos soeurs, nos mères, nos filles, nos amies, nos blondes, nos amoures en prison" (We want no more of our sisters, our mothers, our daughters, our friends, our girlfriends, our romantic partners in prison), the sentence reads. And the repetition of the plural personal possessive "nos" (our), next to "soeurs" (sisters), "mères" (mothers), "filles" (daughters), "amies" (friends), "blondes" (girlfriends), and "amoures" (romantic partners) echoes what the photographs imply: this diverse group speaks out together against the imprisonment of a diverse group of loved ones.

The *Prison Special* cover thus mimics the static layout and mug shot presentation of the Vancouver posters. But the poses the subjects strike on this poster pastiche, the effort each appears to be making to communicate with readers, and the text that headlines each of their photos actively resist and critique the Vancouver poster's static focus on silent and silenced people and on implied criminality. In this way, the *ConStellation* cover implicates a legal system that criminalizes so many of Vancouver's Missing Women in their disappearances. The images and messages included in this *Prison Special* inspire conviviality and solidarity between Stella's readers and members inside and outside of prison walls, and between these people and criminalized and/or incarcerated sex workers across the country.

In addition, the warmth of feeling evoked by words like *mother, sister, friend,* and *romantic partner,* again evoke contemporary memorials to the many missing and murdered sex workers across the country. However, recall that this magazine includes sex workers in its audience first. Thus, the words "On ne veut plus" (We want no more of) and "nos" (our) include the issue's primary readership in this protest while also employing the mother-sister-daughter-friend rhetoric that has proven useful so many times before in garnering public concern for sex workers' plight. The political message communicated through this phrasing and these photos thus contrasts starkly with the pejorative connotations called up by the "prostitutes and drug addicts" phrasing that accompanies the mug shots included on the Vancouver posters. Where Vancouver's posters work to further criminalize and isolate women whom mainstream culture already marginalizes and treats as abject, then, *ConStellation*, like its producers and their allies, works against such dehumanizing symbolic and literal violence.

Other Stella-produced images, included in the "Special Events" page of Stella's website, represent the group's participation in and connections with other national and international sex workers' rights organizations. Significantly, however, as critic Zizi Papacharissi notes, "internet-based technologies enable discussion between people on far sides of the globe, but also frequently frag-mentize political discourse" as too many political realities are brought to bear on a particular issue (9).[28] This reality perhaps explains the absence of such internationally diverse connections on SWAV and SPOC's websites. Nonetheless, photographs like those included on Stella's pages offer evidence that this organization and others like it across Canada do not work in a social or political vacuum. Like contemporary Northern, or Western, feminism, the sex worker activisms work at the local level within particular groups or nations, while also forging global or transnational connections so that activists in different contexts may learn about, confer with, and support one another.

While the above-discussed images and top-billed events on Stella's homepage indicate the organization's specific local concerns and socio-political involvement, other aspects of Stella's site indicate the extensive networks through which Stella and other organizations like them propagate, in transnational contexts, the types of "oppositional ideas and movements" that Kahn and Kellner anticipate. For example, clicking on the navigational button entitled "Press Releases" at one time led site visitors to a substantial list of hyperlinks to reports dating back to 2005.[29] The reports once listed here, like those currently included on the "Special Events" page, recorded Stella's participation in a number of international sex work conferences, activities that were connected, via the accompanying images, to the aforementioned photograph of women marching for sex workers' rights. Other images accessible via Stella's "Special Events" navigation button offer evidence of the relationships the organization has developed with international partners. In one image, we see four women in the foreground of a crowd of protesters. Three of the women foregrounded wear elaborate sequined masks, and all of them wear bright pink T-shirts emblazoned with the slogan "We Are Part of the Solution." The march recorded in this image occurred in Mexico City in August 2008 as part of the 17th International AIDS Conference. Stella representatives were among the "175 sex workers from around the world" who joined 24,000 others for this conference (Stella, "Special Events: Mexico 2008"). On the "Mexico 2008" page, Stella also provides links to documents produced by sex workers at this event, including a poster entitled, "Sex Workers: Training Professionals to Reduce Stigma and Vulnerability to HIV," "Sex Workers' Declaration at the 2008 International AIDS Conference," as well as a short list of links to sex work-related reports, and digital slide and video presentations from the conference.

The sidebar image on the Mexico 2008 page appears to be a photograph of an event banner, the main portion of which is taken up by a large red HIV/AIDS ribbon on a white background. To the viewer's right, below the recognizable red loop, the ribbon becomes the lower portion of a leg at the bottom of which is a foot wearing a high-heeled shoe. Under this modified HIV/AIDS ribbon is the slogan, in black text, "MAKING SEX WORK VISIBLE FOR INCLUSION." A brief consideration of the documents linked on this page, particularly the "Sex Workers' Declaration" noted above (which begins by demanding that sex workers be included in the planning and leadership of future AIDS conferences), poignantly illustrates sex worker marginalization in the global anti-HIV/AIDS movement.

The 2008 image also relates on the symbolic and literal planes to a series of photos documenting Stella's participation in the 16th International AIDS Conference in Toronto in 2006. The repetitive representation in these photos of racially diverse people wearing brightly coloured T-shirts (this time, the same turquoise tees worn by the women who carry the banner in the homepage sidebar image) signals a developing tradition of sex worker activism by Stella. These images also constitute significant public archival records of sex workers' politicized presence in Canada and beyond during a period when such records are largely invisible or significantly marginalized in the Canadian mainstream.

One of these images shows a blue-T-shirted young brown-haired woman standing at a podium in the sunlight on an urban street. In front of her, with their backs to the podium and holding the above-discussed banner facing what we can assume is the protest crowd, stands a racially diverse group of blue-T-shirted women. Another group of blue-T-shirted women stand to their right holding a large white banner with blue text in another language. The text below this photograph on Stella's website (in both English and French) appears to be excerpted from a rallying cry delivered by Stella's Claire Thiboutot at the August 14, 2006 "Marche et ressemblement des femmes et des filles." In English it reads,

> We, sex workers from Quebec, from Canada, from Africa, Asia, Europe, Oceania and from all over the Americas, we are all here this week to tell you and the rest of the world that we won't take it no more! No more of having our human rights taken away mostly because of the criminalization of our lives and work! No more of the hypocrisy of most of our countries' governments who turn a blind eye on us, on our health and safety! No more of the **Bush administration policies** that limit funding to support effective and meaningful HIV/AIDS prevention and care strategies for us, sex workers, in many countries. No more of the condoms supplies shortage in Africa! No more from being infected with HIV and having poor access to treatment, no more of dying of AIDS! ("Toronto 2006," emphasis in original indicates hyperlink)

This call to action and the 2008 "Sex Workers Declaration" function in concert with Stella's other protest photos on three symbolic levels. Together, these textual and visual records reaffirm Stella's mandate to value and support women working in the sex industry by making their voices heard in relevant local and worldwide forums; they affirm the value of Stella's work in the fight against HIV/AIDS; and they fight stigma, marginalization, and invisibility of sex workers in significant public forums by remembering and recording sex workers' contributions to policy-making endeavours at national and international levels.

In addition, site visitors can access Stella's "eXXXpressions" event page by clicking "Forum XXX 2005" on the "Special Events" drop-down menu, then clicking the corresponding hyperlink on the list that appears. Other hyperlinks on the "Forum XXX 2005" page include "Celebrating a Decade of Action. Designing our Future. A Sex Worker Rendezvous" and "250 Sex Workers Call on Government and Public, May 21 2005." The first of these links takes visitors to a page celebrating Stella's tenth anniversary. The second, once the title of a report accessible on the organization's "Press Releases" page, now leads to a blocked page. Records from Forum XXX would appear, currently, to be restricted. The "eXXXpressions" page, however, provides at least an overview of these private events. At the top of this page is an overview entitled "eXXXpressions: Forum XXX Proceedings":

> eXXXpressions is a compilation of presentations, discussions, and perspectives from 250 sex workers from all over the world that converged in Montreal (Canada) on May 18–22, 2005 for the **Forum XXX**. The Forum XXX marked Stella's 10th anniversary and a chance to take collective stock of the sex worker rights movement. eXXXpressions provides insight into sex workers' struggles, challenges, and demand for our human rights.

> **Click here** to download a copy of eXXXpressions: Forum XXX Proceedings. If you have dial up Internet access, downloading this document will require some patience. You can also read **Dear John** on Cybersolidaires. (emphasis in original indicates hyperlink)

The press release, available publicly, began with a similar description of the conference, then went on to explain,

> Participants at the Forum XXX, [sic] have gathered to share diverse stories and come up with an action plan for sex workers' human rights and decriminalization of the sex trade. They have heard successful stories of decriminalization from New Zealand, unionization from Argentina, and organization from Thailand.

> May 21st, at 2:15 pm, 1440 Sanguinet (UQAM's Design Centre), as the **Canadian parliamentary subcommittee on prostitution** prepares for its final round table, 250 sex workers will send a message to be heard from coast to coast and beyond. (emphasis in original indicates hyperlink)

Together with these textual records, what images remain publicly accessible from Forum XXX provide evidence of a variety of national and international sex workers' voices joined, as promised, to send their message. For example, a fifteen-minute digital video entitled *Live eXXXpressions: Sex Workers Stand up in Montreal!* is embedded in the current "eXXXpressions" page. The short promotional blurb above the embedded video describes the video as a reflection on a worldwide sex workers' rights movement and "a glimpse into the Forum XXX, where sex workers' discussion, demands, and struggles for human rights took centre stage." The cover-still on the embedded video shows a woman of colour (whom some of us will recognize—and whom the video later identifies—as Stella's Valérie Boucher), seated at a table facing the camera and speaking into a microphone during a panel discussion at Forum XXX. On her left, also facing the viewer, sits a blonde white woman who looks toward the speaker. The subtitled text in the still reads, "I, as a sex worker, have knowledge and expertise." *Live eXXXpressions*—which at the time of writing may be streamed on Stella's "eXXXpressions" page or on *YouTube*, or downloaded free of charge by clicking a link just below the embedded video on Stella's site—opens with a panoramic view of the city of Montreal while a collection of voices chant "We are here!

We are here! We are everywhere!" The conference proceedings recorded there-after include speakers from Argentina, Australia, Canada, China, Finland, France, India, Israel, New Zealand, Switzerland, Taiwan, Thailand, and the United States of America. The video itself details a conference that was indeed multinational, appreciative of sex worker knowledge and expertise, and intensely focused on human rights and the decriminalization of sex work and sex workers on a global scale.

The eXXXpressions event record—like the records of sex worker involvement in the Toronto 2006 event—thus functions as a significant precursor to Stella's participation in the 2008 International AIDS Conference in Mexico City. Having gathered to solidify relationships among persons from multiple nations, classes, and ethnicities within the movement, sex worker groups harness their combined knowledge and experiences of these relationships in order to make their collective voices heard in other local and international forums.

To date, a combination of locally engaged and transnationally connected politics and praxis continues to be evident throughout Stella's growing web archive. This rich, deep library now contains nearly two decades of sex worker activism that simultaneously highlights local efforts to fight violence against sex workers, and connects these initiatives to a worldwide network of sex workers' rights and anti-violence initiatives. Furthermore, the images included here, like SPOC's, incorporate a wider community into the events in which Stella and their allies participate. Indeed, Stella's on- and offline activism represents sex workers as positive and integral members of their urban neighbourhoods across Canada, and in a virtually connected global movement.

THE BATTLE FOR DECRIMINALIZATION

Despite Stella, SPOC, SWAV, and other similarly mandated groups' substantial efforts, sex worker activists are engaged in an uphill battle for decriminalization and destigmatization of prostitution in Canada. Regardless of growing networks involving sex worker activists and academic researchers, and evidence of tentative reconciliations between sex workers and police, sex work remains a contested element of our society. Police and academic researchers are very divided groups when it comes to their approaches to sex work. In addition, while the websites of groups such as SWAV, SPOC, and Stella are relatively attractive, user-friendly, and information-rich, RCMP and regional police appear to constitute the most substantial online anti-prostitution presence and one of the clearest threats to sex worker activism's on- and offline potential. As a result, partnerships such as those between SWAV, Stella, and the academics of the Sex Trade Advocacy and Research group (STAR), between PACE, PEERS, WISH, and Vancouver's Pivot Legal Society,[30] or between SPOC, lawyer Alan Young, and Toronto Police Sex Crimes Unit former Detective Wendy Leaver[31] are especially important.

A useful case study in these differing approaches to and accumulations of cultural capital are the 2005 proceedings of the joint federal Subcommittee on Solicitation Laws of the Standing Committee on Justice, Human Rights, Public Safety and Emergency Preparedness (referred to in federal documents as the SSLR).[32] The SSLR proceedings constitute an invaluable cultural/political text through which to understand the relationship and influence of sex worker activists to dominant culture. The subcommittee held thirty-five meetings, most of which were public, in cities across Canada, and extended an open invitation to leaders and other community members as well as private-interest groups to speak on the subject of existing prostitution laws and possibilities for legislative change. In addition, the committee extended personal invitations to members of academic, police, lobbyist, and sex-work outreach communities. The ways in which these meetings were organized simultaneously demonstrate and undermine traditional hierarchically structured relationships between sex workers and other politically concerned citizens.

Most meetings opened with the subcommittee's original chair, Liberal MP John Maloney,[33] recognizing the presenters in attendance and inviting each presenter to give a five-minute talk describing their position and making their recommendations to the committee. The meetings then proceeded with two rounds of questions, moderated by the chair, during which committee members in turn addressed questions to presenters in order to facilitate discussion on the topics raised in their presentations. Many groups also provided the SSLR with packages of documents related to their presentations.

Most of the meetings included presentations from a variety of perspectives, enabling, to a certain extent, discussion and debate among academic, private citizen, legal, private-interest group, medical, and police representatives. In this way, for example, anti-prostitution presentations from Gwendolyn Landolt, national vice-president of REAL Women of Canada, Yolande Geedah, an individual researcher in anti-trafficking and anti-prostitution initiatives, or Dr. Richard Poulin of the University of Ottawa, are countered by the pro-sex/decriminalization presentations of Cherry Kingsley, of the Canadian National Coalition of Experiential Women (CNCEW), Valérie Boucher, coordinator for Stella's Forum XXX conference, Dr. Francis Shaver, a Concordia University-based researcher affiliated with STAR, and sociologist and sex work researcher Dr. Deborah Brock of York University. Each of a pre-selected group of presenters had the privilege of being the only presenter at a particular meeting. According to meeting transcripts, no sex activist group was offered this privilege; however, Dr. John Lowman, a contributor to the 1984 Fraser Report on Pornography and Prostitution and member of Pivot Legal Society, was one of these privileged few, as were Catherine Latimer of the Justice Department, and Paul Fraser, chair of the 1984 Special Committee on Pornography and Prostitution.

The structure and content of the discussions undercut this imposed hierarchy to a certain extent. Lowman, Fraser, Shaver, Brock, Pivot's Katrina Pacey, and *Missing Sarah* author Maggie de Vries regularly reference both their own extensive research with sex worker communities and the positions of groups like Stella, PACE, and WISH. In addition, sex worker participants from organizations such as Stella, PACE, WISH, PEERS, and the Canadian National Coalition of Experiential Women endorse the advocacy of these academics in particular, often reporting sex worker experiences in ways that illustrate the accuracy of such research and the efficacy of the legislative changes the academics propose. In this way, despite the obvious influences of whore stigma in the proceedings overall, sex worker activists presented a relatively united front in the battle to make the concerns of sex workers heard in these proceedings.

However, while the SSLR for some represents an encouraging sign that legislative and cultural change is in the wind, for others, the proceedings and report of this committee constitute yet another political exercise undertaken to mollify the public and from which sex workers may expect little. In their March 2005 press release announcing the disbanding of their alliance, SWAV cited the mandate of the SSLR as reason enough for group members to move on to other projects (Sorfleet, "End of an Era"). Despite employing portions of the SSLR findings to relatively good effect in the Ontario constitutional challenge of Canada's prostitution laws, in 2005 SPOC's Valerie Scott was unconvinced of the SSLR's relevance. In an interview that year with *Fab Magazine*, Scott called the SSLR a "charade," telling interviewer Todd Klinck that she's "spoken at many of these forums and public inquiries over the years, and when anything has come out of them, it's been bad for sex workers" ("I Wanted"). In the years since the SSLR's investigation and disappointing final report (in which the strong anti-prostitution position of the federal Conservatives is particularly evident in recommendations for no immediate legislative change, and for further research, particularly into the criminal elements of prostitution), it appears that Scott's seasoned sex activist predictions initially proved uncomfortably true. As *Ottawa Citizen* reporter Dan Gardner records in March 2006, then Conservative Justice Minister Vic Toews told reporters he would oppose any SSLR proposals involving the further decriminalization of prostitution ("Many Faces"). The current Conservative government's resistance to rulings in the Ontario-based constitutional challenge appears to offer further evidence of this commitment to status quo policing and whore stigma on the part of the ruling federal party.

The Ontario-based constitutional challenge to prostitution-related laws, colloquially referred as the *Bedford* case,[34] included three applicants, Valerie Scott and Amy Lebovitch of SPOC, and Terri Jean Bedford, a dominatrix from Toronto. With a legal team headed by Alan Young, and supported by many of the groups and individuals involved in the SSLR hearings, the applicants argued that *Criminal Code* sections 210 (the bawdy house law), 212(1)(j) (living on the avails), and 213(1)(c) (the communicating law) contravene sex workers' rights to liberty and security of the person as they are set out in the *Canadian Charter of Rights and Freedoms*. As noted in Appendix 1, the case was heard before three courts—the Ontario Superior Court (ruling in 2010), the Ontario Court of Appeal (ruling in 2012), and the Supreme Court of Canada (ruling in 2013). Ontario Superior Court Justice Susan Himel struck down all three laws, deeming them unconstitutional. The Attorneys General for Ontario and Canada appealed Himel's decision and, in 2012, a majority decision by the justices of the Ontario Court of Appeal modified Himel's ruling on living on the avails to make exploitation a criminal offence, and reversed her decision on the communicating law, holding that the negative effect of street solicitation on communities justified the limitation of sex workers' rights in this instance. Once more, the provincial and federal governments appealed, taking the case to the Supreme Court. In December 2013, the Supreme Court unanimously upheld Himel's original decision, striking down all three of the impugned laws, and deeming them unconstitutional. The Supreme Court included in their ruling an invitation to Parliament, "should it choose to do so, to devise a new approach [to the regulation of prostitution], reflecting different elements of the existing regime" (Canada v. Bedford, 2013).

Like the SSLR proceedings, the Ontario-based constitutional challenge also offers a rich cultural text through which to understand the relationship and influence of sex worker activists and their allies on dominant (conservative) interests. For example, a number of groups were granted intervenor status at each set of hearings and were thus allowed to submit written documents for the court's consideration, and to have their legal representatives speak before the courts. One of the most consistently outspoken groups siding with government on this case is the so-called Women's Coalition (WC) who spoke on behalf of the Canadian Association of Sexual Assault Centres (CASAC), Native Women's Association of Canada (NWAC), Canadian Association of Elizabeth Fry Societies, Action Ontarienne Contre la Violence Faite Aux Femmes, La Concertation d'Aide et de Lutte Contre les Agressions à Caractère Sexuel, and Vancouver Rape Relief Society. The coalition attained intervenor status in all three courts. Arguing that prostitution constitutes a particularly heinous form of colonial and misogynist violence that must be eradicated, the WC consistently proposed what has been described as the "Nordic Model" of prostitution-related law.[35] Currently in place in Sweden, Norway, and Iceland, this controversial system, criminalizes clients (presumed to be men/male), decriminalizes sex workers (presumed to be women/female), and includes (often forced/coerced) counselling and diversion programs for sex workers with the aim of eradicating sex work entirely (Faraday and Benedict).

An in-depth discussion of the pros and cons of such a model is beyond the scope of this discussion. It is important to highlight, however, that advocates of this approach do not examine international research from all countries; instead, they often focus on problematic research—often from government and police sources—out of Sweden in particular. Significantly, for example, the model the WC proposes ignores evidence from Canadian studies, from the World Health Organization, and from other respected international bodies identifying any form of criminalization of sex workers or their clients as structural violence against already disenfranchised persons (Lazarus and Deering; Rekart; Shannon; WHO).

At the time of writing, responses of the federal Conservative government to the Supreme Court of Canada's decision indicate that, as in each of the

Bedford hearings, and in the months and years to come, sex worker activists and their allies will have to address directly the negative effects of such a model (MacCharles; "Ottawa to Table Prostitution Bill 'Well Before' December Deadline, MacKay Says"). In doing so, we must combat the problematic rhetoric employed by the rescue industry[36] to discount the positionality of sex worker activists and their allies. Such rhetoric is particularly apparent in the WC's argumentation. As feminist theorist and Maggie's ally Mary Bunch rightly notes in response to the 2010 decision,[37] even the label "Women's Coalition" constructs sex workers involved in the constitutional challenge as subaltern, in the Spivakian sense of this word. In its self-definition, the coalition purports to speak with a unified voice for those who identify as women; yet they do so despite the fact that the sex workers in question also identify as women. Employing Spivak's theory of subalternity as a failure of communication (the subaltern can speak, but they cannot be heard because they are understood as subaltern), Bunch eloquently argues that the message of the Women's Coalition as intervenor in this case depended inherently on producing Terri Jean Bedford, Valerie Scott, Amy Lebovitch, and the communities of women they represent (including, not insignificantly, the Native Youth Sexual Health Network) as subaltern, or framing them as self-deluded victims. Even when these sex workers speak, then, as subalterns they cannot be heard on their own terms. Instead, they are rendered transparent, without voice, to be spoken over and for by the Women's Coalition ("Sex Work").

Each of these case studies illustrates that, like Internet technology and CMC, the current socio-political climate both expands and limits the potential influence of sex worker activists. In the context of neoliberal valorization of private enterprise and the subsequent privatization of responsibility for the social welfare of national citizens, there is the potential for private organizations like SWAV, SPOC, and Stella to flourish as their organizers and spokespeople take on the social responsibilities of a formerly social-democratic nation-state. To a select group of marginalized citizens, these organizations offer legal aid programs, social campaigns to facilitate neighbourhood harmony, health clinics, and regularly updated reports on violent offenders who pose a threat to the community.

However, by simultaneously contributing to a social safety net for sex workers and agitating for the decriminalization of prostitution, these groups both undermine and support neoconservative interests in law and order by reducing the risks of violent crime on city streets. Sex worker activism and outreach also directly undermines hegemonic investment in traditional social hierarchies and the elimination of so-called social disorganization in Canadian cities. Additionally, as urbanization and gentrification trends produce citizen and lobby groups whose economic interests are informed by Euro-North American culture's sexually prurient colonial roots, sex worker activists face a monumental task in working for the acceptance and protection of sex workers.

One of the key issues still to be addressed in this struggle is the public relationship—or lack thereof—between sex worker activists and First Nations advocacy groups. Despite the convivial nature of sex worker activism and the work that sex activist groups do to fight the stigma faced by all sex workers, survival or otherwise, the current involvement of these organizations with issues specific to Indigenous women's position in the sex industry appears to be limited. Given the overrepresentation of Indigenous women in the survival sex trade and in the numbers of assaulted, raped, and murdered sex workers, the concerns of these groups in the context of the sex trade must be more clearly addressed. However, even the briefest study of Canadian history will suggest a number of reasons for the tenuousness of current relationships between Aboriginal anti-poverty, anti-violence, and anti-racism groups and the more publicly visible elements of sex worker activism. The next chapter looks specifically at Aboriginal women in the Canadian city and in the street-involved sex trade.

4

AGENCY AND ABORIGINALITY IN STREET-INVOLVED OR SURVIVAL SEX WORK IN CANADA

THIS CHAPTER EXAMINES INTERSECTIONS OF HISTORY, politics, culture, and contemporary fiction, particularly as they converge around Aboriginal women working in the street and/or survival sex trade in Canada, in order to investigate whether and how we might make room for women's agency, even in the survival sex trade, while also taking into account the ways in which the racist misogyny inherent in contemporary dominant culture limits the personal and professional choices of poor Indigenous women. As noted in previous chapters, Aboriginal women are overrepresented in recent serial sex worker assaults and killings across the country. In Vancouver, sixteen of the twenty-six women Robert Pickton was accused of killing are Indigenous; in Edmonton, at least six of the confirmed dead are Indigenous women; in Saskatoon in the early 1990s, a serial killer murdered four Aboriginal women and was suspected of killing at least three others; at the time of writing, upwards of eighty Aboriginal women and girls have been kidnapped and/or murdered in Winnipeg and the surrounding area; and at least eleven Indigenous women have gone missing since the early 1990s along what local residents call the "Highway of Tears": Highway 16 between Prince George and Smithers, British Columbia. Significantly, there are numerous other Aboriginal women whose disappearances are suspected to be associated with these cases.[1] Such statistics poignantly suggest that when centuries-old racism combines with patriarchy, whore stigma, and global capitalism, Aboriginal women, particularly those who live in cities across the country, are among the first to suffer and die. Cases like these do fuel the efforts of groups who struggle to combat the social, political, and economic forces that contribute to increasing extreme violence against sex workers in Canada. However, although many of these groups regularly underscore the high number of Indigenous women involved in the survival sex trade, as well as the overrepresentation of Indigenous women among kidnap, assault, and murder victims in Canada, sex worker activism in Canada remains primarily a white enterprise.

The chapter comprises two complementary discussions. The first section considers sociocultural factors and legislative trends that produce significant distinctions between Aboriginal and other street-involved and survival sex workers. The second section highlights and discusses key portrayals of these forms of sex work in Aboriginal literature, specifically interrogating the portrayal of urban survival sex work in Maria Campbell's *Halfbreed* and Beatrice Culleton Mosionier's *In Search of April Raintree* as the best available choice for disenfranchised and culturally marginalized Aboriginal women. Such representations demand that survival sex work be understood as symptom, not cause, of misogyny as well as of cultural and racial violence, and challenge us to seek a more nuanced approach to survival and/or street sex work than what is typically offered by either sex worker activist groups or Aboriginal urban outreach groups.

COLONIALISM AND ACTIVISM FOR AND BY ABORIGINAL WOMEN IN THE SEX TRADE

Even the briefest consideration of Canada's colonial history provides many reasons why First Nations, Métis,[2] and Inuit women are overrepresented in inner-city populations of women who trade sex for dollar amounts that barely provide sustenance, or that fund debilitating addictions. Such analyses also highlight a number of reasons for divisions between sex worker activists who work from a labour activist or reclaimed whore position and activists who foreground the role of state-sanctioned racism and colonial violence in populating the survival sex industry. The latter of these movements—including the Native Women's Association of Canada (NWAC), the Aboriginal Women's Action

Network (AWAN), and the Aboriginal Healing Foundation (AHF), which funds, among other significant initiatives, a shelter for Inuit, Métis, and First Nations women in downtown Montreal—emphasizes the combined effects of class bias, misogyny, and culturally ingrained racism in the assault, rape, and murder of many survival sex workers. These organizations and the anti-violence, anti-poverty, and anti-prostitution initiatives with which they are involved thus insist that Indigenous sex workers suffer and die *because* they are First Nations, or Inuit, or Métis women whose already precarious cultural status too often becomes difficult to navigate and survive in contemporary urban contexts. Significantly, however, representatives from groups like these also assert that prostitution *causes* rape, poverty, and violence for First Nations women. For example, in 2009, AWAN released a statement opposing the legalization of brothels in Vancouver (proposed in anticipation of the 2010 Olympics). In this statement, AWAN argues that "prostitution is inherently violent," and is "merely an extension of the violence that most prostituted women experience as children.[3] We should aim not merely to reduce this harm, as if it is a necessary evil and/or inescapable, but strive to eliminate it altogether. Those promoting prostitution rarely address class, race, or ethnicity as factors that make women even more vulnerable" ("About Us: AWAN's Statement"). In the recent past, NWAC's position on sex work has been equally unequivocal: in 2003, spokesperson Terri Brown attended a Vancouver public forum organized by Vancouver Rape Relief & Women's Shelter that advocated the end of prostitution. Interviewed about the conference and her views on its subject matter, Brown stated, "Prostitution is slavery, it's rape, it's violence; it's not about choice of occupation" (Borowko). Such claims are echoed in the position of non-Indigenous feminist anti-rape organizations such as the Canadian Association of Sexual Assault Centres (CASAC)[4] and Vancouver Rape Relief.[5]

As noted in the Introduction to this book, though the demographics of persons involved in the street sex trade are not known, poverty, homelessness, and debilitating drug or alcohol addictions seem inevitably to populate the street and/or survival sex industry, especially in inner-city neighbourhoods. Canada's colonial history and continuing systemic racism too often place Aboriginal persons in the bottom levels of urban social and geographical hierarchies. Early settler colonialism ultimately produced laws that sought to eradicate First Nations socio-political structures by assimilating Indigenous peoples into what came to be Euro-Canadian culture. The Indian Acts of 1876 onward offer alarming official evidence of, after more than four hundred years of contact between Indigenous and European cultures, ongoing colonial persecution of Aboriginal and mixed-race populations.

Settler colonialism has both historical and contemporary ramifications for Indigenous women within their own communities. In her 2010 book, *Unsettling the Settler Within: Indian Residential Schools, Truth Telling, and Reconciliation in Canada*, director of research for Canada's Truth and Reconciliation Commission (TRC) on Indian Residential Schools Paulette Regan discusses the need for white settlers in Canada to recognize both the violence of the past and their complicity in its perpetuation in the present: "When I see Indigenous people on the mean streets of the Downtown Eastside, or read about high incarceration rates or the low education success rates for children and youth," Regan writes, "I now understand that much of the social dysfunction, violence, and poverty that exists in communities today is part of the intergenerational legacy of Indian residential schools" (3). With the last residential school in Canada having closed in 1996, Indigenous and non-Indigenous critics—and, to some extent, the Canadian government[6] as well as the Catholic and Anglican churches—now acknowledge and ostensibly regret this "deliberate and systematic process designed to strip" children "of their culture and their Aboriginal identity" (Silver et al. 20). Personal histories of survivors, historical records, and critical analyses from a variety of perspectives extensively document the ramifications of residential schools where Aboriginal students were required to learn English or French, Christian ideology, and a version of their own cultural history that overtly privileged white males and portrayed Indigenous cultures as disadvantaged, anachronistic, and in decline. As the TRC hearings alone make painfully clear, many of the multiple generations of First Nations, Inuit, and Métis children in such schools also suffered physical and sexual abuse at the hands of their teachers and other in-school guardians. Such records also document how, with generation after generation of children legislated into school and away for longer and longer periods from the communities that may otherwise have enabled them to learn their own culture, to parent children, or to address and heal the damage of debilitating abuse, residential schools instead facilitated the erosion of many healthy, self-sustaining First Nations and other Indigenous communities. Significantly, many of these nations included legal, economic, and political systems in which women were treated with a level of respect that remains relatively unknown in Euro-Canadian or Judeo-Christian culture.[7] Among other things, the intergenerational destructive legacies of residential schools effectively illustrate widespread internalization of historical and ongoing systemic racism and policies of colonization on both the individual and the community level.

Moreover, traditional connections between First Nations people and the land, as well as the Indian Acts, treaty rights, and perpetual disputes over Aboriginal land claims, in part suggest why the cityscape can be a particularly fraught setting for Indigenous people in Canada. Indeed, while Indigenous leaders and teachers consistently emphasize the integral connections between the land that is or once was theirs and their cultures, traditional urban imagery—as noted in Chapter 1—sets the modern city up in opposition to capital N Nature. Furthermore, settler cultures' understandings of Indigenous social, cultural, and political structures have stagnated around Romantic, anachronistic (and imaginary) images of First Nations peoples whose "Natural" space of living, being, and governing themselves is necessarily outside of modern cityscapes.

Yet as Thomas King observes, "many Native people now live in cities, with only tenuous ties to a reserve or a nation" (55). Evelyn Peters and O. Starchenko's *Atlas of Urban Aboriginal Peoples* supports King's claim, reporting that only 5 per cent of Aboriginal people lived in Canadian cities in 1901. By 2001, however, 49 per cent of Canada's Aboriginal people were living in urban areas (Peters and Starchenko 1). Census and Statistics Canada report similar findings, noting that only 31 per cent of self-identified Aboriginal persons live on reserves or in other specifically First Nations rural communities (Canada, *Aboriginal Peoples* 1–5). However, it would seem that "the growth of the urban Aboriginal population is less due to an exodus of Aboriginal people from reserves to urban areas—in fact, there is a net movement the other way...—than it is to the relatively high birth rate of urban Aboriginal people and, since 1986, to the increasing numbers of people in urban centres identifying as Aboriginal people" (Silver et al. 15).

As has also been well-documented by this point in colonial history, the cultural and legal status of urban Indigenous people is complicated by the insistence of the federal government, as well as larger Aboriginal organizations such as the Assembly of Manitoba Chiefs, that they are only responsible for registered, on-reserve Aboriginal populations. The needs of non-registered, off-reserve First Nations and Métis populations have thus become the responsibility of the provinces and other political organizations. However, groups that might, for example, address the needs of urban First Nations, Inuit, and Métis people in a "status blind" manner have been slow to emerge. As King points out, "race, culture, language, blood...still form a kind of authenticity test, a racial-reality game that contemporary Native people are forced to play." One of the first questions included in this authenticity test, administered by Aboriginal organizations and non-Aboriginal government institutions alike, is "Were you born on a reserve?" As King explains, "Small, rural towns with high Native populations will do. Cities will not" (55).[8] The legacy of the Indian Act functions, therefore, much like the state apparatuses critical race theorist David Goldberg describes that "sew the variety of modern social exclusions into the seams of the social fabric, normalizing them through their naturalization" (*Racial State* 10).

Ongoing disputes about Indigenous land claims further naturalize aspects of such authenticity tests in contemporary contexts, though it is unlikely the First Nations groups involved intend to reinforce stereotypes of themselves as outsiders or others in modern cityscapes. It is difficult to decide whether the now infamous land conflicts between Mohawk people and golf course owners (and, ultimately, the Quebec government) at Oka/Kanesatake in 1990, and between Six Nations people and suburban developers (and ultimately, the Ontario government) at Caledonia throughout the spring, summer, and fall of 2006 reinforce or begin to dismantle such city/nature binaries in relation to First Nations people. Each of these disputes arose from ostensibly rural First Nations' resistance to urban or suburban development: the planned expansion of a golf course onto sacred Mohawk territory in the Kanesatake instance, and the sale of Six Nations' land to developers for the construction of a subdivision in the case of Caledonia. Each of these land disputes, of course, exemplifies Indigenous nations' ongoing struggle to force white settler society, private developers, and government officials alike, to honour historic treaties and to acknowledge the accompanying land rights First Nations people have under such treaties. Both the Caledonia and Kanesatake disputes, therefore, place Aboriginal peoples in traditional roles: as protectors or stewards of the land, as persons intimately connected to the Natural landscape and whose opposition to its desecration symbolically opposes (sub)urban developers and occupants, or those who would cut down trees, drain or reposition bodies of water, and otherwise re-form, or de-Naturalize, the land. In resisting the effects of suburban sprawl, however, so-called rural Indigenous nations insert themselves and their concerns directly into contemporary urban settler-colonial affairs, insisting that their concerns become the concerns of white settler urban residents. In this way, and through growing urban First Nations populations, Indigenous people in these and other geographical spaces call into question stereotypical understandings of First Nations people as outside of, or anachronistic to, the urban mainstream.

One element of this urban outsidership is the figure of the Aboriginal person as pre-historical. As theorist Terry Goldie discusses, settler-colonial discourse figures First Nations cultures as prehistoric or primitive in relation to Euro-North American cultures, and thus incapable of becoming part of modernity, the urban, etc. (49). The mistreatment of the Six Nations people by police, government officials, and private citizens, alongside their generally unflattering portrayal in mainstream settler-colonial news venues,[9] illustrates perhaps more clearly than any academic argument might just how unreceptive non-Indigenous Canadians are to symbolic and literal intrusions into the cityscapes they perceive as theirs. This cultural assignation of urban outsider status may also begin to explain the violence to which so many urban Aboriginal women are subjected.

Emerging urban communities of First Nations people, in combination with Canada's long history of gendered, racialized cultural violence, and an even longer tradition of whore stigma in Europe and her former colonies, result in the overrepresentation of Aboriginal women in one of urban Canada's simultaneously most visible and most marginalized populations: street and/or survival sex workers. The question of personal agency in the context of the sex trade, particularly in the circumstances through which a woman enters the business, has thus become one of the key points of difference between the most vocal sex worker activist and Aboriginal anti-poverty, anti-violence, and urban outreach groups—though until recently, there was little evidence of public debate between them.

The responses of established national Aboriginal groups (with the noteworthy exception of the NYSHN, discussed below) to Ontario Superior Court Justice Susan Himel's September 2010 decision in favour of SPOC's constitutional challenge of three prostitution-related portions of the Criminal Code illustrate key points of difference between these groups and sex worker activists who advocate the decriminalization of prostitution in Canada. In a statement released in response to Justice Himel's decision, AWAN argues that the court "abandons Aboriginal women and women of colour to pimps" (qtd in Harp). NWAC's response likewise highlights both the overrepresentation of Aboriginal women in the most dangerous parts of the sex trade and the need to protect women involved in the sex trade from violence ("NWAC Questions"). NWAC subsequently became members of a group called the Women's Coalition, which filed for intervenor status in the appeal of Justice Himel's decision that was heard by the Ontario Court of Appeal in June 2011. The coalition advocated the prohibitionist approach to prostitution that is often referred to as the Nordic Model.

However, until joining the Women's Coalition (a process described in the previous chapter), NWAC's position on prostitution, as expressed through Sisters in Spirit (SIS) literature in particular, was significantly less hard-line. In fact, up until their participation in the coalition, I had found no clear anti-prostitution position in SIS documents, presentations, or web materials.[10] Prior to joining the coalition, NWAC appeared instead to read Indigenous women's participation in the sex trade as a symptom of deeply ingrained social injustices. In addition to raising awareness of the growing numbers of missing and murdered Indigenous women across Canada, the SIS Mission Statement and research thus focus on anti-poverty, anti-racism, and anti-violence research and work.

In terms of Aboriginal women's representation in or by sex worker activist organizations, at the time of writing, I could find little evidence either of Indigenous sex worker activism or of direct cooperation between Aboriginal outreach and anti-poverty, anti-violence, or anti-racism groups and sex worker activism and outreach organizations, although WISH, PEERS, and CASAC spokespeople have indicated that the majority of the women who use resources at inner-city shelters are Aboriginal.[11] Nonetheless, a few noteworthy exceptions have emerged in recent years. The first is WISH's Aboriginal health and safety project for women working in the sex trade, delivered in partnership with Vancouver Native Health as well as Vancouver Coastal Health (discussed by WISH Executive Director Kate Gibson at the March 29, 2005 public meeting of the SSLR, mtg. 15, 30). In addition, the nationally focused Native Youth Sexual Health Network (NYSHN)—established in 2009—recently partnered with Toronto-based Maggie's to implement ASWEOP, the Aboriginal Sex Workers Education Outreach Project (Maggie's, "What We Do"; NYSHN, "Collaborative Projects"). Stella's website also includes both a logo and link to the NYSHN website (Stella, "Homepage: July–August 2012" & "Travail du sexe." As this new organization's name indicates, NYSHN's mandate extends beyond sex work. Remarkably, however, the group has been very clear about their support for decriminalization of sex work and sex workers.[12] They also push for more Indigenous representation in sex worker activism. In a 2011 press release from unceded Coast Salish Territory in BC, for example, they declare the following: "Despite heightened statistics of the many realities we face as Indigenous peoples, we are not significantly represented in the leadership or decision making tables of sex work organizations and social justice groups alike. By this we do not mean solely having one Indigenous coordinator or a few outreach workers—we mean meaningful, non-tokenizing, multiple positions and visible leadership roles across organizations, groups, collectives, and at any place where the sex trade is discussed. We are not interested in being included after the fact or having to continuously take a seat at a table we had to fight to be at in the first place—we want to be the centre in which all decisions about our lives are coming from" ("Indigenous Peoples in the Sex Trade—Speaking for Ourselves"). With powerful and important voices like these emerging onto this fraught political terrain, it seems safe to anticipate even more complex and representative sex worker activism to come.

Such activism has, however, hitherto been much more characteristic of organizations that do not identify themselves as representing Indigenous peoples. In another powerfully worded statement, the late Wendy Babcock, law student and former Sex Professionals of Canada spokesperson, once memorably argued that "a blow job is better than no job,"[13] and that, furthermore, sex work is less demeaning than many other forms of employment. SPOC's Mission and Goals, like those of other sex worker activist organizations, outline approaches to prostitution as work that are more nuanced than Babcock's in this instance but similarly affirming. As discussed in earlier chapters of this book, on their websites, Vancouver's PEERS and PACE Society have likewise focused on the legitimacy of prostitution as human labour, asserting that as providers of sexual services for which they receive remuneration, sex workers are contributing citizens of their municipalities and of their respective nations. As such, these groups note, sex workers—particularly those working in the lowest paid and most visible areas of the sex industry (the street-involved and/or survival sex trade, for example)—deserve laws that protect rather than criminalize and fine them, or that violate their civil and human rights.

Nevertheless, in terms of the survival sex trade and many of its poorest and racialized members, such positions may not be especially persuasive or empowering. When, for example, systemic racism, poverty, and any number of other sociocultural factors effectively force a woman to her knees and require that she accept as little as five dollars for services rendered, her agency must be understood as severely limited. If, for example, systemic racism and colonialism—both their historical legacies and their everyday expression—have contributed to an Aboriginal woman's impoverishment or have fuelled her need for cash or drugs, can her participation in the survival sex trade be considered— and respected—as the same manner of "necessary choice" as that of a poor white woman who does the same? Questions like these are rarely addressed directly by sex worker activist groups. On the other hand, positions like those of PACE and SPOC that reject moral condemnations of sex work in favour of a more utilitarian perspective rarely receive due consideration by Aboriginal groups like NWAC/ SIS, AHF, and AWAN, or by feminist anti-violence organizations like Vancouver Rape Relief, CASAC, or the Woman's Coalition.

HALFBREED AND IN SEARCH OF APRIL RAINTREE

This next section explores such questions in one of the few venues through which others have begun to address them: Aboriginal literature. Flagship texts in a growing canon of North American Indigenous literature, Maria Campbell's *Halfbreed* (1973) and Beatrice Culleton Mosionier's *In Search of April Raintree* (1984) unflinchingly examine issues of personal agency within Canada's inner-city survival sex trade. In these novels, Campbell and Mosionier engage stereotypes of degraded and sexualized Aboriginality in the contemporary city, highlighting systemic racism and ongoing colonial violence as well as the cumulative effects of these formidable cultural forces on isolated and marginalized Indigenous women working within the survival sex trade.

In addition, Métis authors Campbell and Mosionier examine key incarnations of the Aboriginal-as-urban-outsider stereotype, particularly as this negative image affects Aboriginal women in recognizably Canadian settings. My analysis therefore takes as its focus the Métis woman protagonists in *Halfbreed* and *In Search of April Raintree* whose cultural isolation, social exclusion, and subsequent impoverishment lead them to the survival sex industry. I turn to these texts and these characters in part because of the ways in which the authors challenge a number of (relatively) dominant positionings of Indigenous women and the sex industry, and in part because of the ways the stories demand that readers acknowledge similarities between real Canadian cities and the cityscapes Campbell and Mosionier describe. Each of these texts interrogates sociocultural circumstances alarmingly similar to those that have facilitated the current serial kidnappings and murders of poor, racialized—in particular, Aboriginal—women in contemporary non-literary Canadian cities. In many ways, Campbell and Mosionier's narratives deny the abjection of the suffering (and Aboriginal) prostitute body that other texts, literary and non-fiction alike, too often facilitate. Indeed, readers' concern for Campbell and Mosionier's marginalized, suffering, even dying protagonists contrasts ironically with the current lack of dominant cultural concern about the plight of so many missing and murdered Indigenous women across the country. Thus, these narratives, like the activism undertaken by Aboriginal anti-violence groups, challenge hegemonic discourses that individualize the plight of the racialized urban poor. Campbell and Mosionier's texts reach beyond the mandates of many of these groups, however, in their thematic treatment of survival sex work as a symptom, not a cause of systemic racism, cultural violence, and misogyny. Indicting systemic forces for the degradation their characters experiences in the survival sex trade, Campbell and Mosionier's narratives call for the end not of prostitution itself but of the state-sponsored and culturally endorsed racial and sexual violence that populates the survival sex industry with Indigenous women.

It is important to note that critics have not always praised these two autobiographical novels for their representation of Aboriginal women. For example, while Anishnaabe scholar Kateri Damm endorses the honest rendering of mixed-race women's experiences in *Halfbreed* ("Dispelling and Telling"), Métis critic Jo-Ann Thom notes many Aboriginal readers' anger with the text because they believe that Campbell's confessions "substantiate the very stereotypes that plague aboriginal women in this country" (299). According to Thom, Aboriginal readers also "feel betrayed by Cheryl's transformation [in *April Raintree*] from proud Métis into a 'gutter-creature' who is the embodiment of every stereotype they encounter" (299). Heather Zwicker suggests yet another reason for criticisms of these two novels, arguing that feminists of the 1990s were tempted to condemn Mosionier's novel and its engagement with real negative stereotypes of First Nations women because Cheryl's demise portrays the death of a stereotype of their own. As Zwicker notes, "we desperately want Cheryl's uncompromising political vision to triumph over April's liberal quiescence....Her death seems so wrong because her politics seem so right" (328).

Yet reading Campbell's heavily edited novel or Mosionier's fictional bildungsroman as thinly veiled representations of real lives and actual events, it has been argued, risks marginalizing these minority authors. Discussing the effects of being defined and defining oneself as Aboriginal, Kokatha/Mirning researcher Sonja Kurtzer notes that Indigenous communities can in fact restrain Indigenous authors by requiring that Aboriginality be "authentically" represented in their writing (qtd in Heiss 207). Focusing on Campbell and Mosionier's narrative authenticity and veracity, or lack thereof—or the authenticity of the authors' identities as Métis women—can and has resulted in their rejection or condemnation by significant segments of readers in and outside of their own communities. Writing for and with the Native Critics Collective in 2008, however, Creek theorist Craig Womack marks a shift in present and future critical reception of the work of cultural producers like Campbell. "For most American Indian artists," Womack writes, "it is impossible to simply walk away from the social ills that threaten our communities to engage in an art that prioritizes aesthetics at the cost of ignoring the things that are killing us" (8). Because of this, Womack explains, "A major dilemma for the Indian artist is commenting in one's art on social policy...while keeping the work artful. Such a conundrum shapes the kind of theory that will be generated by those interested in an ethical criticism. It is our belief that an increased commitment to social realism can actually generate new artistic experimentation rather than shut it down" (8). That said, as Mohawk scholar Patricia Monture argues, to focus on Indigenous writing as resistance is to "place colonialism at the centre of the discussion" and thus to delimit Indigenous people's ability to "be or dream more than resistance and survival" (157). My own analysis of the social realism and colonial resistance inherent in Campbell and Mosionier's cultural critique is produced with the aim of contributing to the ethical criticism Womack anticipates. I humbly acknowledge, however, the need for further critical examination of the ways in which the artfulness of the narratives under consideration interacts with the social criticism so apparent in these texts.

Halfbreed is a coming-of-age story that traces Campbell's life from her impoverished beginnings in rural northern Saskatchewan to her time as a survival sex worker in Vancouver, and then her later struggles as a single mother and her involvement as political activist in the Indigenous rights movement in Calgary. Despite the breadth and richness of Halfbreed's narrative and the significance of its cultural and political commentary, the text remains, I think, under-analyzed in the academy. The small but useful body of literary criticism that has grown up around the book focuses, for the most part, either on identity, discussing its examination of Indigenous, and in particular Métis women's experiences of settler colonialism;[14] or on genre, discussing it in the context of women's and/or postcolonial autobiography.[15] While a few critics appreciatively discuss the "humour, pathos, defiance, and courage" of Campbell's story, such analyses repeatedly return to the ways that the text, in Kate Vangen's words, "has re-created" Campbell's "own history and heritage" (193). And though Armando E. Jannetta points to the ways that characters in the text humorously subvert racial stereotypes by "wearing the mask of the stereotypical image" so that "the Native no longer resembles the stereotypical image of the 'Native'" ("Anecdotal Humour" 6), his reading, like most others, focuses on the first fifteen chapters, or the first half of Maria's life. In fact, the bulk of existing criticism is concerned primarily with Maria's tumultuous and poor but loving family life in rural Saskatchewan, and the historical record she provides of her family and her people, the Métis, or the "Road Allowance people."

Such analyses also highlight Campbell's assertion that she writes to teach and to heal (Lutz 42), but gesture only vaguely toward the darker years of Maria's life in Vancouver as part of the author's learning process—events and experiences from which she recovers and through which she may identify with others, Métis or not, who suffer. For example, Helen Buss argues that in addition to functioning as "a means to help other aboriginal [sic] people,...the autobiography becomes a powerful confessional instrument which Campbell uses to put her own degradation behind her" (165). But Buss offers no further examination of how exactly Campbell works through either her "degradation," or her "confession." Examining Campbell's treatment of Christianity, Ken Derry briefly summarizes Maria's years in Vancouver as characterized by "shame" that "fuels the events of her life as she becomes an addict and a prostitute, living a life of squalor and repeated suicide attempts" (208). Derry further observes that Maria's time as a prostitute haunts and inhibits her from moving on (208)—yet he provides no further analysis of the exact nature of this "haunting" in Maria's life, choosing to focus instead on the events that led up to her time as a prostitute.

For a number of reasons, it is troubling that such analyses offer no extended commentary on the formative years recorded in chapters 16 through 18. First and foremost is the order in which Campbell wrote these sections of her story. Campbell reportedly wrote the first half of the book at the request of her editors who, after discussion that included the editors, the author, and another non-Indigenous reader, reduced her original two-thousand-page manuscript to two hundred pages. They then requested that she write about her earlier years in order to balance out the darkness and anger of the story Campbell initially produced.[16] To focus on the first half of Campbell's story, therefore, is to ignore completely the narrative the author initially intended to be the sole focus of her book.

The body of academic scholarship dealing with *In Search of April Raintree* is small indeed, most often considering Mosionier's examination of racially hybrid identities through April and Cheryl's struggles with the cultural and political consequences of their racial heritage.[17] A significant portion of this criticism discusses the scene in which April is raped as a pivotal moment of self-recognition for April as she comes to identify, finally, with the Aboriginal side of herself. Peter Cumming, for example, argues that the rape scene "performs a critical function in the novel" in terms of April's politicization (313). Helen Hoy describes April's rape as a "critical moment of cross-over" wherein, "with the interchange of protagonists enacted physically....April takes on Cheryl's body, is raped as Cheryl, and thereafter...the sisters trade places regarding Métis pride" (281). And Margery Fee similarly suggests that April's post-rape identity could potentially be positive: "During the brief period between the rape and the final revelations of the trial when April is tentatively thinking of herself as if not Native, at least suffering like one, the sisters bond" (222).

Fee, Hoy, Zwicker, and others subsequently refer to Cheryl's prostitution only in the most general terms, usually within the context of their discussions of Cheryl's "failure" (Zwicker 328), or her "destructive processes of identification" with negative racial stereotypes (Fee 225). I support and appreciate each of these approaches to identity and disidentification in the text, particularly with respect to the extensive analyses critics like these provide of the correspondingly lengthy rape scene in Mosionier's novel. What concerns me, however, is that Mosionier's portrayal of Cheryl's survival sex work and subsequent suicide is equally extensive in this text—but no corresponding body of criticism responds specifically to these aspects of Cheryl's life. The words "whore," "squaw," and "prostitute" are equally applied to Cheryl by implication during the rape scene, and in her own written words thereafter. In addition, Cheryl tells April that she, too, has "prostituted" herself in her marriage (179) and is thus a "hooker," like Cheryl (179). Why, then, is there such scholarly neglect of prostitution in this text? Far more than a straightforward symbol of despair, Mosionier's treatment of sex work in this novel requires thoughtful interrogation.

HALFBREED

As many who analyze Mosionier's novel observe, *Halfbreed* and *In Search of April Raintree* shed light on each other. Throughout the remainder of this chapter, I demonstrate the necessity of reading the sex work portions of Maria's life story, as well as those of Cheryl and April Raintree's story, both individually and in concert. In discussing *Halfbreed*, therefore, I focus specifically on chapters 16 through 18 of Maria's story. In doing so, I argue that the cultural critique Campbell's text offers in fact hinges on the ways that Maria's experiences as a prostitute and criminal in Vancouver compare with her experiences in her family and her rural Saskatchewan community. I also argue that her Vancouver life provides her with a clear understanding of and vision for the activist work she undertakes after she leaves the coastal city. Maria's story subsequently argues that systemic racism breeds violence and hopelessness, that social and political systems are too often racist and corrupt, that crime does pay, and that, for certain female populations in Canada, dreams do not come true. In addition to her survival under such circumstances, however, what makes Maria's story especially remarkable is her encouragement that we continue to dream and struggle to correct these cultural problems in spite of these truths. These themes resonate in Mosionier's novel as well, despite its similarly dark subject matter.

The opening paragraphs of Campbell's autobiography establish the text's settings, both landscape and the buildings contained therein, as key elements in the story that follows. The next fifteen chapters detail the racial history and everyday struggles that result in Maria's decision to leave her rural home. The poverty of this period in her life as well as the happy memories she retains from her childhood remain integral features of her character throughout the story. This early indication of the relationship between the course of Maria's life and the setting in which she lives contributes to the foreboding tone at the beginning of chapter 16. Maria has left her father to marry Darrel, a marriage she has undertaken quickly at fifteen years of age with the belief that such an arrangement will enable her to keep her six little brothers and sisters (whom she refers to as "the kids") with her. But Darrel cares little for Maria's familial concerns, and his telephone call to the welfare office has resulted in the kids' being taken away. Despite the physical and verbal abuse Maria receives from Darrel, and against the advice of her friends, Maria has agreed to travel with him and their new baby, Lisa, to Vancouver, the first city Maria has ever seen.

Having dreamt throughout her childhood of a prosperity she believes is inherent in urban settings, Maria hails Vancouver with excitement akin to a nineteenth-century travel writer viewing a new land for the first time:

> Vancouver! It was raining when we arrived. The city was beyond my wildest imagination! It seemed to go on without end. As we drove along in the cab, I pressed my face against the window and drank in everything around me....The people all looked rich and well-fed. The store windows were full of beautiful displays, lots of food, clothes and all the things a person could possibly need to be happy.
>
> I sat back and thought, "Maybe it's possible to bring the kids here, where everything will be clean and good for them."
> (114)

Though Maria suspects that Darrel intends to leave her soon, she nonetheless manufactures hope, however briefly, as her romantic visions of city life are momentarily confirmed. As the taxi proceeds toward their apartment through the increasingly dilapidated cityscape, however, Maria recalls her shattering disappointment:

> My childhood dreams of toothbrushes and pretty dresses, oranges and apples, and a happy family sitting around the kitchen table talking about their tomorrow came to an abrupt end as I looked out of the window again and saw that we were now in an older part of the

city. The buildings kept getting dirtier and dirtier. I had lived in poverty and seen decay but nothing like what surrounded me now.

The cab pulled up in front of a grimy old apartment block and as Darrel paid the driver I looked about. The street was filthy and I shivered and felt sick as I saw the people who were there. They looked poorer than anyone I'd seen at home; there were drunks, and men who walked aimlessly and seemed not to see anything or anyone; women who appeared as though they had endured so much ugliness that nothing could upset them; and pale, skinny, raggedy kids with big, unfeeling eyes who looked so unloved and neglected. Small as they were, they were frightening. (114)

Maria's suggestion that witnessing ugliness can mark a human being's own appearance is particularly poignant given both the ugliness she has endured in her life to this point and her distress at the "grimy" appearance of her new neighbourhood with its correspondingly "sickening" and "frightening" inhabitants. This brief description of Vancouver thus communicates a clear sense that the evolution of Maria's character throughout her time in Vancouver may not be particularly positive. With the "end" of her dreams of a united family comes a sense of futurelessness in this cityscape.

Thus begins one of the most tragic periods of Maria's already difficult existence. Her claims that her family's impoverished life in Saskatchewan differs significantly from the poverty she sees in Vancouver initially reinforce cross-cultural stereotypes of urban pollution and degeneracy and healthier, or somehow cleaner, rural life. In the next three chapters of the book, however, Campbell explores the effects of a number of collapsing binary systems in Maria's world: stereotyped, or traditional common-sense beliefs about the oppositional relationships between urban and rural, wealth and poverty, criminal and legitimate business, etc. In this way, Maria's life on the urban margins comes to parallel her marginalized existence in the countryside. Later, though she struggles to leave the city in search of the elusive "happiness and beauty" she "had known as a child," she cannot find this home again, anywhere (8). For when she finally returns home years later, she finds even more alcoholism, spousal and child abuse, and poverty than she remembers.

Initially, the difficulty of Maria's life in Vancouver rivals the constant struggle of her life in the countryside—but without the community and family life that made such poverty and desperation bearable. Maria's new neighbours in her dilapidated Vancouver apartment building can barely bring themselves to communicate. In this city, Maria moves alone through what seems to her to be a graveyard of broken dreams from which she repeatedly tries to escape.

Sex work and life in the city are by no means culturally, economically, or emotionally emancipatory for Maria, but neither is entirely oppressive. What description this much-edited section of Campbell's text provides of Maria's experiences in the sex trade makes her agency very clear in these circumstances, framing her sex work as self-exploitation in which she chooses to participate. Subsequently, even as Maria's prostitution traumatizes and degrades her and facilitates the development of her drug addiction, she appears for the most part to be making the best of a very bad situation. Though the chance to support herself and her child through sex work is one that Maria feels she cannot pass up, after she turns her first trick at Lil's house, she recalls, "I lost something that afternoon. Something inside of me died. Life had played such a joke. I had married to escape from what I'd thought was an ugly world, only to find a worse one" (116). The choices Maria makes from this point onward become the only decisions she can imagine taking, as her life circumstances worsen.

Maria's city life thus simultaneously destroys her dreams for the future and gives her a future anyway. The relationships she develops with key figures who live, as she does during her time in Vancouver, outside of mainstream society and the law, are some of the most sympathetic and supportive ones she experiences away from her family. Through Lil and Ray, Maria manages to save herself and her daughter from the hopelessness that initially threatens her in Vancouver. She recalls, "I liked Lil immediately and we talked about all sorts of things—books, clothes and Lisa" (133). Maria also confides in Lil, describing their meeting as the beginning of a friendship, not a business relationship: "I told her how miserable and disappointed I felt about our life in Vancouver. Before we left she gave me her phone number and we agreed to get together some day soon" (133). The business aspect of this new relationship emerges almost immediately after, however, as Maria first explains exactly how broke and alone she is before she resorts to calling Lil for the first time: "After about a week, I knew" Darrel "wasn't ever coming back and I was in a panic. I was back to no money, no groceries, the rent was due and I had no one to turn to. Then I remembered Lil" (133).

The description that follows dispels any expectation that Maria remembers Lil as a friend to whom she may go for advice. "I could say at this point that I was innocent and had no idea what I was getting into," Maria explains, "I have even tried to make myself believe this but that would be lying. I did know. I guess I knew from the moment I picked up the phone and called her" (133). Thus Maria's first friend in the city becomes her first boss, or madame, as Lil finds a convent where Lisa can stay temporarily, gives Maria a makeover and a new wardrobe, and installs her in a room in the house, or brothel, from which she runs her business.

Maria claims what responsibility she can for each of the choices she makes during this period in her life. Her story thus directly challenges archetypal "fallen woman" narrative arcs and completely undercuts the dichotomous relationship critics such as Kim Anderson, Sarah Carter, and Terry Goldie identify between the "Indian maiden" and the "unattractive squaw." Maria occupies each of these roles briefly, but ultimately resists any such clear characterization. Though sex work, however well paid, traumatizes Maria, the arrangements she makes with Lil initially protect both Maria and her daughter in ways that her marriage does not. The nuns who care for Lisa are "gentle and kind and," Maria knows, "she'd be safe with them" (134). Lil takes care of Maria as best she can, given the nature of the work and Maria's unhappiness in it. Despite the isolation Maria recalls between the other women in the house, she also notes, "Lil arranged it so my clientele consisted of older, mature men who thought nothing of spending a small fortune. She was an unusual woman. She was kind in her own way, and I got along well with her" (134). Thus Maria remembers Lil as a businesswoman who offers her a way out—however repugnant Maria finds it—of a desperate situation. And while Maria continues to describe the people she meets in Vancouver as "Lil's girls" (136) or people she has met at Lil's house, Lil herself remains a sympathetic character in Maria's life story.

This sympathetic portrayal of Lil and Maria's relationship significantly separates the circumstances of Maria's sex work from the depth of the sorrow she tries very hard not to feel during this period. As the young woman in the next room at Lil's cries herself to sleep each night, Maria cannot go to her: "It was impossible," she recalls. "I knew, during all that time in Vancouver, that if I shed even one tear, I would fall apart and be finished. I felt that I'd never be able to pull myself together again so I would try to shut out the sounds of her weeping" (135). Maria's description of the relative freedom she experiences after trying some of the pills to which she is introduced at Lil's reveals the source of her sorrow, or what Derry and others term Maria's "degradation," to be not her prostitution in particular, but the hopelessness she feels because of her inability to help her family or to achieve the dreams she chases into the city: "They [the pills] helped me to sleep, they kept me happy, and most of all, I could forget about yesterday and tomorrow" (136). Too long the desperate provider and failing young mother haunted by past losses and responsible for the respective futures of her father's and then her own children, Maria takes pills and then heroin to free herself from the cycles of hope and despair that have brought her to this point in her life. Without a yesterday from which to recover and no tomorrow to plan for, moments of happiness and sleep uninhibited by day-to-day worries become, however briefly, possibilities in Maria's life. As a heroin addict, Maria begins another descent into desperate poverty and spiritual neediness. Ironically, she manages—for a short time at least—to support both herself and her daughter during this period even as she tries to escape these responsibilities.

Given the uniform facelessness of the very poor and very powerful to this point in the urban chapters of Maria's life, those characters whose names are included are all the more remarkable. Ray, the influential businessman who encourages Maria to "get straightened out" and introduces her to the elderly woman who helps her get through heroin withdrawal, is also a well-connected criminal. Maria remembers his kindness to her as well as his sometimes violent dealings with others, noting that this man who occasionally orders the breaking of someone's arms and legs also takes her to parties where she meets "many government people as well as the businessmen" she'd "met before" (140). But Maria remembers no threats in her relationship with Ray. In fact, the only demand he makes of her is that she stop taking heroin if she wishes to continue seeing him; and this demand is accompanied by concerted—and successful—efforts to help her to clean up, get her child back, and even move away from Vancouver.

Campbell portrays Ray as carefully as she portrays Lil, highlighting his criminal activities, but also emphasizing his kindness in comparison to the self-ishness of the influential Vancouver man, referred to only as Mr.-----, of whom

Maria briefly becomes a mistress. Such contrasting depictions of characters like Lil or Ray and Mr.----- or his friends erode divisions between criminal and legitimate citizens in Maria's Vancouver. In fact, Lil, Ray, and Maria herself, the more overtly criminal characters, come to seem more legitimately human or humane alongside Mr.-----, whose purported concern for Maria's well-being, like that of the welfare officials, teachers, and RCMP officers who target Maria's family in her youth, is revealed as cold, even inhumane, and more detrimental than the circumstances in which he intervenes. Unlike Darrel and the welfare people, Ray recognizes and helps Maria to meet her needs and the needs of her child.

During one of her initial unsuccessful attempts to leave her Vancouver life, Maria finds herself alone in Mexico. As she hitchhikes back, a group of Indigenous people in Arizona invite her to stay with them. Demonstrating the extent to which Maria identifies with the culture, traditional social structures, and cultural outsider status of Indigenous people, when Maria leaves the Arizona Natives, she compares them to her own people. The grandmother, who, Maria says, "could easily have been" her "Cheechum" (143), gives her a few dollars for food; and Maria considers for the first time since leaving home how difficult it is for her to stay away from her people, to live on her own and be responsible for no one but herself. Staying away to this point, she says, has been a survival strategy. And once again readers glimpse the depth of her cultural isolation as well as her desolation at the loss of her siblings. She explains how being responsible for others, having to care for others and share responsibility for their fates as well as her own, and the seemingly inevitable losses that accompany such community living, would affect her now: "I knew that as long as I stayed away I would somehow always survive, because I didn't have to feel guilty about taking from white people. With my own people I would have to share. I couldn't survive if I worried about someone else" (143). Thus she continues to deny her desire, or need, for family, for a specifically rural community of her own people, and for home.

Afterwards, upon reaching Vancouver again, a city where she knows at least one way to make a living, Maria begins to blame the Aboriginal men she sees there, men whose circumstances rival her own in terms of desperation, substance abuse, and poverty, for the tragedies of her life and for the lack of education and the poverty that have pushed her to this point. Conceivably recalling her father's desolation and the subsequent erosion of their family life after the Métis political movement he had once been involved in had failed, Maria says, "The drunken

Indian men I saw would fill me with a blinding hatred; I blamed them for what had happened to me...and for all the girls who were on the city streets. If they had only fought back, instead of giving up, these things would never have happened... I hated our men, and yet I loved them" (143–44). But even while she begins what she calls a "really down and out" existence in Vancouver (144), returning to heroin addiction and survival sex work, and living from one fix to the next with Trapper, another addict who beats her, it is the presence of these other Aboriginal people around her that consistently reminds her of her Cheechum.

This time Maria makes her own arrangements for kicking heroin, feeling that her Cheechum is with her throughout the hellish withdrawal period. And when she is clean again, she calls Ray, who picks her up and nurses her back to health, despite his own impending arrest. He also picks Lisa up from the convent, pays the balance owing on her room and board, then makes arrangements for Maria to work as a cook on an Alberta ranch.

Maria experiences severe losses wherever she goes, and the evolution of her thoughts and feelings—or lack thereof—about her future simultaneously reflects these tragedies and signals the dissolution of traditional cultural images of city and country life in Campbell's text. Poignantly commenting on the price she has paid for the decisions she has made in her life to this point in pursuit of what she retrospectively considers "symbols of white ideals and success," Maria says, "I feel an overwhelming compassion and understanding for another human being caught in a situation where the way out is so obvious to others but not to him. Dreams are so important in one's life, yet when followed blindly they can lead to the disintegration of one's soul" (116).

As Maria's feelings of failure when the kids are taken away from her indicate, her expectations for herself are impossibly high, especially given her status in relation to settler-colonial structures and culture. This recognizable pattern, in concert with Maria's earnest selflessness throughout her youth and early adolescence, and the cumulative influences on her life of systemic racism and cultural abuse lead readers to interpret Maria's successes and failures differently than she does. Initially marginalized in her home community because of her race, and isolated and persecuted because of her poverty, Maria's efforts to better her situation in the city leave her feeling even more marginalized and isolated from whatever community she had as a child. Her desolation becomes a tragic inevitability given the course of her life thus far, and her disillusionment is a direct result of her liminal cultural and social status. Thus dreams, in Maria's story, fade and disappear. However, though she encounters more terrible losses after leaving Vancouver, Maria's very survival in Vancouver, the city of her lost dreams, inspires hope and speaks to the strength of the lessons she learns from her Cheechum in her childhood. She survives because, thanks to her Cheechum's refusal to allow Maria to hate her own people, she has happy memories and a desire for the community she has known from which to draw hope during her time as an illegal drug addict and survival sex worker in the city.

In Maria's narration, sex work and other criminal activities become not marginalized, exceptional, or vilified elements of Canadian urban culture, but rather inevitable, even natural developments stemming from the misogynistic, racist, and colonial dominant hegemonic order. Maria's criminal consorts are, she implies, government leaders and captains of industry, the very people who, in mainstream Canadian contexts, currently support and enforce the laws that both separate and draw together (in increasingly unequal relationships) the culturally and politically powerful, and the racialized, criminalized poor. In suggesting that she operates, during her time in Vancouver, from the very cold heart of contemporary culture, Campbell's narrative insists that sex work and addiction constitute viable responses to her difficult life circumstances. In this context, the violence Maria and others like her suffer becomes not random inexplicable acts for which exceptional, culturally marginalized persons are responsible, but rather inevitable expressions of the violent, racist, misogynistic cultural centre.

IN SEARCH OF APRIL RAINTREE

Beatrice Culleton Mosionier likewise invokes this grand-scale reversal of NIMBY (or Not in My Backyard) ideologies in her novel, In Search of April Raintree. Like Halfbreed, In Search of April Raintree is a coming-of-age story told from the perspective of a relatively young Métis woman, April Raintree, who narrates the story of her own and her younger sister Cheryl's lives from early childhood until Cheryl's suicide in her early twenties.

As noted above, much of the criticism of this novel centres on the depictions of racial hybridity, particularly April's journey toward self-acceptance and the role of her rape in this progress, or lack thereof. Very little, however, is said about April and Cheryl's experiences with and responses to prostitution.

As Anderson, Andrea Smith, Goldie, and others note, the "squaw," or sexually available and violable whore, is one of the most pervasive negative stereotypes of Aboriginal womanhood. In denying the abjection of this stereotype, Mosionier, like Campbell, indicts dominant culture, not her prostitute characters, for the degradation Cheryl and, by implication April, experience through survival sex work. Like Campbell, Mosionier sets her most direct re-evaluation of this stereotype in the context of a cityscape with the same name as a real Canadian city.

Despite their initial dreams of happy city life, April and Cheryl, like Maria, quickly learn that the racism, alcoholism, and isolation of their childhood and adolescence surface again, in even more virulent ways, in the city. Also like Maria, Mosionier's heroines experience survival sex work and the stigma-inflected, racialized misogynist violence that Indigenous women in this subsection of the industry too often encounter. The significantly less hopeful and more graphically violent story of April and Cheryl's lives in the city, painful as it can be to read, more overtly communicates its message regarding the effects of systemic racism, as well as the connections between state-sponsored symbolic and literal violence against First Nations and Métis people and the hopelessness, social isolation, physical degradation, and futurelessness too many urban Indigenous people, especially women, experience. Nonetheless, Mosionier's text, like Campbell's, offers hope despite asserting the inevitable death of childhood dreams.

Like Maria, April initially believes that city life offers her freedom from the racism, isolation, and literal and emotional poverty she has known throughout her childhood and adolescence. Having abandoned a half-hearted attempt to find their parents because of the disgust she feels interacting with their impoverished friend in a dirty house in a poor Winnipeg neighbourhood, April resolves to disassociate herself from parents' neglect and alcoholism, as well as her own poverty and ethnicity. As with Maria, city life for April is characterized by pulling away and cutting herself off from her family and her roots. But while Maria does so because she feels her family will be ashamed of what she becomes in the city, April does so for shame of what her family is and for fear that she will be like them.

Though April has also begun to pull away from Cheryl at this point, the sisters' relationship remains strong enough that when Cheryl moves in with her and begins the university social work program for which she has won a scholarship, April describes their first night in the city as, "the real honest Independence Day....That evening, we sat around talking and thinking about the wonderful feeling of being together with no one to control our destinies but us" (101). Nonetheless, settler-colonial racism—external to and internalized by April at this point—in concert with April's determination to keep the truth about their parents from Cheryl and as far away, symbolically, from herself as possible, continue to control the sisters' destinies even after they move to the city.

Significantly, April and Cheryl are treated as outsiders by non-Aboriginals in this urban setting—a marginalization that April connects to a particularly sexualized vulnerability. When she goes out with Cheryl and her Aboriginal friends, April recalls, "Sometimes I'd overhear comments like, 'Who let the Indians off the reservation?' Or we'd be walking home and guys would make comments to us, as if we were easy pick-ups" (107). Though Cheryl and April do not discuss either forms of racism—that of strangers or of April herself—during this time, April's subsequent marriage and move to Toronto with her white middle-class husband finally brings her feelings about Cheryl to the fore in the sisters' relationship.

We later learn that Cheryl does not handle April's rejection well. Just as the intervention of child welfare services in Maria's family destroys the few support structures that keep her from the street, so the Children's Aid Society's separation of Cheryl and April during their childhood ultimately undermines their loving relationship and leaves Cheryl vulnerable to the most threatening and violent aspects of city life and prostitution. Unable to pass, like April does, for white, Cheryl remains in the culturally marginalized, sexually vulnerable social position April's marriage enables her to escape. Shunned by the one person who has always loved and protected her, Cheryl uncovers a number of disturbing truths—about her parents, about the plight of other First Nations and Métis people in the inner city—that she is unable to deal with on her own. Overwhelmed and increasingly hopeless, Cheryl falls into alcoholism and street prostitution.

Thus, survival sex work and urban street life come to represent self-abuse, hopelessness, degradation, and emotional alienation from family and community structures in both Campbell's and Mosionier's texts. However, Maria's happy childhood and her continuing love for her Cheechum make this form of sex work and its accompanying degradations survivable experiences for her. Though Cheryl also experiences survival sex work and a debilitating addiction, she has few happy memories and only a tenuous relationship with April from which to draw hope during this period. Cheryl, therefore, does not survive her experiences in sex work or the alcoholism to which prostitution is so intrinsically connected for her. Her continuing despair, the guilt she feels for her own and her sister's plight, and the shame she feels for her parents, for her people more generally, and as a result of the direction her life has taken ultimately destroy her.

As Cheryl explains to April in the days leading up to her suicide, and in the journals April reads after her death, sex work symbolizes her irreversible descent into a world populated by "gutter-creatures," a term she and April use to describe the urban "Indians" they, like Maria, see staggering or lying drunk along the streets of the poorest neighbourhoods in their city. As Cheryl searches Winnipeg's meanest streets for her parents in the months following her Christmas visit—and argument—with April, her journal entries record both her growing disgust with her people and her increasing knowledge of the systemic reasons for their condition:

> I see more and more of what April sees, broken people with broken houses and broken furniture. The ones I see on Main Street, the ones who give us our public image, the ones I see puking all over public sidewalks, battling it out with each other, their blood smearing up city-owned property, women selling what's left of themselves for a cheap bottle of wine....Sometimes I can't help it, I feel like April does, I despise these people, these gutter-creatures. They are losers. But there is a reason why they are the way they are. Everything they once had has been taken from them. And the white bureaucracy has helped create the image of a parasitic natives. But sometimes I do wonder if these people don't accept defeat too easily, like a dog with his tail between his legs, on his back, his throat exposed forever. (215–16)

Clearly distressed by such hopelessness, Cheryl struggles to hold onto her pride and continues to search for her parents. After discovering that she must count her father among the "gutter-creatures," however, she is overcome by despair:

I walk along Main Street. This is where I belong. With the other gutter-creatures. I'm my father's daughter. My body aches. I enter a hotel. I don't know which one. The word "Beverage" is all I see. I need a drink. A couple of drinks. The depression is bitterly deep....I want to run in front of a car....The creep wants to fondle me and kiss me. He can't wait. "Back off, you ugly old man. I'm no whore, you know?" I don't know why I say that, but I repeat it...."I wanna kiss you. I know what you are. So don't pretend with me. I paid for you."...He gives me a push. I slam into the wall....I open my eyes. I smile dumbly up at the man. He slams his fist into my face.

I wake up. I'm lying on the sidewalk....I notice the garbage cans and garbage bags on either side of me. "Hello there!" I says to them. "I've come home at long last." I chuckle to myself. I think in the morning the garbage men will take us all away, me and my friends. I giggle. I try to get up. I can't. So I stay put. (225–26)

As Cheryl's journal entries make very clear, becoming an alcoholic and a prostitute constitutes a giving over of herself, body and soul, to internalized racism, to the hopelessness and violence precipitated by settler colonialism, and to the repugnant stereotype she and April have struggled to resist since adolescence.

Mrs. Semple, the sisters' first Children's Aid social worker, makes both girls aware of this negative stereotype after their unsuccessful attempt to run away from foster care. After the girls are caught and returned, Mrs. Semple lectures them about "the native girl syndrome." Unfairly dismissing the girls' reasons for leaving the racist, abusive foster household, she explains,

You girls are headed in that direction. It starts out with the fighting, the running away, the lies. Next come the accusations that everyone in the world is against you. There are the sullen uncooperative silences, the feeling sorry for yourselves. And when you go on your own, you get pregnant right away or you can't find or keep jobs.

So you'll start with alcohol and drugs. From there, you get into shoplifting and prostitution and in and out of jails. You'll live with men who abuse you. And on it goes. You'll end up like your parents, living off society....Now, you're going the same route as many other native girls. If you don't smarten up, you'll end up in the same place they do. Skid row! (56–57)

Mrs. Semple's warning follows the girls to the city, where April's rejection of Cheryl and the Native in herself for fear of becoming a "gutter-creature," and both sisters' horror as Cheryl's life deteriorates quite literally to the level of the gutter, illustrate the extent to which this stereotype haunts them, especially in their respective searches for their parents. Fearful of becoming the freeloading national burdens Mrs. Semple describes, chastened and bewildered by the woman's refusal to listen to their legitimate reasons for running away, April and Cheryl learn that the state does not care for them, not really. As Aboriginal wards of the state, April and Cheryl's very presence is already a burden: to their foster families, to the Children's Aid Society, and to the colonial nation-state this agency represents.

That the sisters' efforts to resist such state-sponsored violence are ultimately used against them as evidence of their having set in motion the very forces they set out to resist is insidious indeed. By invoking a longstanding colonial stereotype of Indigenous womanhood to explain April and Cheryl's brief rebellion, and by refusing to see the real mistreatment of the sisters and other similarly situated girls, Mrs. Semple and the state she speaks for render young Indigenous women who would resist such abuse outsiders to mainstream society, outsiders for whose inevitable demise the state holds no responsibility. The necropolitics at work in April and Cheryl Raintree's Canada thus renders the sisters especially vulnerable to the racialized cultural misogyny that fuels the violent assaults they both suffer by suggesting that, by virtue of their race and gender, they deserve—perhaps even invite—such violence. That Cheryl later lies bruised and bleeding in the street and imagines herself to be, quite literally, a cultural waste product is a telling revelation of the sociopolitical forces responsible for setting Cheryl's tragic fall.

It is important to note that Cheryl becomes an alcoholic and a prostitute after learning the truth about her parents and their community of friends. With only negative images of herself to draw from childhood authority figures and from her only family, Cheryl, unlike Maria, appears to fall into sex work and lacks any clear motivation to get herself out, even though she hates what she is doing. Drinking dulls the pain and hopelessness she feels. Hopelessness—and her subsequent alcohol addiction—keep her from working in any other venue. During her reunion with her father, Cheryl recalls him hugging her as she "holds" her "breath against the gutter smell." She describes him stinking of liquor and handing her a beer, which she drinks to assuage her shock and dismay: "All these years, until this very moment, I had envisioned him as a tall straight man....I had made something out of him that he wasn't, never was.... Gratefully, I swallow some beer. Disgust, hatred, shame....yes, for the first time in my life, I feel shame. How do I describe the feeling? I swallow more beer" (218). Learning of her mother's recent suicide devastates Cheryl further, and her despair deepens again when her father demands money from her when she suspects he knows the money comes from sex work.

Perhaps the most striking difference between Campbell and Mosionier's narratives is the degree of violence the texts describe for readers. Campbell's text offers painful but brief records of intoxicated men, Métis and white, beating and raping women outside the bars in her home town, of blank-eyed children and hopeless men and women, Aboriginal and white, in Vancouver, and of her own body, cut and bruised from numerous beatings from Trapper and "anyone else who felt like beating" her (144). Next to Mosionier's documentary-style, detailed descriptions of similarly haunting moments of violence and despair, however, Campbell's treatment of such images is akin to a montage. Maria's narrative thus focuses on the steps she takes, personally and later politically, to save herself and her people from violence, degradation, and hopelessness. For example, a clear and detailed recollection of Maria's agency in leaving Trapper, her addiction, and her street life behind immediately follows her two-sentence recollection of her running sores and layers of bruises from the beatings he administers (144). In contrast, Mosionier's narrative focuses on her protagonists' limited agency in dealing with or preventing devastation in their lives and the lives of their people.

Such relative helplessness is most apparent in the sisters' respective inabilities to recover from and deal effectively with April's rape and the revelations about Cheryl's life that it precipitates. Just as Cheryl's more "Native-looking" features bring to the forefront socially entrenched racisms that hasten the break-up of April's already faltering marriage, Cheryl's reappearance in April's life results in April's learning another, even more unjust and humiliating lesson. Initially refusing to admit the dire circumstances of her life, Cheryl tells April only that she has quit university because volunteering at the Indian Friendship Centre taught her to believe she could not make a difference after all. And as April is kidnapped, beaten, and viciously raped because her attackers mistake her for Cheryl, Mosionier's extended and, literally, blow-by-blow treatment of this terrifying episode demands that readers experience, through April, the realities from which Cheryl has tried to protect her.

Having agreed to pick up Cheryl's things so that Cheryl can avoid running into Mark, her abusive boyfriend and sometime pimp, April heads to the house in what Cheryl describes as "a pretty run down" neighbourhood of Winnipeg (137). But as she reaches the gate by Cheryl's home, three men force her into their car, and drive off. Mosionier unrelentingly records, from April's terrified, angry perspective, every detail of her subsequent beating and repeated rape by these men, effectively requiring, as numerous critics observe, that readers witness April's suffering and her attackers' racist, misogynist verbal and physical abuse. Just as the men assault April, so Mosionier assaults her reader with the horrible details of April's rape. The lengthy rape scene Mosionier provides here is particularly difficult to read because, unlike Campbell's narrative distance and Maria's agency to recover from such events, readers experience this rape from the perspective of a victim whose fear and hatred of her race perhaps rival those of her attackers. Written almost ten years before even the Saskatoon serial murder case made national headlines, this rape scene, its immediacy and its similar abduct-assault-dump-outside-city-limits pattern nonetheless puts the violence of real contemporary kidnappings and gruesome murders of so many Indigenous women in cities across Canada into particularly glaring and painful perspective. As these real events continue to make headlines today, and as reports and responses to them continue both to ignore the ethnicity of so many of the victims and to foreground instead the victims' supposed "responsibility"—through their choices to participate in a "high risk lifestyle or profession" (Project KARE)—for the violence they experience, April's rape in this fictional context and her subsequent blaming of Cheryl for it foreground and interrogate such individualistic necropolitical ideologies in stark and particularly damning ways.

Especially significant, too, are the racial slurs and misogynist threats April endures while the men beat and rape her. The man who assaults April first expresses pleasure when she tries to fight him off, calling her a "real fighting squaw" and telling her, "That's good 'cause I like my fucking rough" (139). Throughout what April calls this "shameful" and torturous night, the men repeatedly call her a "squaw," a "whore," and a "slut" who "wants" the sexual violence that they inflict on her (139–45). April also describes how such verbal abuse consistently follows her efforts to defend herself and is accompanied by more and more debilitating beatings. The consistent and intimate relationship between the racial stereotype the men invoke—the squaw, or "Indian whore"—and the whore stigma and misogyny inherent to both their language and their actions throughout the rape thus constitute yet another significant and disturbing aspect of this prolonged scene. As in her prior efforts to resist racialized abuse and violence, April's resistance is characterized as both in character and inappropriate or deserving of punishment.

Even as April, barely conscious, lies listlessly beneath her first rapist, screaming "long and loud" inside her head and "trying to block everything out," she hears him tell the others, "Hey, she likes this, boys. These squaws really dig this kind of action. They play hard to get and all the time they love it." He then addresses April, telling her, "You love this, don't you, you little cocksucker" (142). That this man later forces his penis into April's mouth and urinates is both horrifying and fully in keeping with his character. Having demonstrated exactly what he thinks of her race, her gender, her supposed profession, and how these elements of her character make April inherently available and violable for him, the most vicious of the rapists ultimately considers her little more than a receptacle for human waste.

April's thought that this man, whom she identifies as the leader of her three attackers, speaks to her as though "he wanted to reduce" her "to nothingness" (140) is particularly haunting both in the context of Cheryl's belief that she might rightly be thrown away with the garbage and in relation to the non-literary kidnappings, rapes, and murders of Aboriginal women that Amnesty International, NWAC, and other groups struggle to bring to the attention of the Canadian public. This struggle becomes, in both contexts, a process of rehumanizing negative stereotypes in relation to persons hegemonic culture has long portrayed as disposable, failing, or lost. For April and Cheryl, this process involves recognizing the painful truths behind the so-called "native girl syndrome," and struggling to understand—or to remember—the many ways that this and other negative stereotypes of Aboriginality are culturally, not individually, produced.

Initially, when April learns that she has been kidnapped and raped because her rapists mistook her for her sister who worked as a prostitute, she unequivocally blames Cheryl for the assault. April refers to herself during this period as "a victim of" her "own sister's folly," and recalls thinking, "Another victim of being native. No matter how hard I tried, I would always be forced into the silly petty things that concerned native life. All because Cheryl insisted on going out of her way to screw up her own life. And, thus, screwing up mine" (183). Later, reading her dead sister's journal, April comes to understand the multiple forces involved in "screwing up" the sisters' lives and the lives of those April comes to recognize as her people, the systemic racism and cultural misogyny that neither the sisters nor any of their friends can resist effectively alone.

That rape, violent abuse, hopelessness, and life in the gutter are inherently connected, for both April and Cheryl, to "being native" (103) is a revealing statement in contemporary non-literary contexts as well. Mosionier's narrative, like Campbell's, enforces a cultural critique of particular relevance now—one that mainstream news media, and even memorialization projects for the missing and murdered women of Vancouver, Edmonton, and elsewhere do not often provide: to be an Aboriginal woman in Canada is to live under the constant threat of sexualized racial violence.

The sisters' arguments in the months leading up to Cheryl's suicide suggest that the rape and the state of Cheryl's life have more to do with "being native" than April initially allows. When, intoxicated and angry, Cheryl tells April she knows she married to get away from her, and that April has thus "prostituted" herself as much if not more than Cheryl has, it is Cheryl's, not April's perspective that rings true. As Cheryl describes the "big white snobs who think they're the superior race. Your white governments, your white churches, sitting back in idle, rich comfort, preaching what ought to be, but making sure it doesn't," April's hatred of the Native in herself emerges as one of the root causes of the sisters' problems (197). And as April waits for Cheryl to continue, feeling that what Cheryl is "on the verge of saying would help solve the mystery of what had made her give up on everything," Cheryl's simultaneous cultural critique and personal indictment of April has solved "the mystery" of her behaviour already (197).

As we eventually learn from Cheryl's final letter to April, settler-colonial racism finally reduces her, in her mind, to nothingness. "We all have the instinct to survive," Cheryl writes: "If that instinct is gone, then we die. April, there should be at least a little joy in living and when there is no joy, then we become the living dead. And I can't live this living death any longer. To drink myself to sleep day in and day out. April, you have strength. Dream my dreams for me. Make them come true for me. Be proud of what you are, of what you and Henry Lee are. I belong with our Mother" (227). As Fee, Hoy, and others note, Cheryl and April's experiences of race and racism connect with and parallel one another especially in the years following April's return to Winnipeg. Thus, while April's giving up on love and her emotional anguish after her rape parallel Cheryl's anguish and giving up on her own loves (rewriting history, helping others, and her child), April's final decision to live as Cheryl would have her live, dreaming her dreams "for" her, is haunting indeed. After all, April's decision to accept her Aboriginal self and to live with hope for her people, working to make their lives better, hinges on Cheryl's death.

Campbell and Mosionier's narratives examine with unflinching determination the ways that central socio-political structures facilitate the social degradation, economic desperation, and racial violence their female protagonists experience. April and Cheryl Raintree's stories especially illustrate the exceptionally violent fate Aboriginal women risk when their participation in the sex trade evokes the historically dehumanizing "squaw" stereotype that too often inspires a toxic combination of misogyny, racial hatred, and colonial violence. As hypervisible "urban outsiders" and supposed embodiments of the sexually available, violable Indigenous body, Maria, April, and Cheryl indeed risk much through prostitution.

However, *In Search of April Raintree* also makes very clear that the different forms of prostitution in which both of the lead characters are involved are symptoms, not causes of larger social problems that make victims out of April and Cheryl. *Halfbreed*, too, works to foreground survival sex work as a symptom rather than the cause of Maria's cultural marginalization, impoverishment, and subsequent social isolation. Her story, like April and Cheryl Raintree's, foregrounds not an anti-prostitution agenda, but rather a pro-urban Aboriginal community mission. About the "Indian" men she once despised on the streets of Vancouver, Maria, like Cheryl and April, comes to believe that blaming them for their plight ignores the complicated web of colonial forces that produce their obvious hopelessness. As Maria writes in chapter 23, "I realize now that the system that fucked me up fucked up our men even worse. The missionaries had impressed upon us the feeling that women were a source of evil. This belief, combined with the ancient Indian recognition of the power of women, is still holding back the progress of our people today" (144). In these closing chapters, Maria describes the uphill battle she fights to establish support networks for urban Aboriginal women, especially those who live and work on inner-city streets. Struggling to make her concerns heard in a variety of social and political settings, she finds Indigenous women must fight harder than their men to find the supportive communities they need. As Maria explains, the racist patriarchal colonial forces that "fuck up" Aboriginal men have even more negative consequences for Aboriginal women: "At one meeting I talked to the AA group about a halfway house for women. I expounded at great length that there were soup kitchens, flop houses and hostels for men throughout Canada. Furthermore, society didn't deal with men on the street as harshly as it did with women. One of the male members said that my problem was that I hated men and that probably what I needed was a good lay. I got so mad and frustrated I walked out" (151). For Maria, as for April and Cheryl, the force to be reckoned with is a system that marginalizes, physically and spiritually brutalizes, and disastrously limits the personal and communal agency of Indigenous people.

RESISTING A DANGEROUS ORDER

In conclusion, I return to the disparate views of sex work—survival or otherwise—taken by sex worker and Aboriginal activists. Is sex work synonymous with slavery, rape, and violence, especially for Aboriginal women, as NWAC's spokespeople once argued? Canada's violent colonial history and present too often place descendants of First Peoples in the bottom levels of urban social and geographical hierarchies. In these contexts, are legal protections and human rights for sex workers enough?

In Campbell and Mosionier's narratives, Aboriginal survival sex workers become not pivotal signifiers of the degradation that is prostitution, but rather street fighters whose daily struggles to survive illustrate the pervasive effects of settler colonialism and misogyny in Canada. How might this relatively rare approach to Indigenous street-involved sex work translate into real-world activist contexts? How might we make room for women's agency, even in the survival sex trade, and take into account the ways that the racist misogyny inherent to contemporary dominant culture limit the personal and professional choices of poor Indigenous women? Might Aboriginal sex workers suffer more if their means of survival is denigrated by First Nations and other social justice and urban outreach groups? How do Aboriginal street-involved and survival sex workers benefit from assertions that their means of subsistence itself constitutes a particularly repugnant form of violence against women?

Throughout this work, I have been arguing that marriage of anti-poverty, anti-racism, anti-violence, and anti-stigma activism might be more effective in terms of acknowledging the personhood, the presence, the agency, and the culturally marginalizing forces that define Aboriginal as well as other sex workers, survival or otherwise. Sex workers, especially Indigenous women in the industry, continue to be taken from city streets; inner-city sex workers, especially Indigenous women in the industry, continue to be assaulted, raped, mutilated, and murdered in greater and greater numbers. How many more deaths do we facilitate by incorporating the forces largely responsible for the murders of so many racialized and marginalized persons into social mobilization that struggles to resist these same forces?

Campbell and Mosionier's texts illustrate the necessity of reading, explaining, undercutting, and struggling against stereotypes of the abject or anachronistic Aboriginal body in the city. By engaging with these texts as they are written, acknowledging the difficult and pervasive stereotypes they tackle, we begin to recognize the groundbreaking work these authors do in humanizing and illustrating the limited personal agency of those women contemporary culture too often dismisses as abject, even deserving, victims. Significantly, these authors do not suggest that assaulted, raped, suffering, addicted, and degraded Aboriginal women are new or exceptional. Rather, they insist that readers look again at these abject stereotypes, and that we understand and resist the cultural forces that perpetuate such suffering and hopelessness.

In addition, Campbell and Mosionier write the city as a space of potential resistance, of emerging community, and of life—but death is everywhere, and acknowledging and building up urban community are important means of preventing more violent death, despair, and degradation. Particularly at a time when political mobilization is happening in Aboriginal and other communities to resist necropolitical forces underlying cases like those in Vancouver, Edmonton, Winnipeg, and elsewhere, it is important to foreground connections between cultural structures and the plight of those who live under state control but not state protection.

CONCLUSION

ON DECEMBER 6, 1989, a young man walked into a university classroom in Montreal, ordered the men out, shot and killed the women in the room, then moved through other halls and classrooms, killing more women and eventually turning the gun on himself. This violent event, often referred to in media reports as the Montreal Massacre, has become a kind of touchstone for feminist anti-violence and commemorative initiatives in Canada for women who have suffered and died as a result of individual and systemic misogyny.

Over the past decade, I have found myself preparing materials for this book on the anniversary of the Montreal Massacre, a day marked by vigils on all of the university campuses on which it has been my privilege to work. This has given me pause.

The Cultural Memory Group (CMG), writers of the critically acclaimed *Remembering Women Murdered by Men*, note that violence against women is too often portrayed as exceptional rather than commonplace in contemporary society. Focus in Montreal Massacre anniversary tributes, for example, vacillates between discussions of violence against women, the ways contemporary Canadian society condones or disguises such violence, and representations of the gunman as a crazed isolated killer whose monstrous actions remain unimaginable and inexplicable in contemporary cultural contexts. Even when fourteen white university students have been publicly and violently murdered because they are women, the Ripper-like serial killer mythos, the tale of the lone, monstrous, homicidal individual, exonerates the wider culture that genders violence male and victimization female. The murderer is thus understood not as the outgrowth of a misogynist and deeply sexist culture, but as an individual maniac moving in from the social margins to inflict otherwise unimaginable violence on women.

However, as some of the controversy arising in response to CMG's work points out, and as a comparison with CMG's projects of memorialization with other examples of commemorative activism make clear, even those feminist projects driven by the best of intentions can reconstitute hegemonic class and racial hierarchies. As I have argued throughout this book, the class, race, professional, and geographical positioning of the missing and murdered street-involved and/or survival sex workers in cities across Canada must inspire critical analyses involving more than issues of violence against women in Canadian society.

ANTI-VIOLENCE ACTIVISM AND FEMINISM

Remembering Women Murdered by Men discusses cross-country efforts to mourn women's violent deaths, to intervene in representations of such violence as exceptional, and to promote cultural change. Many of the commemorative projects, plaques, and monuments discussed in this text are inspired by the events of December 6, 1989. CMG discusses one such monument in the book's first chapter entitled "Vancouver: Missing, Murdered and Counting." *Marker of Change/ À l'aube du changement* is installed in Thornton Park, a mere "half-a-dozen blocks south of the 'cold heart' of Downtown Eastside," Vancouver (CMG 31). A group of women from Capilano College in North Vancouver, headed by media student Christine McDowell, began the *Marker of Change* memorial project because they were "outraged that the whole country knew the name of the [Montreal] women's murderer while the women themselves remained largely unknown" (CMG 34). I have visited *Marker of Change*, walked its circle, read its inscriptions, sat on one of its stone benches, and appreciated its beauty. For me, however, as for others, the signification of this monument vis-à-vis communities of women remains deeply disturbing.

In order to assess the significance of *Marker of Change*, the best place to begin is with CGC's evocative description of this monument:[1]

Here [in Thornton Park] stands a symmetrical ring, 27 metres (90 feet) in diameter and 91 metres (300 feet) in circumference, bordered by fourteen warm pink, construction-grade granite benches, each 1.7 metres (5.5 feet) long and rock-solid like sarcophagi. Each bench is raised 15 centimetres (6 inches) above the ground, each is inscribed with a woman's name protectively facing the centre of the circle and each has a shallow, oval-shaped indentation sandblasted into its top surface, where rain water gathers. Every second bench bears a dedicatory inscription on its outside face in one of seven languages—Chinese, Swahili, French, Chinook, Hindi, Spanish or English:

THE FOURTEEN WOMEN NAMED HERE WERE MURDERED
DECEMBER 6, 1989, UNIVERSITY OF MONTREAL.
WE, THEIR SISTERS AND BROTHERS, REMEMBER, AND WORK FOR A BETTER WORLD.
IN MEMORY AND IN GRIEF FOR ALL WOMEN WHO HAVE BEEN MURDERED BY MEN.
FOR WOMEN OF ALL COUNTRIES, ALL CLASSES, ALL AGES, ALL COLOURS.

...Surrounding the circle of benches is a continuous exterior ring of ceramic brick tiles with over 5,000 names of individuals and groups who donated time or money to the project. Each name is hand letter-punched into the clay—from CÉLÉBRATIONS LESBIENNES to NELSON HOUSE FIRST NATION to MINISTRY OF THE ATTORNEY GENERAL. Tiles inscribed with epitaphs written by the families of the fourteen women are placed across from the benches dedicated to their respective daughters. An orientation stand is located on one corner of the site, closest to the path leading...with key text written in Braille and raised lettering, in both English and French:

THE WOMEN'S MONUMENT, 1990–1997.
A FEMINIST PROJECT REALIZED BY A SMALL GROUP OF WOMEN
IN COLLABORATION WITH CAPILANO COLLEGE
WITH LOVE FOR ALL PEOPLE. (33–34)

Significantly, though none of the fourteen benches directly acknowledges the missing and murdered women of Vancouver, one of the donor tiles reads,

IN LOVING MEMORY
OF THE WOMEN KILLED
ON VANCOUVER'S
DOWNTOWN EASTSIDE
SO MANY WOMEN LOST TO US
WE DREAM
A DIFFERENT WORLD
WHEN THE WAR ON WOMEN
IS OVER.

This tile was included in *Marker of Change* in response to concerns expressed by many DTES residents, local First Nations' groups, and others that the monument reproduced the cultural and racial marginalization of key groups, particularly the groups represented in the growing numbers of missing and murdered women in the DTES. As Marion Dean Dubick, a local victim service worker, argues, "There's people dying every day down here...The fourteen women in Montreal got massacred and that is horrifying, but look at the names on the list. All these women counted. We don't have Canada-wide coverage of all the women that die right here in the Downtown Eastside. Why is that? We're not university students. We're not across the country. We're right here. We're dying every day" (qtd in CGC 38).

In concert with the placement of the single tile dedicated to all of the DTES women outside the circle of fourteen sarcophagi-like benches, Dubick's comments bring into stark relief the ways that even those feminist projects driven by the best of intentions can simultaneously counter and reconstitute hegemonic class and racial hierarchies. In one interview, McDowell explains, "When we started the project, we didn't know about the Downtown Eastside and what was going on there. And we learned about it. Certainly we had meant for the dedication to mean all women. And it does. But I know that the First Nations women in the Downtown Eastside don't feel included in it, and I understand. It's not enough" (qtd in CMG 38). CMG observes that the donor tile for DTES women, "while still not managing explicitly to indicate race, class or economic conditions that make some women more susceptible to men's violence than others, nevertheless opens the monument's community outward in more explicit, located ways and gestures to the need for the more localized memorials" (43).

This need is also evident in the significant controversies—among organizers, and between organizers and city council as well as local groups of Vancouver residents—that emerged during the planning, development, and construction of *Marker of Change*, as CMG records and analyzes. "Vancouver: Missing, Murdered and Counting" begins by describing a number of local commemorative projects, including DTES support workers and activists Carol Martin and Marlene Trick's plan to facilitate the local development of "a lasting memorial to honour all women from the Downtown Eastside who died" (30). CMG documents some of the debates involved in this and other local memorial activism projects, noting that "the stakes in these efforts and disagreements are raw and immediate" and that commemorative initiatives for Vancouver's DTES women raise a number of difficult questions: "how to honour women's lives while marking the violence of their deaths; how to specify individual victims while including all abused women—across lines of race, ethnicity, class, economic situation—in the remembrance; how to acknowledge that these social and cultural conditions put marginalized women at much higher risk; how to make a memorial politically effective, not deflecting from but contributing to the struggle against violence against women" (31). Referencing "a range of memorials" in the DTES, "clustered around a dozen blocks of a deprived neighbourhood, that protest violence against women," CMG suggests that, "above all, these memorials are dedicated to visibility and remembrance as fundamental conditions in keeping alive the struggle to end violence against women, whether the victims are local women working in the sex trade, women murdered 35 kilometres away in a Vancouver suburb or women murdered in a Montreal university 5,000 kilometres across the country" (31).

"Vancouver: Missing, Murdered and Counting," goes on to describe the ways in which a local women's monument committee "continues to both remember and work against" Vancouver's "violent past, vivifying this memorial as a space of possibility and action" by organizing, for example, the 2004 "Peace is Possible" event on the anniversary of the Montreal Massacre, "inviting people to come together in Thornton Park to build a communal peace symbol in the middle of the monument" (45). Such an initiative may give us pause, however, when we learn that those items used to construct the peace symbol—"flowers, quotes, fruits, vegetables...toys, candles, socks and gloves"—in *Marker of Change* are to be left for local "people who need them" (event poster, qtd in CMG 45). I cannot help but think that such an initiative would not be more appropriately located at one of the monuments for local women in the DTES.

One such monument—an inscribed boulder and bench-mounted plaque—is installed in Portside, or CRAB[2] Park, ten blocks away from *Marker of Change* in the DTES. Urban geographer Adrienne Burk,[3] CMG, and others note the contrast between *Marker of Change*'s nationally funded development, its expansive focus, and its relatively elaborate design, and the CRAB Park monument's private funding, local focus and development, and its simple, relatively inexpensive design. The CRAB Park monument "attempts to bridge the local and the universal, but it also insists on inscribing a publicly unacknowledged community of women" (CMG 46), a community of women that *Marker of Change* would seem to acknowledge only very briefly, even as it resides permanently in the neighbourhood from which they have disappeared. The boulder in the CRAB Park monument, placed in 1999 and dedicated by contributors to the Missing People website as well as the CRAB Water for Life Society sits, "surrounded by a clump of bushes, at the dividing line between the park's expanse of green lawn and the beach that curves around the bay" (CMG 46).[4] The inscription on the smooth flat rock face visible from the path nearby reads as follows:

THE HEART HAS

IN HONOR OF THE SPIRIT OF THE PEOPLE

MURDERED IN THE DOWNTOWN EASTSIDE

MANY WERE WOMEN AND MANY WERE NATIVE

ABORIGINAL WOMEN. MANY OF THESE CASES

REMAIN UNSOLVED. ALL MY RELATIONS.

ITS OWN MEMORY

DEDICATED JULY 29, 1997

The plaque on the bench placed a short distance away on the opposite side of the path, reads, "IN MEMORY OF L. COOMBS, S. DE VRIES, M. FREY, J. HENRY, H. HALLMARK, A. JARDINE, C. KNIGHT, K. KOSKI, S. LANE, J. MURDOCK, D. SPENCE & ALL OTHER WOMEN WHO ARE MISSING. WITH OUR LOVE.

MAY 12, 1999." Local activists working to raise awareness of the plight of the disappeared and murdered women of the DTES regularly organize memorial events and protests that often begin, conclude, or otherwise visit the CRAB Park monument. Significantly, "The Memory March," held on March 25, 2007, began at the CRAB Park Memorial Boulder and concluded at *Marker of Change* ("Memory March—Sunday March 25th"). Such literal and symbolic progress from the local to the national/universalized treatment of violence against women poignantly illustrates local activists' willingness to work with other anti-violence feminists, provided the specificities of local contexts are acknowledged.

As CMG points out, again in the first chapter of *Remembering Women*,

> The ambition of the *Marker of Change/À l'aube du changement* to be not just emblematic but "national" is exemplary, raising the status and visibility of the struggle against violence against women. From another perspective, that ambition risks giving deep offence. For many First Nations peoples, the very concept of the national—understood as referring to the latter-day nation-state of the European settler-colony—(re)enacts the violence of the colonization and subjugation of those Nations that preceded Canada and never ceded their claims to indigenous and independent nationhood. The memorials built and performed in memory of murdered and disappeared women from Vancouver's Downtown Eastside have deliberately eschewed any claim to national representation and remain determinedly local. (45)

In the same chapter, CMG briefly discusses other significant local commemorative initiatives, all of which insist that violence against women must be considered in its specific local contexts and many of which resist *Marker of Change*'s universalizing approach to issues of gender violence. Given the differing levels of police and political response, of media attention, and of public outcry apparent in the Montreal Massacre and the series of massacres to which sex workers across the country are being subjected, it would seem particularly important to acknowledge the additional, albeit unintentional, violence done by a nationally funded anti-violence marker that employs fourteen white women university students' murders as symbolic representations of all misogynist violence.

As female members of already marginalized groups, the victims in the multiple ongoing mass or serial murder cases across this country indeed experience a particularly gendered form of cultural violence—but middle-class women and men, as well as some political leaders, police, journalists, and feminists are implicated in this violence. Violence against women is indeed a rubric with the potential to unite disparate classes, races, and geographical populations of feminists who struggle to create a safer, better world, particularly for women. As Burk and CMG note, comparisons between the Montreal and Vancouver cases also have the potential to highlight and critique the class, race, and spatial differences in the two cases that have made martyrs of the Montreal women, and barely recuperable tragic figures of Vancouver's murder victims. As the contrast between inscriptions on Marker of Change and CRAB Park's Missing Women Memorial Boulder make poignantly clear, however, racial and class differences between women cannot be subsumed under the rhetoric of a universalized experience of womanhood in a patriarchal culture. We as anti-violence feminists must remember that racism and class exploitation may not merely be the offspring of a parent system of patriarchy. "Within" the "feminist movement in the West," feminist cultural theorist bell hooks writes, there is an "assumption that resisting patriarchal domination is a more legitimate feminist action than resisting racism and other forms of domination" (19). Stigma-inflected, classed, and racialized violence, as well as the anti-prostitution police and private citizen-driven initiatives this violence has provoked in Canadian inner cities, reify a decidedly anti-feminist position: that certain women deserve, even invite the violence to which they are subjected. Furthermore, we must find means to counter decidedly anti-feminist public responses to mass/serial murder cases that imply that any poor woman—and particularly any Indigenous woman—who stands on an urban street and offers sexual services to passersby in exchange for money or drugs is essentially suicidal and thus shares responsibility for any violence—misogynist, racist, classist, or otherwise—to which she is subjected.

Further analysis of commemorative activism inspired by the violent deaths of disenfranchised women across the country is beyond the scope of this book project. Others have begun this important work, however, determinedly emphasizing the necessity of building bridges between communities who work to memorialize murdered women while also striking that difficult, delicate, controversial, but nonetheless required balance between conversing and talking over, between representing and erasing difference, between facilitating universal concern and highlighting the culturally telling differences between women's lives and their deaths.[5]

PROCEEDINGS FROM AND CONNECTIONS TO THE SSLR

Sex work and sex workers seem always to exist on the front lines of feminist battles, as icons either of feminist resistance to patriarchal control or as the most public expressions of men's oppressive governance over women's bodies and sexuality. Such battles and their associated images of emancipation and oppression are being played out in increasingly public forums—and with increasingly higher stakes for feminists, for women, and for Canadians more generally. The transcribed proceedings and published report of the 2005–2006 federal Subcommittee on Solicitation Laws, inspired as they are by the circumstances leading up to the Vancouver case, are such a public forum. This forum involves a number of key memorial activists—in its proceedings, at least—but has yet to receive the attention it deserves from other feminists. The SSLR's transcribed proceedings and published report may be read as cultural texts—the rhetorical, linguistic, and thematic development of which provocatively illustrate ways that current debates about sex work effectively hobble legislative efforts to protect some of Canada's most vulnerable citizens. Further analysis of exchanges between the committee and academic scholars alongside those of former and current sex workers and sex worker activists highlights the pivotal ways that modes of communication—for example, presentation of empirical data or personal storytelling—as well as the gender, class, and racial status of participants signify in this text.

The SSLR represents a key opportunity for Canadians more generally—politicians, street-involved activists, and academics, as well as private citizens and police—to begin to intervene in the emerging necropolitical order by engaging with the concerns of our most disenfranchised populations and working to address current ideologies and legislation that facilitate a growing number of violent deaths in this country. Such discourse could—and should—acknowledge connections between other national and transnational debates such as existing scholarly interrogations of the Mexican government's inadequate response to the violent murders of hundreds (perhaps even thousands) of women, many of whom were sex workers, in Ciudad Juarez Chihuahua, along the US–Mexico border. Critical examinations of the SSLR proceedings may also effectively draw on postcolonial and critical race theorists' analyses of the South African Truth and Reconciliation Commission proceedings, as well as readings by criminologists, sociologists, and feminist scholars of the published report of Canada's Special Committee on Pornography and Prostitution (the Fraser Committee). As such, we can engage effectively with ongoing international discourse about sex work, violence against racialized and otherwise marginalized women, and human rights that aims to counteract transnational necropolitical trends.

FICTION AND SEX WORK IN CANADA

Literature, fiction in particular, is another means through which critics, activists, and others may engage sex work and other anti-violence and anti-racism activism. More recent fiction in Canada is replete with examinations of the cultural positioning of sex work and sex workers in relation to feminism, to patriarchal class and family structures, to cityscapes, and to issues of race and racism. Historical and contemporary representations of sex work and sex workers in Canadian literature have inspired and developed alongside a variety of socio-political and cultural moments in Canadian and international history. Perhaps because the sexual revolution, the civil rights movement, and second-wave feminism produced a generation of writers concerned with the emancipation of their female characters from restrictive social and moral codes, representations of prostitution in Canadian literature have become increasingly common in the last four decades. Sex workers in texts from the 1970s and 1980s—for example Adele Wiseman's *Crackpot* (1974), Margaret Atwood's *The Handmaid's Tale* (1985), and Daphne Marlatt's *Ana Historic* (1988)—function, in admittedly disparate cultural settings, primarily as symbols of women's political oppression or of feminist resistance.

In the last two decades, a growing body of Canadian and First Nations literature has begun to treat sex work and sex workers as more than a social issue or the embodiment of oppressive socio-political times. As a result, this body of work may be read usefully against Campbell and Mosionier's groundbreaking engagement with damaging colonial, class, and gender stereotypes. For example, Nelly Arcan's novel, *Whore* (published in English in 2004), features a female protagonist who shares the story of her life and work in a Montreal brothel. Arcan's heroine asserts that she finds in her profession means of resisting and undercutting the effects of her suffocating Roman Catholic upbringing and education. Dionne Brand's *At the Full and Change of the Moon* (1999) includes a black protagonist whose experiences in sex work are instrumental in her developing self-love.

Many other contemporary novels constitute important additions to such an analysis. The bildungsroman storyline of Cree writer Tomson Highway's *Kiss of the Fur Queen* (1998) is punctuated by a series of ghastly rapes and murders of female street-involved Aboriginal women in Winnipeg. Rebecca Godfrey's *The Torn Skirt* (2001) features a poor adolescent white girl who becomes a street kid in Vancouver because she idolizes a street-involved sex worker who may or may not be another persona in her increasingly fragmented psyche. Evelyn Lau's *Fresh Girls and Other Stories* (1993) describes the dark and often depressing working conditions in a Vancouver brothel. And Maggie de Vries's *Missing Sarah* (2003) is a pieced-together biography of her sister, Sarah de Vries, a young woman of mixed race who chooses sex work and street life in the DTES over high school and a dysfunctional family life in a white middle-class Vancouver suburb. Analyses—comparative or otherwise—of texts like these have the potential to contribute effectively to initiatives that resist the current dehumanization of sex workers and other marginalized populations in Canada.

"WE'RE DYING HERE"

As contemporary global capitalism continues to facilitate the downward social mobility of larger and wider segments of the population, and as governments here and abroad continue to cut spending on social programs that might otherwise ease the economic and/or cultural desperation of a growing global underclass, privileged classes perhaps work especially hard—as so-called "concerned citizens," as consumers of current politico-economic positions, even as feminists—not to recognize their (our) collective fate in the deaths of those persons who have existed longer on the political, cultural, and economic margins than them/ourselves. As the centre of the nation is defined in increasingly narrow and neoliberal economic terms, and as corporate tax cuts, decreasing job security, record levels of consumer debt, and ongoing colonialism add to the ranks of the underclass, the focus on orderly Canadian cities and the increased policing and protection of a certain increasingly exclusive citizenry by public officials and private citizens alike would seem to facilitate and legalize our own potential disposability. Moreover, if such mass self-destruction is generated at the centre, not the periphery of contemporary culture, the murdered women of Vancouver, Edmonton, Saskatoon, Winnipeg, and other Canadian centres must be seen not as a singularly disposable population, but rather as the first group in an ever-expanding population of citizens-turned-cultural-waste-products.

In working to resist this necropolitical order, as groups such as AHF, CASAC, Maggie's, NWAC, NYSHN, PACE, Pivot, POWER, SPOC, Stella, SWUAV, and SWAV point out, it is essential to listen to and account for the concerns of the persons most directly under attack. As SPOC founder and former Executive Director Valerie Scott told audience members at the "Bawdy House Burlesque" SPOC fundraiser in 2006, current laws and the ideologies that support them have to change because "we're dying here." Her words poignantly echo those of Marion Dean Dubick, the Vancouver DTES service worker quoted above: "We're right here. We're dying every day" (qtd in CMG).

APPENDIX 1

LEGISLATION AND POLICING OF PROSTITUTION AND SOLICITATION IN CANADA

BEFORE 1972

- Street prostitution defined as vagrancy, a summary offence.
- *Criminal Code* s.175(1)(c): "Every one commits a vagrancy who... being a common prostitute or nightwalker is found in a public place and does not, when required, give a good account of *herself*" (emphasis added).

1972

- Vague and sexist s.175(1)(c), or "Vag. C," repealed and replaced with s.195.1, the soliciting law which makes it illegal to solicit for the purposes of prostitution.

1977

- Report of the Special Committee on Places of Amusement urges government to "clean up" Yonge Street in Toronto by legislating closure of bawdy houses and other prostitution-related businesses.
- Police use this report to claim that these businesses facilitate existence of organized crime and illicit drug trade, and thus constitute a serious threat to the community.
- *Criminal Code* sections 210 and 193 (commonly referred to as the bawdy house law/s), further establish and entrench anti–bawdy house legislation. Drawing on nearly a century of related legislation, these laws continue to define "a common bawdy house" (brothel, whore house) as any place used "for the purposes of acts of indecency or prostitution."

1978

- Supreme Court of Canada concludes that charges of soliciting can only be laid if solicitation is "pressing and persistent."
- Soliciting law subsequently becomes toothless.

1983

- In response to growing national concern about street prostitution, Fraser Committee convenes to investigate conditions of and legislation pertaining to prostitution in Canada.

1985

- Fraser Committee Report urges legislature to clarify legal status of prostitution, argues against prohibition, and urges that it be legal for one or two prostitutes to work out of a private dwelling.
- Government ignores Fraser Committee recommendations and instead enacts the communicating law (Bill C-49, *Criminal Code* s.213(1)) prohibiting communication of any kind in a public place for the purposes of prostitution.
- Solicitation law repealed.
- The exchange of sexual services for financial remuneration remains legal.

1990

- Supreme Court of Canada upholds bans on bawdy houses, section 212 (1) of the *Criminal Code* (procuring), part J: "Everyone who lives wholly or in part on the avails of prostitution of another person is guilty of an indictable offense and is liable to imprisonment for a term not exceeding ten years" (s.193), and soliciting in a public place (s.195.1(1)) (Canada, *Reference re: Prostitution*).

1992

- Federal, Provincial, and Territorial Deputy Justice Ministers' Working Group on Prostitution established to review and make recommendations regarding prostitution-related laws, policies, and practices.

- Supreme Court of Canada upholds criminality of "living on the avails of prostitution" (s.212(1) & 212(3)), thus perpetuating isolation and criminality associated with sex work.

1998

- Federal, Provincial, and Territorial Deputy Justice Ministers' Working Group on Prostitution report is released (Canada, *Report and Recommendations in Respect of Legislation, Policy, and Practices Concerning Prostitution-Related Activities*); Report concludes that community harm reduction and reduction of violence against prostitutes should be objectives of these practices; Report advocates elimination of bawdy house law, then government regulation of brothels.
- No legislative change is immediately forthcoming.

2005–2006

- In response to public outcry over the disappearance of numerous Vancouver women, many of whom worked in street prostitution and at least twenty-six of whom were murdered, federal Liberal government strikes Subcommittee on Solicitation Laws of the Standing Committee on Justice, Human Rights, Public Safety and Emergency Preparedness (SSLR); SSLR Report acknowledges the problem of violence against prostitutes and suggests further criminalization of pimps and predators, as well as continuation of current policing strategies; Report also notes significant differences in opinion between Conservative and other SSLR members (Canada, *The Challenge of Change: A Study of Canada's Criminal Prostitution Laws*).
- No legislative change is immediately forthcoming.

2009–2010

- Building on momentum of SSLR hearings, British Columbia's Downtown Eastside Sex Workers United Against Violence Society (SWUAV) and representatives from Ontario's Sex Professionals of Canada challenge portions of the bawdy house (s.210(1)(2) (a) (b)&(c)), living on the avails (s.212(1)(j)), and communicating (s.213(1)(c)) laws before the Superior Courts in British Columbia and Ontario. They argue the laws prevent sex workers from protecting themselves while they engage in legal activity; they argue, therefore, that the laws violate sex workers' human rights under the *Canadian Charter of Rights and Freedoms*.
- The British Columbia court originally denied standing to Vancouver applicants, but "its decision on standing was overturned on appeal and the application was sent back to the trial court to be determined on its merits" (Craig 100, n8; Downtown Eastside Sex Workers United Against Violence Society v. Canada [AG], 2010).
- The Ontario Court, in September 2010, finds in favour of SPOC plaintiffs Terri Jean Bedford, Amy Lebovitch, and Valerie Scott: Justice Susan Himel agrees that the sections in question violate section 7 of the *Canadian Charter of Rights and Freedoms*. Justice Himel strikes down these sections (Bedford v. Canada, 2010). A thirty-day stay is imposed on the decision.
- Attorney General of Canada and Attorney General of Ontario petition Ontario Court to extend stay of Himel's decision pending an Appeal; Appeal is granted and stay is extended.

2011

- Attorney General of Canada and Attorney General of Ontario appeal the Himel decision; a collection of concerned groups file for and are granted intervenor status in the appeal; in June 2011, Ontario Court of Appeal hears the case.
- Stay is extended, again, pending decision of the five Ontario justices.

2012

- Ontario Court of Appeal upholds Himel decision on all but one point: communicating law "remains in full force" (Canada [AG] v. Bedford, 2012).
- Justice J.A. MacPherson, one of the five justices who heard *Canada (AG) v. Bedford*, writes a dissenting opinion, agreeing with Justice Himel's original finding that the communicating law also contravenes the *Canadian Charter of Rights and Freedoms* and should thus be struck down.

2013

- Attorneys General of Canada and Ontario appeal Ontario Court of Appeal's decision to the Supreme Court of Canada; once again, a collection of concerned groups are granted intervenor status in the appeal; in June 2013, Supreme Court of Canada hears the case.
- Supreme Court of Canada overturns Ontario Court of Appeal's decision on communicating law and instead upholds Himel's original decision to strike down all impugned laws, declaring the laws infringe on prostitutes' rights under the *Canadian Charter of Rights and Freedoms* (Canada [AG] v. Bedford, 2013). A one-year stay is imposed on the decision.

APPENDIX 2

Vancouver Reward Poster, 1999. Used by permission.

APPENDIX 3

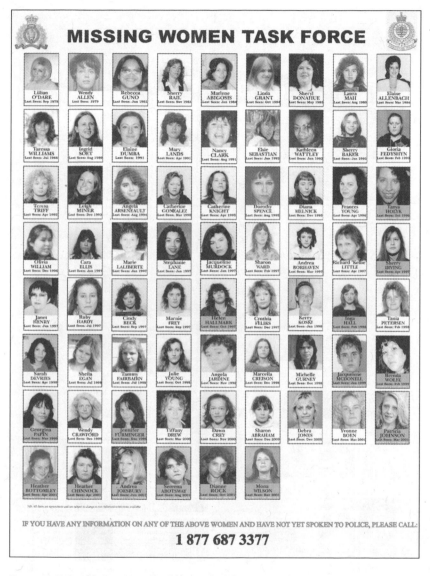

Vancouver Reward Poster, 2004. Used by permission.
In 2006, three of the sixty-nine women pictured here were found alive.

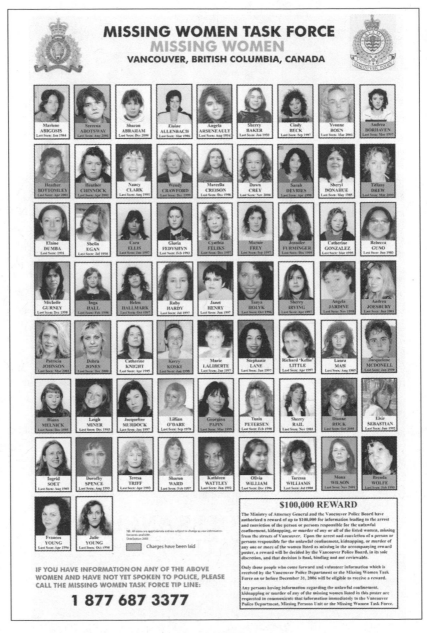

Vancouver Reward Poster, 2007. Used by permission.

Shading beneath a woman's photo indicates that charges were laid in her case.

APPENDIX 5

According to SWAV's online records, this is the textual content and general layout for a 1997 Grandview-Woodlands Neighbourhood Action Group Poster.

---

no more sex on our streets!

Philip Owen, the Mayor of Vancouver, has rejected our petition for

ZERO TOLERANCE on
STREET PROSTITUTION AND DRUG TRADE ACTIVITY.

He refuses to support our demands for enforcement of ZERO TOLERANCE because "it simply results in moving the problem to another neighbourhood."

Do you want your children to walk to school without passing several **hookers**?
Do you want to walk on the street without being propositioned by **johns**?
Do you want to step out your front door without wading through **condoms**?
Do you want your children to play in the park without being stabbed by **needles**?
Do you want to get rid of **rush hour traffic** at midnight on your streets?
Do you want to look out your windows and not see **sex acts** performed in broad daylight?
Do you want your daughters to be recruited by **pimps** at school?
Do you see **drug dealers** selling drugs on your street?
Have you been a victim of **break and enter** recently?
Has your car been stolen or **vandalized**?
Have you been **stalked** as you walk home?

Why THIS neighbourhood? The Mayor has declared our neighbourhood to be the

UNOFFICIAL RED LIGHT DISTRICT FOR VANCOUVER.
NO MORE!!!
*We will **NOT** tolerate this any longer.*

Come to a

ZERO TOLERANCE DEMONSTRATION

Date: Friday June 6th, 1997
Location: On the street at Hastings and Victoria
Time: 6:00 p.m. to 7:00 p.m.

Sponsored by the Grandview Woodlands Neighbourhood Action Group
for more information or to volunteer, phone 254-2482 or 255-9345

NOTES

INTRODUCTION

1. Cultural theorist Rosa-Linda Fregoso draws on Achilles Mbembe's "Necropolitics" in her discussion of this kind of state disavowal of responsibility for the plight of marginalized and excluded populations as a type of rendering of these populations as essentially "attackable" and "disposable" enemies of the state who exist beyond any moral universe of concern ("'We Want'").

2. See, for example, Shannon Bell's critical work, *Reading, Writing and Rewriting the Prostitute Body*, Cosi Fabian's essay "The Holy Whore: A Woman's Gateway to Power," or Tamara Berger's controversial 2004 novel, *The Way of the Whore*.

3. In fact, as Amnesty International notes in *Stolen Sisters: A Human Rights Response to Discrimination and Violence Against Indigenous Women in Canada*, the organization's 2004 report that condemns the Canadian government for its inaction regarding what was then just over five hundred cases of missing and/or murdered Aboriginal women across the country—statistics that the Native Women's Association of Canada's Sisters in Spirit research initiative now places closer to six hundred—"Indigenous women between the ages of 25 and 44 with status under the federal Indian Act, are five times more likely than other women of the same age to die as the result of violence" (23).

4. The identifier or identity of "Métis" is not without its own set of complex significations, histories, debates, and colonial understandings. The term *Métis* (or *métis* or *mestizo*) has been applied, largely in colonial contexts, to delineate all mixed-race persons who trace a portion of their lineage to First Peoples. Throughout this book, I employ the term "Métis" as the Métis National Council currently defines it. As such, Métis citizenship may be rightly claimed via "self-identification as a member of a Métis community, ancestral connection to the historic Métis community whose practices ground the right in question, [or] acceptance by the modern community with continuity to the historic Métis community" ("Citizenship").

5. Regardless of the outcome of such debates—if they are ever truly resolved—many of the missing women of Vancouver, Edmonton, Saskatoon, and others are dead in part because of inaction to combat the dehumanizing effects of whore stigma. And more women who work in the sex trade disappear and die every day. Becoming preoccupied in ideological debates about whether prostitution should or should not exist, do we risk—or even sacrifice—the lives of women in this marginalized and stigmatized industry?

6. Carol Leigh, a.k.a. Scarlot Harlot, writes about the positive effects of this label following its creation in the late 1980s: "This usage of the term 'sex work' marks the beginning of a movement. It acknowledges the work we do rather than defines us by our status. After many years of activism as a prostitute, struggling with increasing

stigma and ostracism from within the mainstream feminist movement, I remember the term 'sex work,' and how powerful it felt to, at last, have a word for this work that is not a euphemism. 'Sex work' has no shame, and neither do I" (230).

7. Deborah Brock discusses this production of prostitution as a social problem in cities across Canada in her book *Making Work, Making Trouble*. See also Becki Ross's "Sex and (Evacuation from) the City: The Moral and Legal Regulation of Sex Workers in Vancouver's West End, 1975–1985."

8. In addition to Amnesty International's damning report (see note 3 above), for further analysis of the disproportionate criminalization and victimization of Aboriginal women in Canada, see the growing body of research by Sisters in Spirit, the Native Women's Association of Canada's research initiative (available at www.nwac-hq.org), and Andrea Smith's *Conquest: Sexual Violence and American Indian Genocide*, as well as selected articles in Gillian Balfour and Elizabeth Comack's collection *Criminalizing Women: Gender and (In) Justice in Neo-Liberal Times*, Annette Burfoot and Susan Lord's collection *Killing Women: The Visual Culture of Gender and Violence*, and Marie-Micheline Hamelin and Katherine McKenna's collection *Violence Against Women: New Canadian Perspectives*.

9. See, for example, Elizabeth Comack's "Making Connections: Class/Race/Gender Intersections" and Nahanni Fontaine's "Surviving Colonization: Anishnaabe Ikwe Gang Participation" in Gillian Balfour and Elizabeth Comack's *Criminalizing Women*, or Rabinovitch's "PEERS," Lakeman's "Linking Violence and Poverty in the CASAC Report," Susan Ship and Laura Norton's "HIV/AIDS and Aboriginal Women in Canada," and Brenda McLeod's "First Nations Women and Sustainability on the Canadian Prairies."

10. Illustrating the extent to which modern Indigenous women continue to feel the effects of such pejorative colonial archetypes, Cree/Métis poet and cultural critic Marilyn Dumont writes in "Squaw Poems,"

> Indian women know all too well the power of the word *squaw*.
> ...As a
> young girl, I held the image of that woman in my mind and she became
> the measure of what I should never be.
> .... squaw is to whore
> as
> Indian maiden is to virgin
> squaw is to whore
> as
> Indian princess is to lady.
> (22–31, emphasis in original)

This sexually available stereotype, with its accompanying legacy of race and gender hierarchy and whore stigma, facilitates ongoing Euro-American colonial projects, simultaneously undercutting women's traditional political and social agency in Indigenous societies and legitimizing sexual violence against Indigenous women more generally.

11. For further examination of the relationship between race and imperial order, see, for example, Ann Stoler's *Race and the Education of Desire*, and Sherene Razack's *Looking White People in the Eye*.

12. Anne McClintock's *Imperial Leather*, as well as Andrea Smith's *Conquest*, provide somewhat of a catalogue of these acts of colonial sexual violence, as well as extensive analyses of the gendered and racialized ideologies that underwrite and normalize these tortures.

13. Smith also notes that while rape and sexual mutilation of Aboriginal people by whites became routine features of colonial conquest, she could find no evidence that Aboriginal warriors similarly assaulted either their foes or their prisoners. In the first chapter of *Conquest*, Smith analyzes several accounts by early white colonials who express surprise that they did not suffer such indignities when captured.

14. Discussing Vancouver's Missing and Murdered People case, critic Laurie McNeill notes that as more women disappeared seemingly without a trace, "the moniker (and group identity) 'Missing Women' was attached to these cases and has stuck, even though, for many of the missing, the name is no longer apt" (378).

15. Participants in ongoing debates about prostitution in Canada generally advocate one of four legislative measures to prevent further violence against sex workers and to eliminate the social nuisance aspects of street-involved prostitution. Two of these proposed initiatives—which may be described as rescue/industry-exit focused and prohibitionism—seek to eradicate prostitution. As a result of this shared goal, groups and individuals taking up these positions often advocate increased funding for the policing of prostitutes and their customers based on existing laws which, at least until the end of 2014 in Canada, criminalize most of the activities associated with prostitution (such as public solicitation, brothel ownership, working out of one's private dwelling, and living on the profits from another person's work in prostitution), if not the actual exchange of money for sex. Each of these positions is at least partly motivated by sympathy for sexually exploited individuals; nonetheless, one of these initiatives requires the overt criminalization of the exchange as well.

    Advocates of both legalization and decriminalization dismiss the possibility of eradicating prostitution; they thus propose to mitigate the problems associated with the sex industry by getting rid of laws that criminalize prostitution-related activities and persons. However, while advocates of legalization push to have new laws put in place to facilitate government regulation and control of the industry, supporters of decriminalization argue that prostitution-specific legislation would make pimps of government and perpetuate the whore stigma. They suggest instead that existing business, criminal, and human rights laws constitute more than adequate regulation for prostitution.

16. My humanities-based training is perhaps most evident in this as well as the following chapter in this book, but the theoretical framework and political focus remains consistent throughout the project.

1 CITY/WHORE SYNECDOCHE AND THE CASE OF VANCOUVER'S MISSING WOMEN

1. In the years since the Vancouver's Missing Women case first made headlines, and particularly since the onset of numerous controversial inner-city cleanup and gentrification projects associated with preparations for Vancouver's hosting of the 2010 Winter Olympics, "Canada's poorest postal code" has become a ubiquitous descriptor of the Downtown Eastside. At the time of writing, a basic Internet search of the phrase returned over 10,000 hits. Each of the more than 200 links that I followed led to discussions—in local and national news sources, blogs by private individuals as well as local activists and politicians, for example—of the DTES. Interestingly, the first link in a *Google.com* search of the phrase leads to a subsection of *Wikipedia*'s "Postal Codes in Canada" entry. In this subsection, entitled "Alternative Uses," the phrase "Vancouver's Downtown Eastside is Canada's poorest postal code" links to another (disputed) *Wikipedia* entry, "Downtown Eastside."

2. At the time of writing, public reports indicate that DNA of thirty-three women has been retrieved from the Pickton farm grounds.

3. A number of cases have emerged over the last decade. There is another case in Edmonton, Alberta where RCMP and Edmonton police formed a task force in 2003 to investigate eighty-three cases of murdered and missing women, many of them street-involved sex workers, dating back to 1982. A serial killer murdered four First Nations women and was suspected of killing at least three others in Saskatoon, Saskatchewan in the early 1990s. Another task force was established in Winnipeg, in 2009, to investigate growing numbers (to date, more than eighty) of missing and murdered Aboriginal women and girls. In addition, at least eleven First Nations women and girls (some estimate this number is as high as thirty-two (Lauren Carter, "Where are Canada's Disappeared Women?") have gone missing since the early 1990s along what local residents call the "Highway of Tears": Highway 16 between Prince George and Prince Rupert, BC. While a task force investigated these disappearances and suggested there was no evidence of a serial killer, local residents remain unconvinced. They compare police and public lack of interest in these missing women to the lack of interest initially shown in the Vancouver case.

4. The *Oxford Dictionary of Literary Terms* defines "synecdoche" as a "common figure of speech (or trope) by which something is referred to indirectly either by naming only some part or constituent of it (e.g., 'hands' for manual labourers) or—less often—by naming some comprehensive entity of which it is a part (e.g., 'the law' for a police officer)" (254). My use of the term *synecdochic* refers to the traditional symbolic connection between sex workers, or "whores," and the Western city such that the image of the individual "whore" may be seen to stand in for the so-called Great Whore, or the industrial city in nineteenth- and early twentieth-century discourse.

5. Drawing on the work of cultural theorists such as Roland Barthes, Edward Said, Stuart Hall, Patrick Brantlinger, Jacques Derrida, and others, Elfriede Fürsich makes a similarly compelling argument regarding the connections between journalism, hegemonic representations, and the potential for reporters to "open" culture rather than

reinforcing dominant exclusions. Noting that much of journalism may be understood as a process representing the Other, Fürsich suggests, "Only self-reflective, open and critical approaches towards traditional-ritualistic reporting and production strategies can help to disentangle problematic media representations" (58).

6. See, for example, Andie Tucher's Froth & Scum: Truth, Beauty, Goodness, and the Ax Murder in America's First Mass Medium (1994), Stuart Hall's "Race, Culture, and Communications: Looking Backward and Forward at Cultural Studies" (1996), John Hartley's Popular Reality: Journalism, Modernity, Popular Culture (1996), Marian Meyers's "Crack Mothers in the News: A Narrative of Paternalistic Racism" (2004), Helga Kristin Hallgrimsdottir, Rachel Phillips, and Cecilia Benoit's "Fallen Women and Rescued Girls: Social Stigma and Media Narratives of the Sex Industry in Victoria, BC, from 1980 to 2005" (2006), Matt Carlson's "Making Memories Matter: Journalistic Authority and the Memorializing Discourse around Mary McGrory and David Brinkley" (2007), and Eval Zandberg's "The Right to Tell the (Right) Story: Journalism, Authority and Memory" (2010).

7. The beginning and endpoint for this research may appear arbitrarily imposed, and to a certain extent, they are. One of the practical challenges of examining contemporary events is their ongoing development and the subsequent need to find a vantage point in a shifting network of events and representations from which to develop a relevant, culturally useful critical analysis. For this reason, then, I chose to limit my investigations to the noted time frame, using the commencement of the Missing People Trial as cut-off point. My ongoing research examines the tenor of public responses to the case at and after this important development.

Another practical reason for my examination of print media in this time frame has to do with research methodology and funding. The latter issue resulted in my having limited time and money for research assistants and myself to pull comprehensive print files for a particular period from "real" and digital databases. In terms of methodology, the last four to five years of technological development have resulted in a shift in the way that news is disseminated. My ongoing research attempts to understand the frameworks and narratives associated with new media, and my methodology has shifted accordingly.

8. For further analysis of the effects of this construction as bare life, and of Aboriginal women's simultaneous invisibility and hypervisibility in what Pratt, by way of Agamben, terms urban "zones of exclusion," see Jennifer England's 2004 article, "Disciplining Subjectivity and Space: Representation, Films, and its Material Effects."

9. David Hugill's analysis of news reporting in Missing Women, Missing News: Covering Crisis in Vancouver's Downtown Eastside (2010) is a particularly in-depth analysis of journalistic responses to culturally produced conditions of exception and violence.

10. In No More Stolen Sisters, Amnesty International notes that all levels of government in Canada have joined "a larger movement in Canada to at long last acknowledge and take responsibility for the violence and discrimination experienced by Indigenous women. In November 2004, a Canadian representative to the United Nations (UN)

acknowledged the *Stolen Sisters* report before the UN General Assembly's Social, Humanitarian and Cultural Committee, stating that 'a great deal of work remains to be done.' Politicians at the federal, provincial and territorial levels have called for action to address this violence. The Canadian Association of Chiefs of Police has urged police forces in Canada to adopt policies and procedures to address the threats faced by Indigenous women. In September 2009, the Province of Manitoba established an 'action group' including Indigenous Peoples' organizations and community agencies to help develop 'new policies to address the crisis of abused and exploited women'" (2). Significantly, however, Amnesty International adds, "despite this acknowledgement, measures to end discrimination and violence against Indigenous women have been piecemeal at best" (4).

11. As I discuss in more detail in Chapter 2, these tropes may be understood as variations on the "savvy criminals and fallen women" as well as the "rescued girls" trope identified by Helga Kristin Hallgrimsdottir, Rachel Phillips, and Cecilia Benoit in their 2006 article, "Fallen Women and Rescued Girls: Social Stigma and Media Narratives of the Sex Industry in Victoria, BC, from 1980 to 2005."

12. Though their website remains functional at the time of writing, PEERS Vancouver lost their funding (a significant portion of which came from governmental sources) and closed its doors in 2012 (Matas, "Vancouver"; Paterson).

13. Dawn Crey was last seen in November 2000. Her DNA was found on the farm in 2004, but police and investigators were unable to retrieve enough evidence to charge Pickton with her murder.

14. See, for example, Kevin Griffin's "Film Goes Beyond Missing Woman's Case" (*Vancouver Sun*, 2 Nov. 2006).

15. Marnie Frey was last seen in 1997. Her name was added to the list of Pickton's murder victims on May 25, 2005.

16. Leigh Miner was last seen in December 1993. At the time of writing, police have not included Miner on their list of missing women.

17. Sarah de Vries, adopted sister of Maggie de Vries, was last seen in April 1998. Her DNA was found on the Port Coquitlam farm in 2002.

18. Lowman makes selected articles publicly available for download from his webpage, *John Lowman's Prostitution Research Page*.

19. It is difficult to decide whether it is worth speculating as to why this switch in victims takes place. Does a blonde white woman's disappearance make the story somehow more tragic? Does the substitution more effectively arouse viewer identification in a mainstream audience that might not otherwise occur? Has the story been "translated" so that white suburban America may better understand the dangers currently inherent in inner-city life?

20. In *Missing Sarah*, de Vries, an influential member of the community Pitman discusses, similarly describes the growth and influence of the missing women's support and advocacy group. Her description of this group's evolution and the actions they forced the mayor and police to take parallel Pitman's analysis.

21. Though articles like Pynn's suggest otherwise, in fact the Pickton farm was not exclusively a pig farm.

22. Emerging research supports de Vries's position on this point. See, for example, Pheterson's critique of influential HIV/AIDS medical study in The Prostitution Prism.

23. Kishtainy analyzes The Epic of Gilgamesh, pointing to the sacred harlot who "civilizes" a man by providing him with days of sexual pleasure (7–11). Shannon Bell offers historical evidence of many respected prostitutes in the ancient (pagan) world: for example, the hetairae in ancient Greece, who "numbered among the philosophers" (1). Roberts points to periods in prehistory in which "culture, religion, and sexuality were intertwined....Sex was sacred by definition, and the shamanic priestesses led group sex rituals in which the whole community participated" (3).

24. See Roberts, chapter 6.

25. For example, Nell Gwyn, "rose from the gutter to become King Charles II's favourite and most long-standing mistress" (Roberts 147), and Olympe de Gouges, a French prostitute formerly of the working classes, was guillotined along with her aristocratic friends and clients during the French Revolution (Roberts 190).

26. In Flesh and Stone: The Body and the City in Western Civilization, Richard Sennett describes this massive urbanization: "In 1850, France, Germany, and the United States, like Britain, were dominantly rural societies; a century later they were dominantly urban, highly concentrated at their cores. Berlin and New York grew at the same headlong rate, roughly, as did London, and both cities grew as the national countryside submitted to the flux of international trade" (320).

27. In Canada, for example, increasingly stringent anti-prostitution policies from the middle of the nineteenth century onward developed alongside middle-class English settlers' xenophobic interactions with French Canadians, as well as class-based antagonism relating to an influx of working-class Irish immigrants—all of which occurred as a result of hegemonic desire for an "orderly" public as the effects of industrialization and urbanization began to be felt (Ball; Brooke M. Taylor).

28. See, for example, Anne McClintock's Imperial Leather and Sherene Razack's edited collection Race, Space, and the Law.

29. See, for example, works by Dr. Alexandre Jean Baptiste Parent-Duchatelet (De la prostitution dans la Ville de Paris, 1836), William Acton (Prostitution, Considered in its Moral, Social and Sanitary Aspects, 1857), and Havelock Ellis (Analysis of the Sexual Impulse, Love and Pain, the Sexual Impulse in Women, 1908; Sexual Inversion, 1908; Sex in Relation to Society, 1910).

30. The term essentialist refers to "a belief in true essence—that which is most irreducible, unchanging, and therefore constitutive of a given person or thing," as Diana Fuss phrases it (2). My discussion is primarily concerned with attempts to locate and express an "authentic" and universal feminine essence in nineteenth-century Western discourse.

31. Poovey describes the re-allocation of social power in this period occurring alongside scientists' "discoveries" and sexologists and other cultural theorists work on innate

characteristics of men and women. "Women became not some errant part of man," she observes, "but his opposite, his moral hope and spiritual guide.... Instead of being articulated upon inherited class position in the form of noblesse oblige, virtue was increasingly articulated upon gender" (10).

32. In "Changing Images of Deviance: Nineteenth-Century Canadian Anti-Prostitution Movements," Richard A. Ball traces the evolution of the construction of the prostitute who, he notes, "was always imaged as the rhetorical antithesis of the Ideal Woman" in the culturally pervasive oppositional economy. In *Imperial Leather*, Anne McClintock discusses the differences between middle-class feminine ideals and the realities of working-class women's lives in various continental and colonial spaces that kept them, like their male counterpart, working outside their homes.

33. See McClintock's *Imperial Leather* for more on imperial instability as it relates to nineteenth-century ideologies of female sexuality and fears of racial miscegenation. See also Sander Gilman's *Difference and Pathology: Stereotypes of Sexuality, Race, and Madness* (1985).

34. Literature from this period is rife with fallen women dying because of their sexual sins. Discussing what he terms the "repentant harlot" trend in nineteenth-century literature, Kishtainy observes a distinctly Judeo-Christian influence in this literature. He notes that Judeo-Christianity allowed "even the repentant harlot, a soul but not a heart. Thus it was very rare for a novelist or dramatist to let a fallen woman rejoin the respectable fold and lead a normal life" (23). And fictional plotlines from this period more often than not exhibit an ominous and unsubtle moral message about the neces-sary cultural restriction of female sexuality. In addition, novels like Elizabeth Gaskell's *Ruth* (1853) and Émile Zola's *Nana* (1880) examine period-specific cultural debates over class purity, the responsibility of the middle classes, especially middle-class women, for the moral education of those around them, and the dangers of even the most fleetingly transgressive female sexuality.

A 1912 German poem describes the autopsy of a beautiful drowned woman. The autopsy reveals a nest of baby rats living "in a bower below the diaphragm," "living off liver and kidneys, / drinking the cold blood" (qtd in Gilman, "'Who?'" 266). The body, that of a fallen woman (a prostitute) who has also literally fallen into the water, perpetuates its own synecdochic relationship with Nature's nightmare: the disease-ridden city, the death-bringing metropolis. Given the common cultural association of prostitution with city life, this woman's fall to her death functions as a cultural indictment of the very city she inhabits. Similarly, the rats living happily inside her corpse suggest Nature gone terribly wrong as one symbol of urban disease and death (the prostitute body) effectively feeds another (the rats)—thus communicating a synecdochic doomsday message for modern cities.

35. An extensive body of academic and popular work examines this case. Gilman's "'Who Kills Whores?' 'I Do,' Says Jack" provides a useful introduction to the class, gender, and racial issues surrounding the Whitechapel murders. In addition, Walkowitz's *City of Dreadful Delight* provides both a thorough contextualization and

fascinating analysis of the case and a comprehensive list of historical popular and academic documents related to the so-called Ripper slayings.

36. Polly Nichols, Annie Chapman, Catherine Eddowes, Elizabeth Stride, and Mary Jane Kelly were all killed within a three-month period in 1888. It was suspected that there were other victims, but these murders remain the ones most clearly linked to "Jack."

37. For discussion of subsequent similar campaigns in North America see Jane Caputi's *The Age of Sex Crime*, Kirsten Pullen's *Actresses and Whores: On Stage and in Society*, Kristin Luker's, "Sex, Social Hygiene, and the State: The Double-edged Sword of Social Reform," Julia O'Connell-Davidson's *Prostitution, Power and Freedom*, Nickie Roberts's *Whores in History: Prostitution in Western Society*, Geralyn Marie Strecker's "Reading Prostitution in American Fiction, 1893–1917," as well as Mary Louise Adams's "Youth, Corruptibility, and English-Canadian Postwar Campaigns Against Indecency, 1948–1955," Helen Boritch's *Fallen Women: Female Crime and Criminal Justice in Canada*, Sarah Carter's *Capturing Women: The Manipulation of Cultural Imagery in Canada's Prairie West*, Nick Larsen's "Canadian Prostitution Control between 1914 and 1970: An Exercise in Chauvinist Reasoning," Pivot Legal Society Sex Work Subcommittee's *Voices for Dignity: A Call to End the Harms Caused by Canada's Sex Trade Laws*, Joan Sangster's "Incarcerating 'Bad Girls': The Regulation of Sexuality through the Female Refuges Act in Ontario, 1920–1945," and Mariana Valverde's *The Age of Light, Soap and Water: Moral Reform in English Canada, 1885–1925*.

38. For more information on this murder case, see, for example, Baron Boulos and Liz Stanley's *The Yorkshire Ripper: A Case Study of "The Sutcliffe Papers,"* Paul Mason and Jane Monckton-Smith's "Conflation, Collocation and Confusion: British Press Coverage of the Sexual Murder of Women," and Alexandra Warwick's "The Scene of the Crime: Inventing the Serial Killer."

39. For discussion of what continue to be deep divisions between feminists on the subject of prostitution, see Janice Dickin-McGinnis's comprehensive "Whores and Worthies." See also Francis Shaver's "Avoiding the Morality Traps," Julia O'Connell-Davidson's "The Rights and Wrongs of Prostitution," Gail Pheterson's *The Prostitution Prism*, Jill Nagle's Introduction to *Whores and Other Feminists*, or—for a Canadian case study— Deborah Brock and Valerie Scott's "Getting Angry, Getting Organized," an account of the many conflicts between sex worker and non-sex worker feminists organizing the seminal 1985 Canadian conference entitled "Challenging Our Images: The Politics of Pornography and Prostitution."

40. In chapter 15 of *Whores in History*, Roberts analyzes similar trends in popular representations of and feminist responses to the serial murder of seventeen women, all of whom were sex workers, in Los Angeles during the South Side Slayer case of the 1980s.

41. In the American collection *Whores and Other Feminists* (1997), for example, Nagle insists that sex worker feminists speak *"as insiders to feminism"* (italics in original, 3). See also the proceedings from the 1985 "Challenging Our Images" Canadian conference entitled *Good Girls/Bad Girls: Feminists and Sex Trade Workers Face to Face*. The essays in this collection significantly problematize the perceived distinctions between sex workers and

feminists and explore the potential for political action that accompanies the recognition of women's personal agency within the sex industry. Even in the more conservative British collection *Rethinking Prostitution: Purchasing Sex in the 1990s* (1997), editors Graham Scambler and Annette Scambler advocate "a presumption of wilful rationality" such that any useful analysis of prostitution begins with the "respectful attribution of agency" to those within the industry under scrutiny (xv). In the more recent collections *Sex Workers in the Maritimes Talk Back* (2006), and *Sex Work Matters: Exploring Money, Power and Intimacy in the Sex Industry* (2010), editors acknowledge more overtly the connections between those who work in the industry and those who study it. As *Sex Work Matters* editors Alys Willman and Antonia Levy explain, their text is "a product of conversations among sex workers, academics, activists, and those who fit all three categories" (3).

42. See Hainsworth, "Family of Missing Woman Wants Serial Killer Doll Removed from Vancouver Store."

43. These gruesome renderings of torture and violent death have been played and replayed in the many books and films made about the Ripper case.

44. Gilman and, to some extent, Walkowitz discuss the repercussions of similar efforts to contain the Whitechapel murders within this significantly larger socio-economically depressed neighbourhood of London. However, the notorious Jack the Ripper persona exceeds this important case detail and the Ripper is thus routinely portrayed as the infamous murderer who terrorized the city of London.

2 ANTI-PROSTITUTION REPORTING, POLICING, AND ACTIVISM IN CANADA'S GLOBAL CITIES

1. Ferris, "Restorative Street Justice: *Victims, All of Us, Street Youth*, and Sex Work."

2. Abuses such as failure to receive payment for months, even years of work with little hope of legal redress, illegally long, ill-paid, labour-intensive shifts, and refusal by employers of promised assistance with immigration processes as well as sexual exploitation are suffered by illegal immigrant workers in restaurants, cleaning businesses, textile factories, and private homes in cities across Canada. See Roxana Ng's "Freedom from Whom? Globalization and Trade from the Standpoint of Garment Workers" (2002), Alejandro Bustos's "Workers Cheated, Sexually Exploited" (2005), and Luis Aguiar's "Janitors and Sweatshop Citizenship in Canada" (2006).

3. Moreover, as researcher and activist Elya M. Durisin reminds us, "conceptualizing prostitution as work can also make visible the role violence plays in the sex industry by connecting violence—sexual, physical, and economic—that women working in the sex industry experience to violence against women workers within the workplace, particularly as experienced by colonized and racialized women in Canada and transnationally" (128).

4. As activists make particular efforts to disseminate stories and images of sex workers as living persons with communities, personalities, and lives beyond the street, a small collection of projects analyzing the growing number of memorials to murdered experiential women across Canada have emerged. Such projects examine the benefits and disadvantages of this form of activism, emerging as it does within a violent

sociocultural framework. See, for example, Amber Dean's "The Politics of Cultural Memory: Remembering Vancouver's Murdered and Missing Women," the Cultural Memory Group's *Remembering Women Murdered by Men: Memorials across Canada*, and issue 53 of *West Coast Line: Representations of Murdered and Missing Women*.

5. For some other relatively extreme examples of this imagistic trope in mainstream news reporting, see also Saunders and Thompson (2002), Hume (2003), Girard (2005), and Matas and Fong (2006).

6. Developing a point similar to Kaun's regarding the inability for these mug shot-like images to compel public concern for the Missing Women, Dean notes that, despite the boundaries imposed by the frames of the individual photos in the posters and in the news reports that reproduce them, "the arrangement of the photographs into a grid invites the mug shots to spill out of their frames to the other, more familial photographs, linking them with visible markers of poverty, of criminality, of addiction (already broadly associated in many imaginings with the neighbourhood of the Downtown Eastside or with "the streets")—in essence, with the sorts of markings that contribute to rendering certain lives ungrievable to many, particularly to those whose only encounter with the women is through these photographs" ("Hauntings" 137).

7. Both Sarah de Vries and Marnie Lee Frey disappeared in Vancouver in 1997.

8. Janet Henry disappeared in June 1997. She is among the forty women still considered missing in the Vancouver case.

9. This series was accessible online until at least July 2012, the last time I visited the "Deadly Streets" pages on CBC Edmonton's site. Almost a decade of public availability is significant, despite the series' eventual disappearance from the site and web archive.

10. Ellie-May Meyer, last seen alive on April 1, 2005, was found dead on May 6, 2005. In 2008, Project KARE charged an already incarcerated man with Meyer's murder. Rachel Quinney was found dead on June 11, 2004. In 2007, Project KARE charged a local man with her murder. Monique Pitre's body was found on January 8, 2003. Melissa Munch's body was found on January 12, 2003. Debbie Lake, last seen alive on November 4, 2002, was found dead on April 12, 2003. Charlene Gauld, last seen alive on April 8, 2005, was found dead on April 16, 2005. Sylvia Ballantyne, last seen alive on April 27, 2003, was found dead on July 7, 2003. Edna Bernard was found dead on September 23, 2002. Samantha Berg, last seen alive in late December 2004, was found dead on January 25, 2005. Basic details of each woman's disappearance and murder can be found on the Project KARE website.

11. This in direct contrast to nineteenth-century moralists' portrayals of white working-class prostitutes as having black, or low, "Negro" attributes (McClintock 56).

12. While there are no statistics regarding the numbers of people who work in the sex industry, researchers who work closely with sex workers, such as Cecilia Benoit and Alison Millar (affiliated with UBC and PEERS), John Lowman and Katrina Pacey (of the Vancouver-based sex worker and human rights advocate Pivot Legal Society) estimate that street-involved sex work constitutes only 20 per cent of the sex trade as a whole.

13. See, for example, sex worker comments in Benoit et al.'s *Dispelling Myths and Understanding Realities*, or Pivot Legal Society's *Voices for Dignity*.

14. Highlighting the ways this report mimics reporting on Vancouver's missing women, CBC anchor Peter Mansbridge introduces Piercey's piece as a "story about murder" that has "a disturbing and familiar ring." Mansbridge continues, "Some of the victims worked in the sex trade. All had high-risk lifestyles. Then they went missing." Having thus included the far from unusual implication that sex workers, as participants in "high-risk lifestyles," put themselves in harm's way and must therefore share responsibility for the violence to which they are subjected, Mansbridge turns the story over to Piercey.

    The report that follows focuses on the disappearance and murder of five Edmonton women who are thought to have been involved in the street-involved sex trade. Beginning with a ride-along with a man who helps police record pertinent information about street sex workers to aid in body identification in murder investigations, Piercey then interviews two grieving mothers, two young sex workers, RCMP and Edmonton police supervisors, and criminologist John Lowman about police performance in the current murder cases. While images of lone nightwalkers, sometimes facing the camera, are interspersed throughout the report, faces of interviewed sex workers do not appear. Instead, a series of edited clips show the women's shadows against the wall next to concerned-looking Piercey, and foreground one woman's short skirt and bare legs as she discusses the case with the demurely dressed reporter.

    Repeatedly including such juxtapositions of sex workers and others involved in these cases, Piercey's report consistently contrasts the comments of these two women with those of the mothers of murder victims and police, using Lowman to critique police procedures but not to support the women's claims: although the two sex workers interviewed suggest that women like themselves work together to protect each other on the street, especially since these high-profile murder cases, none of the "street life" clips included here reflect this reality.

15. Until recently, interviews with sex workers by journalists, academics, social workers, and the like since at least the time of Dr. Parent-Duchatelet (see Chapter 1, note 29) have routinely featured questions such as how many men a single woman services in a particular time period, or what, exactly, such services entailed.

16. A "stroll" is a street, usually a particular segment of a street, where sex workers are known to work.

17. As numerous critics have noted, this criminalizing and victimizing discourse around prostitution is evident in the Canadian penal system as well. Jacqueline Lewis's "Shifting the Focus: Restorative Justice and Sex Work" examines Canadian prostitution-related harm reduction initiatives that construct neighbourhoods or communities as the primary victims in prostitution-related crimes. In such cases, Lewis argues, sex workers are constructed as (secondary) hapless victims who are then forced into diversion programs (290–92). Stephen Bittle's "From Villain to Victim: Secure Care and Young Women in Prostitution" outlines some of the contemporary classed, aged, raced, and gendered implications of this discourse in relation to

neoliberal provincial and federal legal policies. See also Gillian Balfour and Elizabeth Comack's collection in which Bittle's essay is included, *Criminalizing Women: Gender and (In)Justice in Neo-Liberal Times.*

18. Such collaborative approaches to sex workers and communities are regularly endorsed by criminologists and other legal scholars (by John Lowman and Katrina Pacey, for example, as well as Pivot Legal Society). As law professor Elaine Craig writes in a 2011 issue of *Review of Constitutional Studies*, "detailed recommendations regarding the municipal regulation of sex work should be developed in full consultation with the sex workers operating in the community in which such laws will apply. The objectives of this piece are more modest: to demonstrate how the principles identified in *Bedford* also apply to municipal law and to argue that, at the local level, in revisiting current regulations or developing new ones (in response to decriminalization for example), these principles require municipal lawmakers to accommodate the safety interests of the sex workers in their communities" (99). One wonders, then, why and how municipal police and community-level activists continue to disregard collaborative approaches to the issue of sex work in their neighbourhoods.

19. Discussion in Chapter 3 takes up this theme of sex workers as everyday people, examining both the whore stigma-inspired cultural threat and the radical potential for sex worker destigmatization inherent to such portrayals.

20. This term is used by Brenner and Theodore in "Cities and the Geographies of 'Actually Existing Neoliberalism.'" In this paper, Brenner and Theodore discuss what they term "contemporary neoliberalization processes as catalysts and expressions of an ongoing creative destruction of political-economic space at multiple geographic scales" (349). They present "the concept of creative destruction...as a useful means for describing the geographically uneven, socially regressive, and politically volatile trajectories of institutional/spatial change that have been crystallizing under these conditions" (349).

21. It is also noteworthy that zero-tolerance policing has little positive influence on crime rates. In fact, as a San Francisco-based study found in 1999, approaches to crime that "adopted less strident law enforcement policies that reduced arrests, prosecutions and incarceration rates...registered reductions in crime that exceed or equal comparable cities and jurisdictions—including New York" (Maccallair 1). In fact, according to Parenti, zero-tolerance policies place more members of disenfranchised populations in jail, where they become what he terms "raw material" in America's "prison industrial complex"—referring to the use of prisoners in privately owned jails as cheap labour (211–45). At the time of writing, Canada has undertaken one unsuccessful experiment with a privately owned and operated prison in Penetanguishene, Ontario. Although this prison was taken over by government, again, in 2006, after only five years of privatization, there are those who believe the current federal Conservatives anticipate further privatization of Canadian prisons. (See, for example, Donalee Moulton's "Can Private Jails Come to Canada?" (2012), Andrew Mayeda's "Canada Studying Private Firms for Prisons as Budgets Fall" (2012), and Alex Roslin's "Stephen Harper Opens Door to Prison Privatization" (2007).

22. While the Conservative plan, perhaps inevitably using language that reflects their
     support base in rural Canada, focuses on "communities" instead of cities, a brief
     appraisal of, for example, the Conservative Party's 2006 election platform, reveals a
     number of similarities between the Harper and Martin approaches to "community"
     investment.

23. Discussing Vancouver's municipal plan, *A Framework for Action: A Four-Pillar Approach to
     Drug Problems in Vancouver*, published in 2001, University of Victoria-based researcher
     Susan Boyd writes, "In 2001 the city of Vancouver recommended education/prevention,
     the development of harm reduction initiatives, expansion of drug treatment services,
     and an increased police presence to disrupt the open drug scene in the DTES. Even
     before Canada's Conservative government and Vancouver's Mayor Sam Sullivan were
     elected, it was clear that the enforcement pillar and the reduction of public 'disorder'
     in the DTES was a top priority" ("Community-Based Research" 21).

24. This law, Bill C-49, *Criminal Code* s.213(1), prohibits communication of any kind in a
     public place for the purposes of prostitution. In December 2013, the Supreme Court of
     Canada ruled the communicating law unconstitutional and struck it down (Canada v.
     Bedford, 2013).

25. Put another way, as Sherene Razack argues, "Predictably, space becomes important in
     determining who is policed and how, since the objective is not to dissolve the relations
     between spaces as much as it is to prevent seepage from the space of the prostitution
     to the space of respectability" ("Race, Space, and Prostitution" 373).

26. In fact, as Becki Ross, principal investigator in Vancouver's *West End Sex Work History
     Project* records, "CROWE's ability to frame and tactically manage the conflict was later
     emulated by similar organizations from Victoria to Edmonton, and from Toronto to
     Halifax" ("Sex and (Evacuation from) the City" 200). The *West End Sex Work History
     Project* is ongoing. Its objectives include the recording and commemoration of West
     End sex worker histories from 1975 to 1985; further analysis of related archival
     materials; contribution to and support of related contemporary research, debates,
     and legal actions; establishment of a permanent memorial to displaced West End
     sex workers from the 1980s ("Objectives").

27. The Grandview-Woodlands Neighbourhood Action Group published a poster entitled
     "No More Sex on Our Streets" (Appendix 5). During CROWE's anti-prostitution
     campaign, hand-written posters were stapled to telephone poles in the DTES that
     read, "Warning: Street Prostitutes From: 700, 800, 900 Block East Pender, Hastings &
     Cordova Residents. Move out or face the consequences by July 15/93 and thereafter."
     In addition, an open letter appeared in the *Vancouver Sun* in April 1986 that invited
     movie star Clint Eastwood to come to Mount Pleasant, a neighbourhood the author
     says has been "invaded by street prostitutes and other criminals," and to bring his gun
     (qtd in Lowman, "Violence" 17).

28. See, for example, "Halifax Undercover Police Clamp Down on Prostitution" (*CBC.ca*);
     A Sex Trade Reality Check (distributed by Winnipeg Police Service Morals Unit, or
     available for download in PDF form on the WPS website); and "Government Targets

Prostitution" (*CBC.ca*). See also Part III of the 1998 report on "Prostitution-Related Activities" by the federal Department of Justice detailing various actions against johns and their motor vehicles in cities across Canada.

29. CEASE's current homepage features a scrolling banner that includes three different images with accompanying headings and short blurbs describing the organization's anti-prostitution focus and related initiatives. A list of working links for CEASE programs appears below the banner on this homepage. At the time of writing, these links are entitled: "COARSE: Creating Options Aimed at Reducing Sexual Exploitation: A Court Diversion Program for Women," "'john school': Also known as Prostitution Offender Program: A Court Diversion Program for Men," "Heal the Harm: Therapists are available to those who have experienced sexual exploitation," and "Victim Advocates: Support, Transition, Action, Recovery: Victim Advocates—Peer Support."

30. Lowman notes, "The term 'pimp' does not appear anywhere in the criminal code. Technically, anyone who lives on the avails of prostitution is a 'pimp.' However, the term is usually reserved for men who manage street prostitutes, particularly African-American men" ("Violence" n9).

31. According to Graeme Smith's article in the May 10, 2004 *Globe and Mail*, unlike KARE's, the VPD sex worker registry program garnered little support or participation from local sex workers ("Prostitutes Wary").

32. In the 2012 version of this page, the text that once appeared as "HIGH RISK MISSING PERSONS" (HRMP) appears as "High Risk Missing Persons."

33. Interestingly, Canadian Blood Services has begun to make connections between professions involving personal risk. For example, in the organization's most recent informational brochure for blood donors, though people who have received payment for drugs or sex are listed among those who may be at risk of contracting HIV, flight crews, scuba divers, bus drivers, and heavy equipment operators are listed as persons involved in hazardous jobs (*Blood*).

3 TECHNOLOGIES OF RESISTANCE: SEX WORKER ACTIVISM ONLINE

1. SWAV is not to be confused with SWUAV, the Downtown Eastside Sex Workers United Against Violence Society, a non-profit society run by and for street-involved sex workers in Vancouver. At the time of writing, SWUAV is partnering with Pivot Legal Society in another constitutional challenge to Canada's prostitution laws that began in British Columbia and is potentially headed to the Supreme Court of Canada. (For more information, see Pivot's blog *Pivot Points*, as well as the Supreme Court of Canada's case information (available online) for *Canada v. Downtown Eastside Sex Workers United Against Violence Society*, et al.)

2. Comparatively speaking, with the exception of CEASE/PAAFE, non-sex worker citizen groups have next to no significant presence on the Internet. Of the other neighbour- hood association websites I managed to uncover, most were relatively limited in content, a number loaded inconsistently or were missing links, and all included at least one working link to a significantly more user-friendly police website.

3. Not without controversy in a variety of fields in and outside of the academy, "Web 2.0" is a term popularly employed to mark "the shift of websites from being static information repositories to being interactive, dynamic places—wikis, forums and communities are all part of this" (*Wikipedia Talk: Web 2.0*).

4. This turn to the Internet for political ends mirrors sex workers' increased Internet use for professional activities. Studying this phenomenon in the US, Scott Cunningham and Todd Kendall note that "the internet has exponentially increased the ability of sex workers to: (a) reach large numbers of potential clients with informative advertising, (b) build reputations for high-quality service, and (c) employ screening methods to reduce the risk of discovery and avoid undesirable clients" ("Prostitution 2.0").

5. See, for instance, Alliance Féministe Solidaire Pour les Droits des Travailleuses/rs du Sexe's Facebook page, 23 May 2011, Facebook; PACE Society's Facebook page, 23 May 2011, Facebook; SWAT: Sex Workers Alliance of Toronto's Facebook page, 23 May 2011, Facebook.

6. See the Ontario Court of Appeal's March 2012 ruling on *Canada (AG) v. Bedford*, 2012. Having heard the case in June 2013, the Supreme Court of Canada upheld Himel's decision and struck down the three impugned laws.

7. Detailed lists including as much information as possible about clients who have robbed, assaulted, or otherwise threatened sex workers. Many lists include dates, times, and geographical locations of assaults as well as physical descriptions, telephone numbers, service preferences, and modus operandi for assailants.

8. I continue to hope that future analyses of photographic self-representation by sex worker activist groups will include Vancouver's PACE Society. At the time of writing, however, this organization is running out of funding and may have to close its doors (PACE Society. "Funding Crisis at PACE: Facebook." *Facebook*. 30 Aug. 2010. Web. 24 May 2011). It's unclear whether the PACE website would remain if this comes to pass. Members of this organization have begun to self-represent strategically via photographs; however, PACE is outside the scope of my discussion here as I am interested, in this chapter, in groups who have self-represented through photographs on the web over the longer term.

9. See, for example, Steven Best and Douglas Kellner's *The Postmodern Adventure: Science, Technology and Cultural Studies at the Third Millennium* (2001).

10. At time of writing, interested readers can click on the first link, entitled "Sex Workers Alliance of Vancouver: End of an Era," at the top of SWAV's homepage to read former SWAV coordinator Andy Sorfleet's March 16, 2005 media release explaining why the organization disbanded.

11. *Lurkers* is a term used to describe those who become members of a particular online community—usually in a chat room, on a listserv, or on an interactive blog—who rarely, if ever, contribute to ongoing discussions or attend events organized by other members.

12. Over the past century, Canada has established and entrenched *Criminal Code* sections 210 and 193, sections that outlaw bawdy houses. Under these laws, a "common bawdy house" (brothel, whore house) is any place used "for the purpose of

prostitution or the practice of acts of indecency." Increased government funding in the 1970s facilitated police crackdowns on brothel-based prostitution that continued into the 1980s in cities across Canada.

13. See Becki Ross's *Burlesque West: Showgirls, Sex, and Sin in Postwar Vancouver*, and "Sex and (Evacuation from) the City" for more extensive analysis of the historical and contemporary resonance of these events for the Vancouver sex trade and beyond.

14. See Debi Brock and Valerie Scott's "Getting Angry, Getting Organized: The Formation of the Canadian Organization for the Rights of Prostitutes" in academic journal *Fireweed*'s Spring 1999 issue.

15. See *Toronto Star* reporter Debra Black's article of August 4, 2005, "Prostitutes Identify 'Bad Dates' on Website."

16. Given this professionalization of the organization, SPOC's more recently added "Be a Good Client" button, which links to a list of guidelines for sex worker clients who want to get the most out of their time with a "sex pro," is particularly fitting.

17. See Dean's "Hauntings: Representations of Vancouver's Disappeared Women."

18. John Bonnar is a Toronto-based independent journalist with a particular interest in social justice issues. His photos of SPOC's March 3, 2005 rally were included in his Smugmug copyrighted photo archive in 2005. At the time of writing, however, these photos no longer appear in the Smugmug collection.

19. The W.H.O.R.E. acronym stands for "Women Helping Ourselves to Rights and Equality" (16 May 2011).

20. Goodhandy's is a Toronto nightclub that bills itself as "Toronto's Pansexual Playground" (*Goodhandys.com*).

21. When SPOC first began publishing their Bad Client List, they published as much information as possible about Bad Dates, including any photographs or phone numbers available. This decision was not without controversy. In 2005, following a legal challenge by a man who dropped his suit after sex workers came forward to testify against him, Valerie Scott told *Toronto Star* reporter Debra Black that SPOC would continue to post this information. "We truly do believe this is the right thing to do," Scott is quoted as saying. "I don't want to invade anyone's privacy. And we would never just publish someone's name for being a date. But I figure you forfeit your privacy when you're violent" ("Prostitutes"). At the time of writing, a notice at the top of SPOC's Bad Client List page reads, "Due to legal reasons, we can now only publish partial names, phone numbers or addresses of most bad clients. However we can publish the full information of some of them. SPOC does have more information on each bad client. If you are a sex workers and want this info, do not hesitate to email us at welcome@spoc.ca" (19 May 2011).

22. In the Spring 2005 issue of *ConStellation*, an author identified as "Sylvie" provides a history of the Stella logo and name. About the logo, she explains, "Dans les années 1980, pour pouvoir danser à Ottawa, il fallait avoir une carte d'identification pour sortir dans les bars après avoir travaillé (dehors les chiens pas de médailles!). Moi ma carte c'était une bien belle carte. À côté de ma photo, c'était écrit que j'étais artiste.

J'ai fait de la frime...j'étais plus seulement une «topless», j'étais une artiste! Sur cette petite carte, il y avait une belle fille avec un boa qui me rendait plus sexy et fière. En 1995, j'ai été engagée chez Stella à cause de mon vécu. Là, on avait besoin d'un logo sexy et féminin alors j'ai pensé à ma carte de danseuse. Depuis ce temps c'est devenu le logo de Stella. Nous sommes sexy, fières et solidaires" ("Saviez-vous que?"). [In the 1980s, in order to dance in Ottawa, you had to have an ID card before you could go into the bars after having worked (keep out the riffraff!). My card was really nice. Beside my photo, it said that I was an artist. I was swanky! I wasn't just a "topless dancer" anymore, I was an artist! On that little card was a beautiful girl with a boa that made me look more sexy and proud. In 1995, I was hired at Stella because of my experience. They needed a sexy and feminine logo, and I thought of my dancer's card. From that moment it became Stella's logo. We are sexy, proud, and united.]

23. Former and current sex workers regularly report such discriminatory practices. One of many who describe such experiences, then PAAFE chairperson Dawn Hodgins writes, in a letter to the editors of the *Canadian Medical Association Journal*, "CMAJ has...missed a concern that lies at its own front door: systematic discrimination from doctors and other health care professionals. Having lived within the trade myself for over a decade and having talked with hundreds of women formerly and currently involved in 'the life,' I have heard countless stories of judgmental bedside manners by members of the medical profession."

24. See, for example, Pheterson's discussion in the chapter entitled "The Category 'Prostitute' in Scientific Inquiry," in *The Prostitution Prism*.

25. British Parliament passed the first of three controversial Contagious Diseases Acts in 1864. The acts required the medical inspection of prostitutes for contagious diseases in military outposts in England and Ireland. Walkowitz further notes that under the Contagious Diseases Acts, "Special controls were placed on the female body in that prostitutes, not their male clients, were identified as the primary source of disease and pollution. This medical and police supervision in turn created an outcast class of 'sexually deviant' females, forcing prostitutes to acknowledge their status as 'public' women" (*Prostitution* 5).

26. Organizations such as Stella, Spectre de Rue, and Rézo in Montreal appear to receive government funding primarily for (or because of) their disease prevention and education-related initiatives.

27. In fact, each person pictured is speaking the word, syllable, or letter sound that appears above their photo. This was meant as a (virtually) embodied statement of solidarity with local and international sex workers negatively affected by criminalizing laws (personal communication).

28. It is important to remember, however, that limited or lack of access to technology both in local and other contexts worldwide significantly limits the overall effectiveness of Internet activism, particularly among street-involved sex workers, persons who are culturally marginalized in many nations around the globe.

29. At the time of writing, this page on both the French and English versions of the website is under construction.

30. Pivot Legal Society, currently directed by lawyer and increasingly influential human rights advocate Katrina Pacey, maintains a rich online archive of Pivot's research and other related publications. They are a vocal advocate for the decriminalization of prostitution. Contributors to their 2006 Annual Report, *Beyond Decriminalization: Sex Work, Human Rights and a New Framework of Law Reform*, include Pacey, criminologist John Lowman, and BC lawyer Mary Childs.

31. Prior to Detective Wendy Leaver's retirement, the "Resources" section of SPOC's website endorsed the Toronto Police Sex Crimes Unit, and Leaver in particular: "SPOC recommends calling and/or going to see the people at the Toronto Sex Crimes Unit. Over the past 2 years, Sex Crimes has been doing a lot of work with Sex Pro organizations, including SPOC, in a genuine effort to help Sex Pros regarding bad clients.... They've been understanding about the fact that not all of us can go through a public trial. Sex crimes is interested in, and now keeps a data base on reported bad clients, so that if you are unable to charge him, someone else down the road may be. All reports are important in helping them build cases against bad clients. The best go-to person at sex crimes is **Detective Wendy Leaver**. (Note to Det. Leaver, please do not retire.) Sex Crimes phone number is **416-808-7474**. Also, they now have a Bad Date hotline. It's an anonymous voicemail" (May 2006, emphasis in original).

32. Vancouver East NDP Member of Parliament Libby Davies has also consistently called for change to current prostitution-related laws to prevent any further victimization of the women in her riding. Davies's efforts resulted in the striking of a joint federal committee, the 2005–2006 federal Subcommittee on Solicitation Laws of the Standing Committee on Justice, Human Rights, Public Safety and Emergency Preparedness (the SSLR). The committee was dropped by Stephen Harper's Conservative government shortly after the 2006 federal election; but they managed to publish a truncated report in December 2006. Transcripts of SSLR open meetings as well as the published report are available online.

33. In the SSLR's final report, *The Challenge of Change*, both John Maloney and Conservative MP Art Hanger are listed as committee chairs.

34. The case was originally indexed by the Ontario Superior Court alphabetically by applicant surname: *Bedford v. Canada*. Despite the importance of Lebovitch, for example, as the only currently working sex worker applicant, the case is identified by Bedford's surname.

35. In fact, "Nordic Model" is somewhat of a misnomer as two of the five Nordic countries have debated and ultimately decided not to criminalize sex workers' clients.

36. The term *rescue industry* was coined by UK-based sex work researcher and author of the *Naked Anthropologist* blog Laura August in her seminal work, *Sex at the Margins: Migration, Markets and the Rescue Industry*.

37. Paper delivered at the Canadian Women's Studies Association's annual conference at the University of Waterloo in May 2012.

4 AGENCY AND ABORIGINALITY IN STREET-INVOLVED OR SURVIVAL SEX WORK IN CANADA

1. See, for example, Amnesty International's *Stolen Sisters* and *No More Stolen Sisters*.

2. See Introduction, note 4.

3. Francis Shaver's research, which she presented before the 2005–2006 federal Subcommittee on Solicitation Laws (the SSLR), examines the personal histories of female sex workers and women working in other service industries such as hairdressing and nursing. Her findings suggest that survivors of childhood sexual abuse are not overrepresented in the sex trade (SSLR, mtg. 005).

4. See Lee Lakeman's "Linking Violence and Poverty in the CASAC Report."

5. See "Prohibition of Prostitution" on the "Issues" page of Vancouver Rape Relief's website.

6. Despite the recent Settlement Agreement the Canadian Government has made with former residential school students who suffered "sexual or serious physical abuse" (News Release, 10 May 2006) in these institutions, the government continues to evade responsibility for the cultural violence this system perpetuated. As of June 2006, the "Residential School System Historical Overview" published by the Office of Indian Residential Schools Resolution of Canada records that the government became involved in the administration of these "missionary" efforts "to meet legal obligations under the Indian Act, as well as to assist with the integration of Aboriginal people into the broader Canadian society." Indian Affairs further qualifies its admission of wrongdoing in claims such as this one: "While it is not uncommon to hear some former students speak about the positive experience in these institutions, their stories are overshadowed by disclosures of abuse, criminal convictions of perpetrators and the findings of various studies such as the Royal Commission on Aboriginal Peoples, which tell of the tragic legacy that the residential school system has left with many former students" ("Residential School System").

7. A number of recent publications have explored, celebrated, and interrogated women's roles in Indigenous cultural, political, economic, and familial structures past and present. Many of these same publications analyze (dis)connections between Indigenous and non-Indigenous feminisms. See, for example, Kim Anderson's *Life Stages and Native Women* (2011); Jessica Yee's edited collection *Feminism for REAL: Deconstructing the Academic Industrial Complex of Feminism* (2011); Cheryl Suzack, Shari Huhndorf, Jeanne Perreault, and Jean Barman's collection *Indigenous Women and Feminism: Politics, Activism, Culture* (2010); Eric Guimond, Gail Guthrie Valaskakis, and Madeline Dion Stout's collection *Restoring the Balance: First Nations Women, Community, and Culture* (2008); Joyce Green's collection *Making Space for Indigenous Feminism* (2007); and Kim Anderson and Bonita Lawrence's collection *Strong Women Stories: Native Vision and Community Survival* (2003).

8. Mohawk scholar Audra Simpson similarly discusses formalized racial tests of authenticity, or what she terms "the problem of recognition" in "Paths toward a Mohawk Nation: Narratives of Citizenship and Nationhood in Kahnawake."

9. For example, in the first weeks of the Caledonia conflict, CBC Radio news reported on the actions of "the Natives" versus "area residents" or "citizens."

10. Terms such as *sex work* and *prostitution* are rarely used on the SIS webpages, or in the research documents, pamphlets, newsletters, and "Toolkits" linked to these pages. Although some of the missing and murdered Indigenous women whose disappearances and violent deaths SIS investigates were involved in the sex industry, many were not. However, as discussed in the Introduction, the conflation of Aboriginal womanhood and prostitution is a significant negative effect of colonization in Canada. Such conflation occurs regularly in mainstream media reports on these cases (see, for example, Jiwani and Young's "Missing and Murdered Women: Reproducing Marginality in News Discourses"). SIS researchers appear to be well aware of this fact and work to resist this conflation in their research and education initiatives.

11. See also Cecilia Benoit, Dena Carroll, and Munaza Chaudhry's "In Search of a Healing Place: Aboriginal Women in Vancouver's Downtown Eastside"; or Michelle Oleman's *First Nations Drum* report "Conference Tackles Missing Women Crisis."

12. See NYSHN's press releases (currently available for download from their website) "Indigenous Peoples in the Sex Trade—Our Life, Our Bodies, Our Realities" (2012), "Indigenous Peoples in the Sex Trade—Speaking for Ourselves" (2011), and "Decriminalization of Sex Work and Indigenous Youth and Communities—a Response from the Native Youth Sexual Health Network on the Recent Ontario Superior Court Decision" (2010).

13. Babcock made this statement at SPOC's "Bawdy House Burlesque Show," an SPOC fundraising event held at Toronto's Gladstone Hotel on August 16, 2006.

14. See, for example, Kristina Fagan, Stephanie Danyluk, Bryce Donaldson, Amelias Horsburgh, Robyn Moore, and Martin Winquist's "Reading the Critical Reception of Maria Campbell's *Halfbreed*," or Cheryl Suzack's "Law Stories as Life Stories: Jeannette Lavell, Yvonne Bédard, and *Halfbreed*."

15. See, for example, Helen M. Buss's "The Different Voice of Canadian Autobiographers," Armando E. Jannetta's "Métis Autobiography," or (again) Suzack's "Law Stories as Life Stories."

16. See Campbell's interview with Hartmut Lutz, or Barbara Godard's "Voicing Difference: The Literary Production of Native Women."

17. See, for example, Janice Acoose's "The Problem of 'Searching' for April Raintree," or Sharon Smulders's "'What is the proper word for people like you?': The Question of Métis Identity in *In Search of April Raintree*."

CONCLUSION

1. Although I have visited *Marker of Change*, I nonetheless employ CMG's description because I appreciate its attentiveness and beauty. In short, CMG finds words and phrases better than any I could put together to communicate a sense of this monument.

2. CRAB (Create a Real Available Beach) is an acronym that reflects other ongoing demands that the needs of DTES residents be met by the municipality.

3. See Burk's important analyses, "In Sight, Out of View: A Tale of Three Monuments" and *Speaking for a Long Time: Public space and Social Memory in Vancouver*.

4. Once again, though I have visited the CRAB Park boulder and bench, I employ CMG's simple, elegantly worded description. (See note 1 above.)

5. See, for example, Christine Bold, Rick Knowles, and Belinda Leach's "National Countermemories: Feminist Memorializing and Cultural Countermemory: The Case of Marianne's Park"; Adrienne Burk's scholarship (see note 3 above); Dara Culhane's "'Their Spirits Live Within Us': Aboriginal Women in Downtown Eastside Vancouver Emerging into Visibility"; Amber Dean and Anne Stone's special issue of *West Coast Line: Representations of Murdered and Missing Women*; Amber Dean's "Hauntings: Representations of Vancouver's Disappeared Women" and "Representing and Remembering Murdered Women: Thoughts on the Ethics of Critique"; Mariane Hirsch and Valerie Smith's "Feminism and Cultural Memory: An Introduction"; Laurie McNeill's "Death and the Maidens: Vancouver's Missing Women, the Montreal Massacre, and Commemoration's Blindspots"; Roger I. Simon, Sharon Rosenberg, and Claudia Eppert's *Between Hope and Despair: Pedagogy and the Remembrance of Historical Trauma*.

WORKS CITED

Acoose, Janice. "The Problem of 'Searching' for April Raintree." Suzack, *April Raintree*
    227–36. Print.

Adams, Mary Louise. "Youth, Corruptibility, and English-Canadian Postwar Campaigns
    Against Indecency, 1948–1955." *Journal of the History of Sexuality* 6.1 (July 1995):
    89–117. Print.

Aguiar, Luis L.M. "Janitors and Sweatshop Citizenship in Canada." *Antipode* 38.3 (2006):
    441–62. Web.

AHF: *Aboriginal Healing Foundation*. Aboriginal Healing Foundation. Web. 26 Oct. 2006.

Althusser, Louis. "Ideology and Ideological State Apparatuses: Notes towards an
    Investigation." *Lenin and Philosophy and Other Essays*. Trans. Ben Brewster. New York:
    Monthly Review, 2001. Transcribed by Andy Blunden. *Marxists Internet Archive*. Web.

America's Most Wanted. Fox Television. 31 July 1999. Television.

Amnesty International Canada. *No More Stolen Sisters: The Need for a Comprehensive Response
    to Discrimination and Violence against Indigenous Women in Canada*. London: Amnesty
    International, 2009. *Amnesty International*. Web.

———. *Stolen Sisters: A Human Rights Response to Discrimination and Violence against Indigenous
    Women in Canada*. Amnesty International Canada. 4 Oct. 2004. Web. 19 July 2010.

Anderson, Kim. *Life Stages and Native Women*. Winnipeg: U of Manitoba P, 2011. Print.

———. *A Recognition of Being: Reconstructing Native Womanhood*. Toronto: Sumach, 2000. Print.

Anderson, Kim, and Bonita Lawrence, eds. *Strong Women Stories: Native Vision and Community
    Survival*. Toronto: Sumach, 2003. Print.

Armstrong, Jane. "Police Alter Missing Women Theory." *Globe and Mail*. 21 Aug. 2001.
    A3. Print.

Attorney General of Canada v. Downtown Eastside Sex Workers against Violence Society,
    et al. 2012 SCC 33981. Supreme Court of Canada. *CanLII*. Web.

AWAN: Aboriginal Women's Action Network. "About Us: AWAN's Statement Opposing
    Legalized Prostitution & Total Decriminalization of Prostitution." *Aboriginal Women's
    Action Network*. 1 Mar. 2009. Web.

Ayers, Michael D. "Comparing Collective Identity in Online and Offline Feminist Activists."
    McCaughey and Ayers 145–64.

Babbage, Maria. "Murder Rate Increase Skewed by Case of Missing Women; Overall Crime
    Rate Steady." *Ottawa Citizen*. 24 July 2003. Web.

Babcock, Wendy. "Me and My Insane Friends." *W.H.O.R.E.: Women Helping Ourselves to Rights
    and Equality*. 6 Sept. 2006. Web. 24 May 2011.

Bains, Camille, and Greg Joyce. "Relatives Await News as Police Search Farm in Missing BC
    Women Case." Canadian Press, 7 Feb. 2002. Web. 6 Nov. 2009.

Balfour, Gillian, and Elizabeth Comack, eds. *Criminalizing Women: Gender and (In)Justice in
    Neo-Liberal Times*. Halifax: Fernwood, 2006. Print.

Ball, Richard A. "Changing Images of Deviance: Nineteenth-Century Canadian Anti-Prostitution Movements." *Deviant Behavior* 33.1 (2012): 26–39. Web. 15 June 2012.

Bauman, Zygmunt. *Globalization: The Human Consequences.* New York: Columbia UP, 1998. Print.

———. *Work, Consumerism and the New Poor.* Philadelphia: Open UP, 1998. Print.

BC Coalition of Experiential Communities. 1 Mar. 2011. Web. 23 May 2011.

"BC Court Rejects Robert Pickton's Appeal." *thestar.com.* Toronto Star Magazines, 25 July 2009. Web. 2 Jan. 2010.

"BC Police Search Farm in Missing-women Case." Canadian Press. 7 Feb. 2002. *Missingpeople.net.* Web. 22 July 2010.

Bedford v. Canada. 2010 ONSC 4264. Ontario Supreme Court. *CanLII.* Web.

Bell, Laurie, ed. *Good Girls/Bad Girls: Feminists and Sex Trade Workers Face to Face.* Seattle: Seal, 1987. Print.

Bell, Shannon. *Reading, Writing and Rewriting the Prostitute Body.* Bloomington: Indiana UP, 1994. Print.

Benoit, Cecilia, Alison Millar, Prostitutes' Empowerment and Resource Society, BC Health Research Foundation, and Capital Health Region (BC). *Dispelling Myths and Understanding Realities: Working Conditions, Heath Status, and Exiting Experiences of Sex Workers.* Victoria, BC: Dept. of Sociology, U of Victoria, 2001. Google Books. Web.

Berger, John. *Ways of Seeing.* New York: Viking, 1973. Print.

Berger, Tamara. *The Way of the Whore.* Toronto: Gutter, 2004. Print.

Best, Steven, and Douglas Kellner. *The Postmodern Adventure: Science, Technology and Cultural Studies at the Third Millennium.* New York: Routledge, 2001. Print.

Bittle, Steven. "From Villain to Victim: Secure Care and Young Women in Prostitution." Balfour and Comack 195–213.

Black, Debra. "Prostitutes Identify 'Bad Dates' on Website." *Toronto Star.* 4 Aug. 2005. Web. 5 Oct. 2005.

Blood: What You Must Know to Give Blood. Canadian Blood Services, 2005. Print.

Bold, Christine, Rick Knowles, and Belinda Leach. "National Countermemories: Feminist Memorializing and Cultural Countermemory: The Case of Marianne's Park." *Signs* 28.1 (2002): 125–48. Web. 1 Jan. 2012.

Boritch, Helen. *Fallen Women: Female Crime and Criminal Justice in Canada.* Toronto: Nelson, 1997. Print.

Borowko, Whitney. "The Bottom Line: On Prostitution." *e.Peak* 9.115 (27 Oct. 2003). Web. 29 Oct. 2006.

Boulos, Baron, and Liz Stanley. *The Yorkshire Ripper: A Case Study of "The Sutcliffe Papers."* Manchester: U of Manchester P, 1983. Print.

Boyd, Susan C. "Community-based Research in the Downtown Eastside of Vancouver." *Resources for Feminist Research* 33.1/2 (2008): 19–43. Web. 10 June 2012.

Brenner, N. and Theodore, N. "Cities and the Geographies of 'Actually Existing Neoliberalism.'" *Antipode* 34.3 (2002): 349–79. Print.

Brock, Deborah. *Making Work, Making Trouble: Prostitution as a Social Problem.* Toronto: U of Toronto P, 1998.

Brock, Deborah, and Valerie Scott. "Getting Angry, Getting Organized: The Formation of the Canadian Organization for the Rights of Prostitutes." *Sex Work*. Spec. issue of *Fireweed* 65 (1999): 8–21. Print.

Bunch, Mary. "Sex Work and the Justice to Come: Feminist Coalition Building at a Crossroads." Annual Conference of the Canadian Women's Studies Association. University of Waterloo, Ontario. 27 May 2012. Conference Paper.

Burfoot, Annette, and Susan Lord, eds. *Killing Women: The Visual Culture of Gender and Violence.* Waterloo, ON: Wilfrid Laurier UP, 2006. Print.

Burk, Adrienne. "In Sight, Out of View: A Tale of Three Monuments." *Antipode* 38.1 (2006): 41–58. Web. 20 Dec. 2011.

———. *Speaking for a Long Time: Public Space and Social Memory in Vancouver.* Vancouver: UBC P, 2010. Print.

Buss, Helen M. "The Different Voice of Canadian Feminist Autobiographers." *Biography* 13.2 (Spring 1990): 154–67. Print.

Bustos, Alejandro. "Workers Cheated, Sexually Exploited: Employers Threaten Deportation, Immigration Officials Admit to Problem." *Toronto Star.* 15 Aug. 2005. Print.

Butler, Judith. *Gender Trouble: Feminism and the Subversion of Identity.* 1991. New York: Routledge, 1999. Print.

———. *Precarious Life: the Power of Mourning and Violence.* New York: Verso, 2004. Print.

Cameron, Stevie. "The Pig Farm: a Work in Progress for Knopf Canada." *Missingpeople.net.* 2003. Web. 25 Aug. 2010.

Campbell, Larry. "Inaugural Address." *Vancouver City Council: City Clerk's Site.* 2 Dec. 2002. Web. 14 Oct. 2005.

Campbell, Maria. *Halfbreed.* Halifax: Seal, 1973. Print.

Canada. *Aboriginal Peoples in Canada: First Nations People, Métis, and Inuit. National Household Survey, 2011.* Statistics Canada. 2013. Web.

———. *Criminal Code.* (R.S.C., 1985, c. C-46). Minister of Justice. 5 May 2011. Web. 24 May 2011.

———. Federal/Provincial/Territorial Working Group on Prostitution. *Report and Recommendations in Respect of Legislation, Policy, and Practices Concerning Prostitution-Related Activities.* Department of Justice. 1998. Web. 10 June 2007.

———. House of Commons. Subcommittee on Solicitation Laws of the Standing Committee on Justice, Human Rights, Public Safety and Emergency Preparedness (SSLR). *The Challenge of Change: A Study of Canada's Criminal Prostitution Laws. Report of the Standing Committee on Justice and Human Rights* (Chair Art Hanger). *Report of the Subcommittee on Solicitation Laws* (Chair John Maloney). Parliament of Canada. Dec. 2006. Web. 11 June 2011.

———. House of Commons. Subcommittee on Solicitation Laws of the Standing Committee on Justice, Human Rights, Public Safety and Emergency Preparedness (SSLR) (Chair John Maloney). *Proceedings of the Subcommittee on Solicitation Laws of the Standing Committee on Justice, Human Rights, Public Safety and Emergency Preparedness.* 15 July 2005. Web. 5 Aug. 2010.

———. Special Committee on Pornography and Prostitution (Chair Paul Fraser). *Report of the Special Committee on Pornography and Prostitution* (Fraser Committee Report). 1998. Web. 10 June 2007.

———. Supreme Court of Canada. *Reference re: Prostitution*. By Justice Dickson. 1990. Web.

Canada (AG) v. Bedford. 2012 ONCA 186. Ontario Court of Appeals. *CanLII*. Web.

Canada (AG) v. Bedford. 2013 SCC 72. Supreme Court of Canada. *CanLII*. Web.

"Canada's Poorest Postal Code." *Wikipedia: The Free Encyclopedia*. 28 Jan. 2010. Web.

Canclini, Néstor García. *Consumers and Citizens: Globalization and Multicultural Conflicts*. Trans. George Yúdice. Minneapolis: U of Minnesota P, 2001. Print.

Caputi, Jane. *The Age of Sex Crime*. Bowling Green, OH: Bowling Green State U Popular P, 1987. Print.

Carlson, Matt. "Making Memories Matter: Journalistic Authority and the Memorializing Discourse around Mary McGrory and David Brinkley." *Journalism* 8 (2007): 165–83. Web.

Carroll, William K., and Robert A. Hackett. "Democratic Media Activism through the Lens of Social Movement Theory." *Media, Culture & Society* 28.1 (2006): 83–104. Web.

Carter, Lauren. "Where are Canada's Disappeared Women?" *Herizons* 19.2 (2005): 20–23, 45–46). Web. 1 May 2012.

Carter, Sarah. *Capturing Women: The Manipulation of Cultural Imagery in Canada's Prairie West*. Montreal: McGill-Queen's UP, 1997. Print.

CBC News Online. "In Depth: Pickton." News Archive. 2 Mar. 2006. Web. 1 June 2006.

———. "The Missing Women of Vancouver." 2 Mar. 2006. Web. 1 June 2006.

CEASE. "About." *CEASE: Centre to End All Sexual Exploitation*. 2011. Web. 12 July 2012.

———. "Homepage." *CEASE: Centre to End All Sexual Exploitation*. 2011. Web. 12 July 2012.

Comack, Elizabeth. "Making Connections: Class/Race/Gender Intersections." Balfour and Comack 58–72.

Comack Elizabeth, and Maya Seshia. "Bad Dates and Street Hassles: Violence in the Winnipeg Street Sex Trade." *Canadian Journal of Criminology and Criminal Justice* 52.2 (2010): 203–14. Web. 1 June 2012.

Conservative Party of Canada. *Stand Up for Canada: The Conservative Party of Canada Federal Election Platform 2006*. Web.

Craig, Elaine. "Sex Work By Law: Bedford's Impact on Municipal Approaches to Regulating the Sex Trade." *Review of Constitutional Studies* 16.1 (2011): 97–120. Web. 15 May 2012.

"Crime Statistics." *The Daily*. Statistics Canada. 21 July 2005. Web.

CSIS: Commercial Sex Information Service. 15 Jan. 1996. Web. 23 May 2011.

Culbert, Lori. "Children of Vancouver's Missing Women." *Vancouver Sun*. 28 Jan. 2006. *Missingpeople.net*. Web. 26 Nov. 2006.

———. "'Nothing's Changed' in Vancouver's Drug-plagued Downtown Eastside." *Vancouver Sun. Missingpeople.net*. 25 Feb. 2008. Web.

———. "Sketches Express Softer Side of Missing Women." *Vancouver Sun*. 17 Dec. 2005. *Missingpeople.net*. Web. 20 Dec. 2005.

Culbert, Lori, and Neal Hall. "Family, Friends Attend Court Opening." *Vancouver Sun*. 31 Jan. 2006. *Missingpeople.net*. Web. 4 Feb. 2006.

Culhane, Dara. "'Their Spirits Live Within Us': Aboriginal Women in Downtown Eastside Vancouver Emerging into Visibility." *American Indian Quarterly* 27.3–4 (2000): 593–606. Web. 15 Aug. 2009.

The Cultural Memory Group. *Remembering Women Murdered by Men: Memorials across Canada.* Toronto: Sumach, 2006. Print.

Cumming, Peter. "'The Only Dirty Book': The Rape of April Raintree." Suzack, *April Raintree* 307–22.

Cunningham, Scott, and Todd D. Kendall. "Prostitution 2.0: The Changing Face of Sex Work." *Journal of Urban Economics* 69.3 (2011): 273–87. Web. 13 Mar. 2011.

Damm, Kateri. "Dispelling and Telling: Speaking Native Realities in Maria Campbell's *Halfbreed* and Beatrice Culleton's *In Search of April Raintree.*" *Looking at the Words of Our People: First Nations Analysis of Literature.* Ed. Jeannette Armstrong. Penticton: Theytus, 1993. 95–114. Print.

Dauvergne, Mia. "Crime Statistics in Canada, 2007." *Juristat: Canadian Centre for Justice Statistics* 28.7 (July 2008): 1–17. 31 July 2009. Web. 2 Nov. 2009.

Davis, Mike. *City of Quartz: Excavating the Future in Los Angeles.* New York: Verso, 1990. Print.

"Deadly Streets." *CBC Edmonton: Features. CBC.ca.* 17 June 2005. Web. 18 Aug. 2010.

Dean, Amber. "Hauntings: Representations of Vancouver's Disappeared Women." Diss. U of Alberta, 2009. Web. 10 Jan. 2009.

———. "'Just Another Day / Just Another Death': Ungrievability and Vancouver's Missing Women." Unpublished MS.

———. "Representing and Remembering Murdered Women: Thoughts on the Ethics of Critique." *ESC: English Studies in Canada* 34.2/3 (2008): 229–41. Web. 11 Jan. 2012.

———. "The Politics of Cultural Memory: Remembering Vancouver's Murdered and Missing Women." Cultural Studies Now: An International Conference. U of East London. London, UK. 20 July 2007.

De Vries, Maggie. "The Harm That the Media Can Do." *Vancouver Sun via Missingpeople.net.* 2 Nov. 2004. Web. 20 June 2011.

———. *Missing Sarah: A Vancouver Women Remembers Her Sister.* Toronto: Penguin Canada, 2003. Print.

Derry, Ken. "Religion and (Mimetic) Violence in Canadian Native Literature." *Literature and Theology* 16.2 (2002): 201–19. Print.

Dickin-McGinnis, Janice. "Whores and Worthies: Feminism and Prostitution." *CJLS: Canadian Journal of Law and Society* 9.1 (1994): 105–26. Print.

Ditmore, Melissa Hope, Antonia Levy, and Alys Willman, eds. *Sex Work Matters: Exploring Money, Power and Intimacy in the Sex Industry.* New York: Zed, 2010. Print.

"Downtown Eastside." *Wikipedia: The Free Encyclopedia.* 28 Jan. 2010. Web. 21 June 2011.

Downtown Eastside Sex Workers United Against Violence Society v. Attorney General (Canada). 2008 BCSC 1726. British Columbia Supreme Court. Web.

Downtown Eastside Sex Workers United Against Violence Society v. Canada (AG). 2010 BCCA 439. British Columbia Court of Appeals. *CanLII.* Web.

Dumont, Marilyn. "Squaw Poems." *An Anthology of Canadian Native Literature in English.* 2nd ed. Ed. Daniel David Moses and Terry Goldie. Don Mills, ON: Oxford UP, 1998. 386–88. Print.

Durisin, Elya. "Perspectives on Rape in the Canadian Sex Industry: Navigating the Terrain between Sex Work as Labour and Sex Work as Violence Paradigms." *Canadian Woman Studies* 28.1 (2009/2010): 128–35. Web. 20 May 2012.

England, Jennifer. "Disciplining Subjectivity and Space: Representation, Films, and Its Material Effects." *Antipode* 36.2 (2004): 295–321. Web.

Entman, Robert. "Cascading Activism: Contesting the White House's Frame After 9/11." *Political Communication* 20.4 (2003): 415–32. Print.

Ettema, James S. "Crafting Cultural Power: Imaginative Power in Everyday Journalism." *Journalism* 6.2 (2005): 131–52. Web. 17 Apr. 2010.

Fabian, Cosi. "The Holy Whore: A Woman's Gateway to Power." Nagle 44–54.

Fagan, Kristina, Stephanie Danyluk, Bryce Donaldson, Amelias Horsburgh, Robyn Moore, and Martin Winquist. "Reading the Critical Reception of Maria Campbell's *Halfbreed*." *Canadian Journal of Native Studies* 29.1/2 (2009): 257–81. Web. 15 July 2012.

Fahmi, Wael Salah. "Bloggers' Street Movement and the Right to the City. (Re)claiming Cairo's Real and Virtual 'Spaces of Freedom.'" *Environment and Urbanization* 21.1 (2009): 89–107. Web. 7 Mar. 2011.

Faraday, Fay, and Janine Benedict. "Factum of the Intervenor Women's Coalition." Court of Appeal for Ontario. Toronto, 2011. Web. 21 June 2011.

Fee, Margery. "Deploying Identity in the Face of Racism." Suzack, *April Raintree* 211–26.

Ferris, S. "Restorative Street Justice: *Victims, All of Us*, Street Youth, and Sex Work." Cultural Studies Now: International Conference. U of East London. London, UK. 20 July 2007.

Fong, Petti. "Pictures Provide the Clues to a Daughter's Lost Life." *Globe and Mail.* 28 Jan. 2006. *Missingpeople.net.* Web. 23 June 2010.

Fontaine, Nahanni. "Surviving Colonization: Anishnaabe Ikwe Gang Participation." Balfour and Comack 113–29.

Fraser, Nancy. *Justice Interruptus: Critical Reflections on the "Postsocialist" Condition.* New York: Routledge, 1997. Print.

Fregoso, Rosa-Linda. "'We Want Them Alive!': The Politics and Culture of Human Rights." *Social Identities* 12.2 (2006): 109–38. Web.

Fürsich, Elfriede. "How Can Global Journalists Represent the 'Other'?: A Critical Assessment of the Cultural Studies Concept for Media Practice." *Journalism* 3.1 (2002): 57–84. Web.

Fuss, Diana. *Essentially Speaking: Feminism, Nature, and Difference.* New York: Routledge, 1989. Print.

Galusky, Wyatt. "Identifying with Information: Citizen Empowerment, the Internet, and the Environmental Anti-toxins Movement." McCaughey and Ayers 185–208.

Gardner, Dan. "Courting Death: Parts 1 & 2." *Ottawa Citizen.* 15 June 2002. *Missingpeople.net.* Web. 19 July 2010.

———. "How Cities License Off-Street Hookers." *Ottawa Citizen*. 16 June 2002.
    Missingpeople.net. Web. 29 July 2010.

———. "The Many Faces of Prostitution." *Ottawa Citizen*. 20 Mar. 2006. Web.

Gaskel, Elizabeth. *Ruth*. 1853. New York: Oxford UP, 1985. Print.

Gilman, Sander. *Difference and Pathology: Stereotypes of Sexuality, Race and Madness*. Ithaca, NY:
    Cornell UP, 1985. Print.

———. "'Who Kills Whores?' 'I Do,' Says Jack: Race and Gender in Victorian London."
    Death and Representation. Ed. Sarah Webster Goodwin and Elizabeth Bronfen.
    Baltimore: Johns Hopkins UP, 1993. Print.

Gill, Alexandra. "Prostitutes, Addicts, Too Strung Out to Care." *Globe and Mail*. 9 Feb. 2002.
    A5. Print.

Gilroy, Paul. *Postcolonial Melancholia*. New York: Columbia UP, 2005. Print.

Girard, Daniel. "BC Murder Case Grows: Now There are 27." *Toronto Star*. 26 May 2005:
    A1. Print.

Giroux, Henry A. *The Terror of Neoliberalism: Authoritarianism and the Eclipse of Democracy*.
    Boulder, CO: Paradigm, 2004. Print.

Goldberg, David. *The Racial State*. Oxford: Blackwell, 2002. Print.

———. *Racist Culture: Philosophy and the Politics of Meaning*. Cambridge, MA: Blackwell,
    1993. Print.

Goldie, Terry. *Fear and Temptation: The Image of the Indigene in Canadian, Australian, and
    New Zealand Literatures*. Montreal: McGill-Queen's UP, 1989.

Gonzalez, Vernadette V., and Robyn Magalit Rodriguez. "Filipina.com: Wives, Workers, and
    Whores on the Cyberfrontier." *Asian America.Net: Ethnicity, Nationalism, and Cyberspace*. Ed.
    Rachel C. Lee and Sau-ling Cynthia Wong. New York: Routledge, 2003. 215–34. Web.

"Government Targets Prostitution." *CBC.ca*. 7 Nov. 2000. Web. 6 Aug. 2006.

Grant, Dianne. "Sexin' Work: The Politics of Prostitution Regulation." *New Proposals: Journal
    of Marxism and Interdisciplinary Inquiry* 2.1 (2008): 61–74. Web. 15 May 2012.

Green, Joyce, ed. *Making Space for Indigenous Feminism*. Toronto: Sumach, 2007. Print.

Greenaway, Norma, and Chad Skelton. "Supreme Court Rejects Serial Killer Robert
    Pickton's Bid for a New Trial." *Postmedia News* and *Vancouver Sun*. 30 July 2010. Web.
    30 July 2010.

Guimond, Eric, Gail Guthrie Valaskakis, and Madeline Dion Stout, eds. *Restoring the Balance:
    First Nations Women, Community, and Culture*. Winnipeg: U of Manitoba P, 2008. Print.

Hainsworth, Jeremy. "Family of Missing Woman Wants Serial Killer Doll Removed from
    Vancouver Store." *Maclean's*. Rogers Digital Media, 30 Dec. 2004. Web. 10 Feb. 2005.

"Halifax Undercover Police Clamp Down on Prostitution." *CBC.ca*. 4 May 2000. Web.
    6 Aug. 2005.

Hall, Stuart. "Race, Culture, and Communications: Looking Backward and Forward at
    Cultural Studies." *What is Cultural Studies? A Reader*. Ed. John Storey. London: Arnold,
    1996. Print.

Hallgrimsdottir, Helga Kristin, Rachel Phillips, and Cecilia Benoit. "Fallen Women and Rescued Girls: Social Stigma and Media Narratives of the Sex Industry in Victoria, BC, from 1980 to 2005." *Canadian Review of Sociology and Anthropology* 43.3 (2006): 265–80. Web.

Hara, Noriko, and Zilia Estrada. "Analyzing the Mobilization of Grassroots Activities Via the Internet: A Case Study." *Journal of Information Science* 31.6 (2005): 503–14. Web. 13 Mar. 2011.

Harding, Katherine. "The Edmonton Killings: Who is Responsible for the Deaths of 15 Women?" *Globe and Mail*. 18 May 2006: A7. Print.

Harp, Rick. "Has Ontario Court Ruling Made Life Safer or Riskier for Aboriginal Sex Workers?" *Media Indigena*. 11 Oct. 2010. Web. 6 Nov. 2010.

Hartley, John. *Popular Reality: Journalism, Modernity, Popular Culture*. London: Arnold, 1996. Print.

Harvey, David. "Consent to Coercion." *The New Imperialism*. New York: Oxford UP, 2003. 183–212. Print.

Heiss, Anita. "Aboriginal Identity and Its Effects on Writing." *(Ad)dressing Our Words: Aboriginal Perspectives on Aboriginal Literatures*. Ed. Armand Ruffo. Penticton, BC: Theytus, 2001. 205–32.

Highway, Tomson. *Kiss of the Fur Queen*. Toronto: Doubleday Canada, 1998.

Hirsch, M., and V. Smith. "Feminism and Cultural Memory: An Introduction." *Signs* 28.1 (2002): 1–19. Web. 1 Jan. 2012.

Hodgins, Dawn. "Dealing with Prostitution in Canada." *CMAJ: Canadian Medical Association Journal* 172.1 (2005): Web.

"Homeless in Whitechapel." *Illustrated London News*. 1888. *British Library Images Online Collection*. British Library, 20 May 2005. Web. 6 Aug. 2005.

hooks, bell. "Feminism: a Transformational Politic." *Talking Back: Thinking Feminist, Thinking Black*. Cambridge, MA: South End, 1989. 19–27. Print.

"How Police, Street Workers and Families Are Dealing with the Murders of Edmonton Women." Rep. Judy Piercey. *The National*. CBC Television. 1 Sept. 2003. Web.

Hoy, Helen. "'Nothing but the Truth': Discursive Transparency in Beatrice Culleton." Suzack, *April Raintree* 273–94.

Hugill, David. *Missing Women, Missing News: Covering Crisis in Vancouver's Downtown Eastside*. Halifax: Fernwood, 2010. Print.

Huhndorf, Shari M. and Cheryl Suzack. "Indigenous Feminism: Theorizing the Issues." Suzack, Huhndorf, Perrault, and Barman, eds. 1–17.

Hume, Mark. "15 Lives Lived Dangerously." *National Post*. 11 Jan. 2003. *Missingpeople.net*. Web. 17 July 2010.

Inglewood Community League Newsletter. Inglewood Community League of Edmonton, 10 Oct. 2005. Web.

Ipsos Canada. "Vancouver Mayor and Council—One Year Review." 4 Dec. 2003. Web. 1 Apr. 2006.

Jannetta, Armando E. "Anecdotal Humour in Maria Campbell's *Halfbreed* (1973)." *Journal of Canadian Studies* 31 (1996): 62–75. Print.

———. "Métis Autobiography: The Emergence of a Genre amid Alienation, Resistance and Healing in the Context of Maria Campbell's *Halfbreed*." *International Journal of Canadian Studies* 12 (1995): 169–81. Print.

Jeffrey, Leslie Ann, and Gayle MacDonald. *Sex Workers in the Maritimes Talk Back*. Vancouver: UBC P, 2006. Print.

Jiwani, Yasmin. "Race and the Media: A Retrospective and Prospective Gaze." *Canadian Journal of Communication* 34.4 (2009): 735–40. Web. 1 June 2012.

Jiwani, Yasmin, and Mary Lynn Young. "Missing and Murdered Women: Reproducing Marginality in News Discourses." *Canadian Journal of Communication* 31 (2006): 895–917. Web. 21 June 2011.

John Howard Society of Alberta. *Prostitution*. John Howard Society of Alberta. 2001. Web. 11 June 2011.

John Howard Society of Canada. "About Us." *John Howard Society*. 6 Nov. 2001. Web. 11 June 2011.

Joyce, Greg. "Intense Interest in Pickton Trial Declines Markedly After First Day." Canadian Press. 1 Feb. 2006. Web. 15 May 2006.

Kahn, Richard, and Douglas Kellner. "New Media and Internet Activism: from the 'Battle of Seattle' to Blogging." *New Media & Society* 6.1 (2004): 87–95. Web. 21 June 2011.

King, Thomas. *The Truth about Stories: A Native Narrative*. Toronto: Anansi, 2003. Print.

Kishtainy, Khalid. *The Prostitute in Progressive Literature*. New York: Allison, 1982. Print.

Klinck, Todd. "I Wanted to Be a Saloon Girl: Interview with Valerie Scott." *Fab Magazine* 266 (April 2005): Web. 21 June 2011.

Kristeva, Julia. *Powers of Horror: An Essay on Abjection*. Trans. Leon S. Roudiez. New York: Columbia UP, 1982. Print.

Lakeman, Lee. "Linking Violence and Poverty in the CASAC Report." *Canadian Woman Studies* 23.3–4 (2003): 57–62. Print.

Larsen, Nick. "Canadian Prostitution Control between 1914 and 1970: An Exercise in Chauvinist Reasoning." *CJLS: Canadian Journal of Law and Society* 7 (1992): 140–55. Print.

Lazarus, L., and Deering, K. "Occupation Stigma as a Primary Barrier to Health Care for Street-based Sex Workers in Canada." *Culture, Health & Sexuality* 14.2 (2012): 139–50. Web.

Leigh, Carol [Scarlot Harlot]. "Inventing Sex Work." Nagle 225–31.

Lewis, Jacqueline. "Shifting the Focus: Restorative Justice and Sex Work." *Canadian Journal of Criminology* 52.3 (2010): 285–301. Web. 8 July 2012.

Liberal Party of Canada. "Issues: Cities and Communities." *Liberal Party of Canada*, 10 Mar. 2006. Web.

Lippert, Randy. "Urban Revitalization, Security, and Knowledge Transfer: The Case of Broken Windows and Kiddie Bars." *CJLS: Canadian Journal of Law and Society* 22.2 (2007): 29–53. Web. 15 June 2012.

Live eXXXpressions: Sex Workers Stand up in Montreal! Dir. Mirha-Soleil Ross. Stella: "eXXXpressions" & YouTube. Stella, 2005. Web. 15 July 2012.

Lowman, John. "Deadly Inertia: A History of Constitutional Challenges to Canada's
Criminal Code Sections on Prostitution." *John Lowman's Prostitution Research Page.*
John Lowman, 10 Oct. 2009. Web. 1 June 2011.

———. *John Lowman's Prostitution Research Page.* John Lowman, 2009. Web. 19 July 2010.

———. "Prostitution Law Reform in Canada." *Toward Comparative Law in the 21st Century.*
Ed. Institute of Comparative Law in Japan. Tokyo: Chuo UP, 1998. 919–46. Web.

———. "Violence and the Outlaw Status of (Street) Prostitution in Canada." *Violence Against
Women* 6.9 (2000): 987–1011. Print.

Lowman, John, M.A. Jackson, T.S. Palys, and S. Gavigan, eds. *Regulating Sex: An Anthology of
Commentaries on the Findings and Recommendations of the Badgley and Fraser Reports.*
Burnaby: Simon Fraser University School of Criminology, 1986. Print.

Luker, Kristin. "Sex, Social Hygiene, and the State: The Double-Edged Sword of Social
Reform." *Theory and Society* 27 (1998): 601–34. Print.

Lutz, Hartmut. *Contemporary Challenges: Conversations with Canadian Native Authors.* Saskatoon:
Fifth House, 1991. Print.

Maccallair, Daniel. "Shattering 'Broken Windows': An Analysis of San Francisco's Alternative
Crime Policies." (US) Center on Juvenile and Criminal Justice. Oct. 1999. Web.

MacCharles, Tonda. "Peter MacKay Rules Out Legalization, Municipal Regulation of
Prostitution." *thestar.com.* Toronto Star Newspapers, 20 Jan. 2014. Web. 9 Feb. 2014.

Maggie's: Sex Work Is Real Work. 2011. Toronto. 10 Jan. 2004. Web. 19 June 2011.

———. "What We Do." *Maggie's.* Toronto. 2011. Web. 20 June 2011.

Mason, Paul, and Jane Monckton-Smith. "Conflation, Collocation and Confusion: British
Press Coverage of the Sexual Murder of Women." *Journalism* 9.6 (2008): 691–710. Web.
20 July 2010.

Masse, Mark H. "Creative Nonfiction: Where Journalism and Storytelling Meet." *Writer*
108.10 (Oct. 1995): Web. 21 June 2011.

Masson, Dominique. "Economic Globalization, Regionalization, and Women's Movement
Organizing in Québec." *Canadian Woman Studies* 23.3/4 (2003): 171–74. Print.

Masthead. "*Saturday Night* Earns Most NMA Nominations." Masthead Online. 18 Apr. 2000.
Web. 26 Aug. 2010.

Matas, Robert. "Pickton Set to Plead Not Guilty." *Globe and Mail.* 28 Jan. 2006. A9. Print.

———. "Vancouver Prostitutes to Lose Agency That Helps Them Leave the Trade."
Globe and Mail. 14 Nov. 2011. Web. 23 Jan. 2014.

Matas, Robert, and Ingrid Peritz. "Canada's Poorest Postal Code in for an Olympic
Clean-up?" *Globe and Mail: National.* Globeandmail.com. 15 Aug. 2008. 7 Jan. 2010. Web.

Matas, Robert, and Petti Fong. "27." *Globe and Mail.* 26 May 2006: A1. Print.

Mayeda, Andrew. "Canada Studying Private Firms for Prisons as Budgets Fall."
Bloomberg: News. 10 July 2012. Web. 12 July 2012.

Mbembe, Achilles. "Necropolitics." *Public Culture* 15.1 (2003): 24. Print.

McCaughey, Martha, and Michael D. Ayers, eds. *Cyberactivism: Online Activism in Theory and
Practice.* New York: Routledge, 2003. Print.

McClintock, Anne. *Imperial Leather: Race, Gender and Sexuality in the Colonial Contest*. New York: Routledge, 1995. Print.

McElhinney, Lora. "Memorial March, 2007." *West Coast Line 53: Representations of Murdered and Missing Women* 41.1 (2007): 70–73. Print.

McKinnon, J.B. "Crime: The Big Sweep." *Vancouver Magazine*. 3 June 2003. Web. 20 Mar. 2006.

McLeod, Brenda. "First Nations Women and Sustainability on the Canadian Prairies." *Canadian Woman Studies* 23.1 (2003): 47–54. Print.

McNeill, Laurie. "Death and the Maidens: Vancouver's Missing Women, the Montreal Massacre, and Commemoration's Blindspots." *Canadian Review of American Studies* 38.3 (2008): 375–98. Print.

Meikle, Graham. *Future Active: Media Activism and the Internet*. New York: Routledge, 2002. Print.

"Memory March—Sunday March 25th, 2 pm, Crab Park, Vancouver, BC." *Missingpeople.net*. Mar. 2007. Web.

Merrifield, Andy. *Metromarxism: A Marxist Tale of the City*. New York: Routledge, 2002. Print.

Mertyl, Steve. "Pressure Led to Stepped-up Investigation into Missing Vancouver Women." *Canadian Press. Missingpeople.net*. 7 Feb. 2002. Web.

Métis National Council. "Citizenship." *Métis National Council / Ralliement National des Métis*. Web. 15 July 2012.

Meyers, Marian. "Crack Mothers in the News: A Narrative of Paternalistic Racism." *Journal of Communication Inquiry* 28.3 (2004): 194–216. Print.

Miller, David. "New Deal Speech." *Mayors' Summit*. 22 Jan. 2004. Web.

Milloy, John. *A National Crime: The Canadian Government and the Residential School System, 1879–1986*. Winnipeg: U of Manitoba P, 1999. Print.

"Missing Women's Families Remember Their Loved Ones." *Vancouver Sun*. 26 May 2005. *Missingpeople.net*. Web. 23 July 2010.

Mojica, Monique. *Princess Pocahontas and the Blue Spots*. Toronto: Women's, 1991. Print.

Monture, Patricia A. "Women's Words: Power, Identity, and Indigenous Sovereignty." *Canadian Woman Studies* 26.3/4 (2008): 154–59. Web. 15 July 2012.

Moore, Dene. "Sarah de Vries: Poet, Artist, Drug Addict, Fallen Angel of the Downtown Eastside." *Missing Lives: A Special Report from the Canadian Press*. CBC, 16 Jan. 2007. Web. 29 June 2010.

Morton, Heather, Carolin Klein, and Boris B. Gorzalka. "Attitudes, Beliefs, and Knowledge of Prostitution and the Law in Canada." *Canadian Journal of Criminology and Criminal Justice* 54.2 (2012): 229–44. Web. 3 July 2012.

Mosionier, Beatrice Culleton. *In Search of April Raintree*. 1984. Critical Edition. Ed. Cheryl Suzack. Winnipeg: Portage & Main, 1999. Print.

Moulton, Donalee. "Can Private Jails Come to Canada?" *The Lawyer's Weekly*. 20 Jan. 2012. Web. 12 July 2012.

Moyes, Lianne. "Introduction." *Tessera: Contemporary Feminist Baroque féministe contemporain* 24 (Summer 1998): 8–23. Print.

Nagle, Jill. "Introduction." Nagle 1–18.

Nagle, Jill, ed. *Whores and Other Feminists*. New York: Routledge, 1997. Print.

Native Youth Sexual Health Network. NYHSN. 2009. Web. 15 July 2012.

———. "Collaborative Projects." NYHSN. 2009. Web. 1 June 2011.

———. "Decriminalization of Sex Work." NYHSN. 6 Oct. 2010. Web. 15 July 2012.

———. "Indigenous Peoples in the Sex Trade—Our Life, Our Bodies, Our Realities. NYSHN. 14 Feb. 2012. Web. 15 July 2012.

———. "Indigenous Peoples in the Sex Trade—Speaking for Ourselves." NYHSN. 11 Apr. 2011. Web. 15 July 2012.

"The Nemesis of Neglect." *Punch, or the London Charivari*. 29 Sept. 1888. British Library Images Online. 20 May 2006. Web.

Ng, Roxana. "Freedom from Whom? Globalization and Trade from the Standpoint of Garment Workers." *Canadian Woman Studies* 21/22 (4&1) (2002): 74–81. Print.

Nordstrom, Carolyn. "Visible Wars & Invisible Girls, Shadow Industries, and the Politics of Not-Knowing." *Atlantis: A Women's Studies Journal* (2003): 71–84. Print.

Nowakowska, Patricia. "Brain Candy: Are Sex Workers Not Human?" *The McGill Daily*. 28 July 2005. Web.

NWAC: Native Women's Association of Canada. "Departments: Sisters in Spirit." *Native Women's Association of Canada Website*. 22 Sept. 2007. Web. 20 July 2010.

———. "NWAC Questions if Landmark Ruling Will Increase Safety in Prostitution." *NWAC: Media Centre*. Ottawa. 30 Sept. 2010. Web. 1 Mar. 2011.

———. *What Their Stories Tell Us: Research Findings from the Sisters in Spirit Initiative*. Native Women's Association of Canada Website. 31 Mar. 2010. 19 July 2010. Web.

NWAC, and CAEFS. "Women and the Canadian Legal System: Examining Situations of Hyper-Responsibility." *Canadian Woman Studies* 26.3/4 (2008): 94–104. Web. 17 June 2010.

"Objectives." *West End Sex Work History Project, 1975–1985*. Web. 20 June 2014.

OCAP: Ontario Coalition Against Poverty. Immigration Archive. Web. 26 Nov. 2006.

O'Connell-Davidson, Julia. *Prostitution, Power and Freedom*. Cambridge: Polity, 1998. Print.

———. "The Rights and Wrongs of Prostitution." *Hypatia* 17.2 (2002): 84–98. Print.

Oleman, Michelle. "Conference Tackles Missing Women Crisis." *First Nations Drum: News From Canada's Native Communities* (Summer 2006): Web.

———. "Young Hearts, Young Lives: Profiles of the Highway of Tears' Missing Girls." *First Nations Drum: News From Canada's Native Communities* (Summer 2006): Web.

PAAFE. "John School: Prostitution Offender Program: Course Outline." *PAAFE: The Prostitution Awareness and Action Foundation of Edmonton*. 2005. Web. 6 Aug. 2005.

———. *PAAFE: The Prostitution Awareness and Action Foundation of Edmonton*. Dawn Hodgins, 2005. Web. 6 Nov. 2006.

———. "Welcome to the Prostitution Awareness and Action Foundation of Edmonton." *PAAFE: The Prostitution Awareness and Action Foundation of Edmonton*. 15 Apr. 2011. Web. 11 June 2011.

PACE Society. "About Us." *PACE Society: Prostitution Alternatives, Counselling and Education*. 2014. Web. 18 June 2014.

———. "Violence Prevention." *PACE Society: Prostitution Alternatives, Counselling and Education.* 15 Dec. 2006. Web. 1 June 2011.

Papacharissi, Zizi. "The Virtual Sphere: The Internet as Public Sphere." *New Media & Society* 4.1 (2002): 9–27. Web.

Parenti, Christian. *Lockdown America: Police and Prisons in the Age of Crisis.* New York: Verso, 1999. Print.

Parker, Mark. "Sex in the City." *Here* [Saint John, New Brunswick]. 16–23 June 2003. 13. Print.

Paterson, Jody. "Two BC Sex-worker Organizations Shutting Doors." *A Closer Look: Jody Paterson.* Blog. 16 Nov. 2011. Web. 23 Jan. 2014.

PBS. "Local News: If It Bleeds, It Leads." PBS. 3 Jan. 2010. Web. 23 May 2011.

PEERS: *The Prostitutes, Empowerment, Education, and Resource Society.* 1 Dec. 2007. Web. 20 May 2011.

PEERS Vancouver: *The Prostitutes, Empowerment, Education, and Resource Society of Vancouver.* 20 Jan. 2010. Web. 21 May 2011.

Pendleton, Eve. "Love for Sale: Queering Heterosexuality." Nagle 73–82.

Peters, Evelyn J., and O. Starchenko. *Atlas of Urban Aboriginal Peoples.* U of Saskatchewan, 2005. Web.

Peterson, Gail. *The Prostitution Prism.* Amsterdam: Amsterdam UP, 1996. Print.

———, ed. *A Vindication of the Rights of Whores.* Seattle: Seal Press, 1989. Print.

Phillips, Robert Anthony. "Mayor: No Reward in Missing Hookers Case." *APB News.* APBnews.com, 9 Apr. 1999. Web. 10 Feb. 2005.

Pitman, Beverley A. "Re-mediating the Spaces of Reality Television: *America's Most Wanted* and the Case of Vancouver's Missing Women." *Environment and Planning A* 34 (2002): 167–87. Print.

Pivot Legal Society. *Beyond Decriminalization: Sex Work, Human Rights and a New Framework for Law Reform.* Ed. Naomi Brunemeyer, Karen Mirsky, and Sean Rossiter. Vancouver: Pivot Legal Society, 2006. Web. 17 Mar. 2006.

———. "Sex Work, Access to Justice and the Supreme Court of Canada." *Pivot Points: Blog.* Pivot. 2012. Web. 12 July 2012.

Pivot Legal Society Sex Work Subcommittee. *Voices for Dignity: A Call to End the Harms Caused by Canada's Sex Trade Laws.* Vancouver: Pivot Legal Society, 2004. Web. 4 Jan. 2006.

Poovey, Mary. *Uneven Developments: The Ideological Work of Gender in Mid-Victorian England.* Chicago: U of Chicago P, 1988. 1–22. Print.

Pratt, Geraldine. "Abandoned Women and Spaces of the Exception." *Antipode* 37.5 (2005): 1052–1078. Web. 21 June 2011.

Prison Special. Spec. issue of *ConStellation* 9.1 (2005). Print & Web.

Project KARE: Unsolved Homicides / High Risk Missing Persons. 6 Jan. 2006. Web. 11 June 2011.

Project KARE. "Information: Proactive Initiative." *Project KARE.* 6 Jan. 2006. Web. 1 Mar. 2006.

———. "Information: Proactive Initiative." *Project KARE.* 2012. Web. 12 July 2012.

———. "Information: Project Mandate." *Project KARE.* 2006. Web. 6 Jan. 2006.

———. "Information: Project Mandate." *Project KARE.* 2011. Web. 5 June 2011.

———. "Information: Project Mandate." *Project KARE.* 2012. Web. 12 July 2012.

————. "Information: Safety Tips." *Project KARE.* 2006. Web. 6 Jan. 2006.

————. "Information: Safety Tips." *Project KARE.* 2011. Web. 5 June 2011.

————. "Information: Safety Tips." *Project KARE.* 2012. Web. 12 July 2012.

"Prostitutes Form Political Party." (Canadian Press) *Ottawa Citizen.* 3 July 2000. Web.

"Prostitution Laws: Health Risks and Hypocrisy." Editorial. *CMAJ: Canadian Medical Association Journal* 171.2 (2004): Web.

Pullen, Kirsten. *Actresses and Whores: On Stage and in Society.* New York: Cambridge UP, 2005. Print.

Pynn, Larry. "Ottawa Rates Health Risk from Human Remains in Farm Meat." *Vancouver Sun.* 29 Oct. 2004. *Missingpeople.net.* Web. 5 Nov. 2004.

Raban, Jonathan. *Soft City.* London: Harvill, 1974. Print.

Rabinovitch, Jannit. "PEERS: The Prostitutes' Empowerment, Education and Resource Society." *Prostitution, Trafficking, and Traumatic Stress.* Ed. Melissa Farley. Binghampton, NY: Haworth, 2003. Print.

Razack, Sherene. "Gendered Racial Violence and Spatialized Justice: The Murder of Pamela George." Razack 121–56.

————. *Looking White People in the Eye: Gender, Race and Culture in Courtrooms and Classrooms.* Toronto: U of Toronto P, 1998. Print.

————. "Race, Space, and Prostitution: The Making of the Bourgeois Subject." *Canadian Journal of Women and the Law* 10.2 (1998): 338–76. Print.

————, ed. *Race, Space, and the Law: Unmapping a White Settler Society.* Toronto: Between the Lines, 2002. Print.

Regan, Paulette. *Unsettling the Settler Within: Indian Residential Schools, Truth Telling, and Reconciliation in Canada.* Vancouver: UBC P, 2010. Print.

"Regions, Cities, & Routes: Vancouver." *HelloBC.com.* Tourism British Columbia. Web. 4 July 2010 & 15 May 2012.

"Regions, Cities, & Routes: Vancouver Neighbourhoods." *HelloBC.com.* Tourism British Columbia. Web. 4 July 2010 & 15 May 2012.

Rekart, M.L. "Sex-work Harm Reduction." *The Lancet* 366.9503 (2005): 2123–2134. Web.

"Residential School System Historical Overview." *Indian Residential Schools Resolution of Canada.* Office of Indian Residential Schools Resolution of Canada, 2005. Web. 8 Jan. 2006.

Rézo: Santé mieux-être des hommes gais et bisexuels. 2011. Web. 6 June 2011.

Roberts, Nickie. *Whores in History: Prostitution in Western Society.* London: Grafton, 1993. Print.

Roslin, Alex. "Stephen Harper Opens Door to Prison Privatization." *Straight.com: News and Views: News Features.* 22 Nov. 2007. Web. 12 July 2012.

Ross, Becki. *Burlesque West: Showgirls, Sex, and Sin in Postwar Vancouver.* Toronto: U of Toronto P, 2009. Print.

————. "Sex and (Evacuation from) the City: The Moral and Legal Regulation of Sex Workers in Vancouver's West End, 1975–1985." *Sexualities* 13.2 (2010): 197–218. Web. 15 May 2012.

Sangster, Joan. "Incarcerating 'Bad Girls': The Regulation of Sexuality through the Female Refuges Act in Ontario, 1920–1945." *Journal of the History of Sexuality* 7.2 (Oct. 1996): 239–75. Print.

Sassen, Saskia. *Cities in a World Economy*. 2nd ed. Thousand Oaks, CA: Pine Forge, 2000. Print.

Saunders, Philip. "The Missing Women of Vancouver." *CBC News: Indepth Backgrounder*. 7 Feb. 2002. Web. 10 Jan. 2003.

Saunders, Philip, and Justin Thompson. "The Missing Women of Vancouver." 7 Feb. 2002. Updated 23 July 2003. *CBC News: Indepth Backgrounder*. Web. 22 Oct. 2003.

Scambler, Graham, and Annette Scambler, eds. *Rethinking Prostitution: Purchasing Sex in the 1990s*. London: Routledge, 1997. Print.

———. "Foreward: Understanding Prostitution." *Rethinking Prostitution: Purchasing Sex in the 1990s*. Ed. Graham Scambler and Annette Scambler. London: Routledge, 1997. xi–xviii. Print.

Sennett, Richard. *Flesh and Stone: The Body and the City in Western Civilization*. New York: Norton, 1994. Print.

Sex Work. Spec. issue of *Fireweed* 65 (1999). Print.

Shannon, Kate. "The Hypocrisy of Canada's Prostitution Legislation." *CMAJ: Canadian Medical Association Journal* 182.12 (2010): 1388. Web.

Shaver, Frances M. "Prostitution: On the Dark Side of the Service Industry." *Post-Critical Criminology*. Ed. Thomas O'Reilly-Fleming. Toronto: Prentice-Hall Canada, 1996. 42–55. Print.

———. "The Regulation of Prostitution: Avoiding the Morality Traps." *CJLS: Canadian Journal of Law and Society* 9.1 (1994): 123–45. Print.

———. "Sex Trade Advocacy and Research Workbook: Materials for a Two-day Training Workshop with Community Partners." *Head, Heart and Hand: Partnerships for Women's Health in Canadian Environments Volume 2*. Ed. P. Van Esterick. National Network on Environments and Women's Health, 2003. Print.

Ship, Susan Judith, and Laura Norton. "HIV/AIDS and Aboriginal Women in Canada." *Canadian Woman Studies* 21.2 (2001): 25–31. Print.

Silver, Jim, Joan Hay, Darlene Klyne, Parvin Ghorayshi, Peter Gorzen, Cyril Keeper, Michael MacKenzie, and Freeman Simard. *In Their Own Voices: Building Urban Aboriginal Communities*. Halifax: Fernwood, 2006. Print.

Simpson, Audra. "Paths toward a Mohawk Nation: Narratives of Citizenship and Nationhood in Kahnawake." *Political Theory and the Rights of Indigenous Peoples*. Ed. Duncan Ivison, Paul Patton and Will Sanders. Cambridge: Cambridge UP, 2000. 113–36. Print.

Six Nations Caledonia Resource Page. *The Autonomy and Solidarity Website*. 26 Oct. 2006.

"Six Whitechapel Murders." *The Illustrated Police News: Law Courts and Weekly Record*. 8 Dec. 1888. *British Library Images Online Collection*. British Library. Web. 20 May 2006.

Smith, Andrea. *Conquest: Sexual Violence and American Indian Genocide*. Cambridge, MA: South End, 2005. Print.

Smith, Graeme. "Prostitutes Wary of Police DNA Database." *Globe and Mail*. 10 May 2006. Web.

Smulders, Sharon. "'What is the proper word for people like you?': The Question of Métis Identity in *In Search of April Raintree*." *English Studies in Canada* 32.4 (2006): 75–100. Web. 15 July 2012.

Sorfleet, Andrew. "Sex Workers Alliance of Vancouver: End of an Era..." SWAV Media
    Release. 15 Mar. 2005. Web. 21 June 2011.

Sorfleet, Andrew, and Raigen D'Angelo. "'Pimps' and 'Predators': A Letter to Janet
    Steffenhagen, City Editor, *Vancouver Sun*, 19 Feb. 1996." *SWAV: Sex Workers Alliance of
    Vancouver*. Web. 10 Jan. 2004.

Spectre de Rue: Organisme communautaire au service de la collectivité. 2007–2011. Web. 6
    June 2011.

Spicer, Andrew. "Stephen Harper's New Deal for Cities, Provinces, and Communities."
    Andrew Spicer's Weblog. 24 Mar. 2004. Web. 10 Mar. 2006.

Spigel, Lynn. *Welcome to the Dreamhouse: Popular Media and Postwar Suburbs*. Durham, NC:
    Duke UP, 2001. Print.

SPOC: *Sex Professionals of Canada*. 15 Nov. 2005. Web. 15 July 2012.

SPOC. "Bad Client List." SPOC: *Sex Professionals of Canada*. Web. 15 July 2012.

———. "Editorials by SPOC: Why a Public Bad Client List?" SPOC: *Sex Professionals of Canada*.
    Web. 24 May 2011.

———. "Holiday Pimp Chocolate." SPOC: *Sex Professionals of Canada*. 17 Dec. 2005. Web.
    15 July 2012.

———. "Red Light Night June 10th 2007." SPOC: *Sex Professionals of Canada*. 10 June 2007.
    Web. 15 July 2012.

———. "Sex on Trial: the Constitutional Challenge of Canada's Prostitution Laws."
    SPOC: *Sex Professionals of Canada*. 8 Feb. 2010. Web. 15 July 2012.

———. "Sex Professionals of Canada in the News." SPOC: *Sex Professionals of Canada*. Web.
    15 July 2012.

———. "'Traffic Stopping Hookers'–International Day to End Violence against Sex
    Workers." SPOC: *Sex Professionals of Canada*. Mar. 2005. Web. 24 May 2011.

STAR: *Sex Trade Advocacy and Research*. Lewis. 10 July 2006. Web. 28 Nov. 2006.

Stella. "Homepage: About Stella." *Stella*. 31 May 2005. Web. 31 May 2011.

———. "Homepage: July–August 2012: At Stella." *Stella*. Web. 15 July 2012.

———. "Medical Clinic." *Stella*. 7 June 2011. Web. 15 July 2012.

———. "Par et pour les travailleuses du sexe / By and For Sex Workers." *Stella*. Chezstella.org.
    n.d. Web. 24 May 2011.

———. "Press Releases." *Stella*. 29 May 2011. Web. 7 June 2011.

———. "Press Releases: 250 Sex Workers Call on Government and Public." *Stella*.
    21 May 2005. Web. 7 June 2011.

———. "Special Events: Forum XXX 2005." *Stella*. Web. 15 July 2012.

———. "Special Events: Forum XXX 2005: eXXXpressions." *Stella*. Web. 15 July 2012.

———. "Special Events: Mexico 2008." *Stella*. Web. 7 June 2011.

———. "Special Events: Toronto 2006: Marche et rassemblement des femmes et des
    filles–14 août." *Stella*. 29 May 2011. Web. 15 July 2012.

———. "Travail du sexe: Un mouvement international de défense des droits humains."
    Stella. 29 May 2011. Web. 6 June 2011.

Stella of Montreal. n.d. 15 May 2005. Web. 26 Oct. 2009.

Stepping Stone. Halifax, 2008. Web. 26 Oct. 2009.

Stoler, Anne. *Race and the Education of Desire.* Durham, NC: Duke UP, 1997. Print.

Strecker, Geralyn Marie. "Reading Prostitution in American Fiction, 1893–1917." Diss. Ball State U, 2001. DAI 62 (2001): DA3013182.

STWC: Sex Trade Workers of Canada. 20 Dec. 2005. Web. 26 Oct. 2009.

Sullivan, Sam. "Inaugural Speech." Vancouver City Council. City Clerk's Site. 5 Dec. 2005. Web. 10 Mar. 2006.

Suzack, Cheryl. "Law Stories as Life Stories: Jeannette Lavell, Yvonne Bédard, and *Halfbreed.*" *Tracing the Autobiographical.* Ed. Marlene Kadar, Linda Warley, Jeanne Perrault, and Susanna Egan. Waterloo, ON: Wilfrid Laurier UP, 2005. 117–42. eBook.

———, ed. *In Search of April Raintree.* Winnipeg: Portage & Main, 1999. Print.

Suzack, Cheryl, Shari Huhndorf, Jeanne Perreault, and Jean Barman, eds. *Indigenous Women and Feminism: Politics, Activism, Culture.* Vancouver: UBC P, 2010. Print.

SWAT: Sex Workers Alliance of Toronto. 12 Sept. 2005. Web. 23 May 2011.

SWAV: Sex Workers Alliance of Vancouver. 15 Oct. 2005. Web. 26 May 2011.

———. "Canada Day 2000: One Whore's Birthday Suit Salute!" *SWAV.* 1 July 2000. Web. 12 July 2012.

———. "Historical Sites in Vancouver: Mescaleros." *SWAV.* Mar. 2005. Web. 12 July 2012.

———. "Historical Sites in Vancouver: The Penthouse." *SWAV.* Mar. 2005. Web. 12 July 2012.

Sylvie. "Saviez-vous que?: L'histoire du logo de Stella." *ConStellation* 4.2 (Spring 2005): Web. 7 June 2011.

"Synecdoche." *The Concise Oxford Dictionary of Literary Terms.* 2nd ed. 2001. Web. 21 June 2011.

Taylor, Brooke M. *Promoters, Patriots and Partisans: Historiography in Nineteenth-Century English Canada.* Toronto: U of Toronto P. 1989. Print.

Thom, Jo-Ann. "The Effect of Readers' Responses on the Development of Aboriginal Literature in Canada: A Study of Maria Campbell's *Halfbreed,* Beatrice Culleton's *In Search of April Raintree,* and Richard Wagamese's *Keeper'n Me.*" Mosionier 295–306.

Trade Secrets: Health and Safety in the Sex Industry. 14 Jan. 2011. Web. 23 May 2011.

"Trials of the Sex Trade: A Survival Guide to Canada's Legal Jungle." *CSIS: Commercial Sex Information Service.* 27 Dec. 2000. Web. 1 Dec. 2005.

Tucher, Andie. *Froth & Scum: Truth, Beauty, Goodness, and the Ax Murder in America's First Mass Medium.* Chapel Hill: U of North Carolina P. 1994. Print.

"Twenty-third Annual National Magazine Award Winners." *Sources* 46 (Winter 2000). Web. 26 Aug. 2010.

"Two More Whitechapel Murders." *The Illustrated Police News: Law Courts and Weekly Record.* 6 Oct. 1888. British Library Images Online Collection. British Library. Web. 20 May 2006.

Valverde, Mariana. *The Age of Light, Soap and Water: Moral Reform in English Canada, 1885–1925.* Toronto: McClelland & Stewart, 1991. Print.

———. "Moral Capital." *CJLS: Canadian Journal of Law and Society* 9.1 (1994): 213–32. Print.

Van Brunschot, Erin Gibbs, Rosalind A. Sydie, and Catherine Krull. "Images of Prostitution: The Prostitute and Print Media." *Women & Criminal Justice* 10.4 (2000): 47–72. Print.

Vancouver Police Services. "Vancouver Police Department Strategic Plan 2004–2008." *The Vancouver Police Department* 15 Oct. 2004. Web.

Vancouver Rape Relief & Women's Shelter. 25 Feb. 2009. Web. 20 Feb. 2011.

Vangen, Kate. "Making Faces: Defiance and Humour in Campbell's *Halfbreed* and Welch's *Winter in the Blood.*" *The Native in Literature.* Ed. Thomas King, Cheryl Cates, and Helen Hoy. Winnipeg: ECW, 1987. 188–205. Print.

Walkowitz, Judith R. *City of Dreadful Delight.* Chicago: U of Chicago P, 1992. Print.

———. *Prostitution in Victorian Society.* Cambridge: Cambridge UP, 1980. Print.

Walsh, Christine, dir. *Finding Dawn.* National Film Board of Canada, 2006. Film.

Ward, Doug. "Morality Takes Back Seat to Violence." *Vancouver Sun.* 3 May 2003. *Missingpeople.net.* Web. 19 July 2010.

Warwick, Alexandra. "The Scene of the Crime: Inventing the Serial Killer." *Social & Legal Studies* 15.4 (2006): 552–69. Web. 10 Sept. 2009.

"Web 2.0 Is a Cultural Phenomenon and Should Be Documented as Such." *Wikipedia Talk: Web 2.0.* 11 Jan. 2011. Web. 15 July 2012.

Webster Goodwin, Sarah, and Elizabeth Bronfen, eds. *Death and Representation.* Baltimore: Johns Hopkins UP, 1993. Print.

West End Sex Work History Project, 1975–85. Westendsexworkhistory.com. Web. 20 June 2014.

WHO: World Health Organization. *Toolkit for Targeted HIV/AIDS Prevention and Care in Sex Work Settings.* Geneva, 2005. Web.

Willman, Alys, and Antonia Levy. "Introduction: Beyond the Sex in Sex Work." *Sex Work Matters: Exploring Money, Power and Intimacy in the Sex Industry.* Ed. Melissa Hope Ditmore, Antonia Levy, and Alys Willman. New York: Zed, 2010. 1–6. Print.

Winnipeg Police Service Morals Unit, Sage House, the Salvation Army, and the Province of Manitoba. *A Sex Trade Reality Check. Winnipeg Police Service.* 11 July 2011. Web. 26 June 2012.

WISH: Women's Information Safe House. 20 Oct. 2009. Web. 10 May 2011.

Womack, Craig S. "A Single Decade: Book-Length Native Literary Criticism between 1986 and 1997." *Reasoning Together: The Native Critics Collective.* Ed. Craig S. Womack, Daniel Heath Justice, and Christopher B. Teuton. Norman: U of Oklahoma P, 2008. 3–104. Print.

Wood, Daniel. "Missing: Vancouver's Missing Prostitutes." *Elm Street* (Nov. 1999): 2–10. Web.

Yang, Guobin. "Online Activism." *Journal of Democracy* 20.3 (2009): 33–36. Web. 13 Mar. 2011.

Yee, Jessica, ed. *Feminism for REAL: Deconstructing the Academic Industrial Complex of Feminism.* Ottawa: Canadian Centre for Policy Alternatives, 2011. Print.

Zandberg, Eyal. "The Right to Tell the (Right) Story: Journalism, Authority and Memory." *Media Culture Society* 32.5 (2010): 5–24. Web. 20 Aug. 2010.

Zola, Émile. *Nana.* 1880. Trans. George Holden. New York: Viking Penguin, 1972. Print.

Zwicker, Heather. "The Limits of Sisterhood." Suzack, *April Raintree* 323–38.

INDEX

OTHER TITLES FROM THE UNIVERSITY OF ALBERTA PRESS

THE IMPORTANCE OF BEING MONOGAMOUS
Marriage and Nation Building in Western Canada
to 1915
SARAH CARTER

400 pages | B&W photographs, notes, bibliography, index
978–0–88864–490–9 | $34.95 (T) paper
Copublished with AU Press at Athabasca University
Canadian History/Gender Studies/Politics

DISINHERITED GENERATIONS
Our Struggle to Reclaim Treaty Rights for First Nations
Women and their Descendants
**NELLIE CARLSON & KATHLEEN STEINHAUER, AS TOLD TO LINDA GOYETTE
FOREWORD BY MARIA CAMPBELL**

216 pages | 20 B&W photographs, notes, appendices, index
978–0–88864–642–2 | $24.95 (T) paper
978–0–88864–804–4 | $19.99 (T) PDF
Native Studies/Human Rights/Women's Studies/Oral History

OVERCOMING CONFLICTING LOYALTIES
Intimate Partner Violence, Community Resources
and Faith
IRENE SEVCIK, MICHAEL ROTHERY, NANCY NASON-CLARK & ROBERT PYNN

296 pages | Introduction, bibliography, notes, index
978–1–77212–050–9 | $34.95 (T) paper
978–1–77212–063–9 | $27.99 (T) EPUB
978–1–77212–064–6 | $27.99 (T) Kindle
978–1–77212–065–3 | $27.99 (T) PDF
Domestic Violence/Religion/Social Work